T5-AQR-437

A VIRGINIA WOOLF CHRONOLOGY

A Virginia Woolf Chronology

EDWARD BISHOP

G.K.HALL &CO.
70 LINCOLN STREET, BOSTON, MASS.

Published 1988 in the United States by
G. K. HALL & CO.
70 Lincoln Street
Boston, Massachusetts 02111

First published 1989 by
THE MACMILLAN PRESS LTD
Houndmills, Basingstoke
Hampshire RG21 2XS

Printed in Hong Kong

Library of Congress Cataloging-in-Publication Data
Bishop, Edward L.
A Virginia Woolf chronology.
(Macmillan author chronologies)
Includes index.
1. Woolf, Virginia, 1881–1941—Chronology. I. Title.
II. Series.
PR6045.072Z556 1989 823′.912 88–4097
ISBN 0–8161–8982–X

Contents

General Editor's Preface

Most biographies are ill adapted to serve as works of reference – not surprisingly so, since the biographer is likely to regard his function as the devising of a continuous and readable narrative, with excursions into interpretation and speculation, rather than a bald recital of facts. There are times, however, when anyone reading for business or pleasure needs to check a point quickly or to obtain a rapid overview of part of an author's life or career; and at such moments turning over the pages of a biography can be a time-consuming and frustrating occupation. The present series of volumes aims at providing a means whereby the chronological facts of an author's life and career, rather than needing to be prised out of the narrative in which they are (if they appear at all) securely embedded, can be seen at a glance. Moreover, whereas biographies are often, and quite understandably, vague over matters of fact (since it makes for tediousness to be forever enumerating details of dates and places), a chronology can be precise whenever it is possible to be precise.

Thanks to the survival, sometimes in very large quantities, of letters, diaries, notebooks and other documents, as well as to thoroughly researched biographies and bibliographies, this material now exists in abundance for many major authors. In the case of, for example, Dickens, we can often ascertain what he was doing in each month and week, and almost on each day, of his prodigiously active working life; and the student of, say, *David Copperfield* is likely to find it fascinating as well as useful to know just when Dickens was at work on each part of that novel, what other literary enterprises he was engaged in at the same time, whom he was meeting, what places he was visiting, and what were the relevant circumstances of his personal and professional life. Such a chronology is not, of course, a substitute for a biography; but its arrangement, in combination with its index, makes it a much more convenient tool for this kind of purpose; and it may be acceptable as a form of 'alternative' biography, with its own distinctive advantages as well as its obvious limitations.

Since information relating to an author's early years is usually scanty and chronologically imprecise, the opening section of some volumes in this series groups together the years of childhood and adolescence. Thereafter each year, and usually each month, are dealt with separately. Information not readily assignable to a specific month or day is given as a general note at the beginning of a year's or month's entry. The first entry for each month carries an indication of the day of the week, so that when necessary this can be readily calculated for other dates. Each volume also contains a list of persons frequently referred to, with brief relevant details, and a bibliography of the principal sources of information. In the chronology itself, the sources of many of the more specific items, including quotations, are identified, in order that the reader who wishes to do so may consult the original contexts.

Norman Page

Introduction and Acknowledgements

Since Quentin Bell's 1972 biography of Virginia Woolf, the amount of information available to the common reader has increased enormously: we now have the five volumes of diaries, the six volumes of letters, and the letters of Vita Sackville-West to Virginia Woolf; we have previously unpublished memoirs and essays, manuscript drafts of several novels, and a detailed guide to Woolf's reading notebooks. Whole books have been devoted to the composition of individual novels, and a steady flow of biographical studies continues to elaborate, modify and contest the received view of Woolf in terms of her status as woman, wife, patient and writer. All of which makes it difficult to keep the broad outlines of Woolf's working life clear. This volume is designed to enable the scholar to trace quickly the arc from conception to completion of a given novel, to chart the relation of her fiction to her journalism, and to place Woolf's writing in the context of her reading, her work at the Hogarth Press, and her social life.

The Chronology records the stages of composition of her books, and it indicates the authors she was reading (for Sterne and Proust had the power to bend her own sentences), the people she was meeting (such as T. S. Eliot, who inhibited *Jacob's Room*, and Ottoline Morrell, who stimulated *Mrs Dalloway*), and her illnesses (which were sometimes welcomed – as when she was writing *The Waves* – for the fertile, almost 'mystical' states they could bring). The Chronology lists the first appearance of her reviews and essays during her lifetime, and it also lists the works published by the Hogarth Press from the date of its inception until 1938, the year in which Virginia Woolf sold her interest. She did not read all of the manuscripts, and many of the political titles are clearly Leonard Woolf's choices rather than hers, but the entries indicate works that she would have been aware of, and heard discussed, even if she did not read them at the time – as with those of Freud, which Leonard read in 1914 and the Hogarth Press began to publish in 1922, and which Virginia records reading only in 1939.

The outlines of her friendships with such figures as Clive Bell, Violet Dickinson, T. S. Eliot, Lytton Strachey, Katherine Mansfield and Vita Sackville-West are sketched here, but dinner parties of regular guests and the constant visits with her sister Vanessa, in London and in Sussex, have had to make way for entries more immediately connected with her work. And, though the Woolfs' travels are recorded, the focus (as with their very literary honeymoon) is on the reading and writing, rather than the sightseeing, accomplished *en route*. The twice-yearly migrations from London to Monk's House, their summer home in Rodmell, Sussex, have been noted, but the frequent weekend visits omitted.

The primary sources of information for this Chronology have been Quentin Bell's biography, *Virginia Woolf*, B. J. Kirkpatrick's *Bibliography*, J. Howard Woolmer's *Checklist of the Hogarth Press, 1917–1938*, Majumdar and McLaurin's *Virginia Woolf: The Critical Heritage*, and the *Diary*, ed. Anne Olivier Bell and Andrew McNeillie, and *Letters*, ed. Nigel Nicolson and Joanne Trautmann; I am greatly indebted to the meticulously researched footnotes by the editors of both the letters and the diary. Dates for the composition of novels, when they have not been taken from the diary or letters, come from the published editions of the manuscripts by Louise DeSalvo, Susan Dick, Ellen Hawkes, John Graham, Mitchell Leaska, Jeanne Schulkind, Brenda Silver and Madeline Moore. Dates for *Jacob's Room* and *Mrs Dalloway* are from the manuscripts in the Berg Collection, New York Public Library, the Monk's House Papers at the University of Sussex, and the manuscripts in the British Library. For the 'Events and Letters' sections I have relied on Bernard Grun's *The Timetables of History* and the chronologies in Bradbury and McFarlane's *Modernism* and S. P. Rosenbaum's *The Bloomsbury Group*. I have used Brenda Silver's guide to the *Reading Notebooks*, and the biographical studies of Gordon, Poole, Rose, Trombley, and Spater and Parsons, the Leonard Woolf Papers at Sussex and the Charleston Papers at Trinity College, Cambridge; and I owe a debt to the authors and editors of the biographies, memoirs, letters and studies of the period that I consulted in cross-checking references, but which are too numerous to mention here.

For permission to quote from the *Letters* and *Diary* of Virginia Woolf, I wish to thank the Estate of Virginia Woolf, The Hogarth Press, and Harcourt Brace Jovanovich, and for permission to quote from *Virginia Woolf: The Critical Heritage* I thank Routledge and Kegan Paul. I wish to acknowledge the Research Fellowship from the Social Sciences and Humanities Research Council of Canada, and the Mactaggart Fellowship from the University of Alberta, which enabled me to consult the manuscripts in New York and England. I am indebted to the staff of the manuscript collections at Trinity College, Cambridge, the Berg Collection in New York, and the University of Sussex for their assistance, and my thanks go to Elizabeth Inglis for her hospitality in Lewes. I am grateful to Gerald Wandio, Gail Sorenson, Joene MacArthur, Glennis Stephenson and Audrey Bishop for their help in tracking down obscure dates and checking the typescript, to Marjorie Campbell for her encouragement, and to Norman Page for his guidance. I am of course responsible for any errors in the text.

List of Abbreviations and Works Cited

Persons frequently referred to

Individuals are referred to by their first and last names for the first entry; subsequent entries list them by initial and last name. With Adrian and Ann Stephen, James and Julia Strachey, and Pernel and Philippa Strachey, I have used the initial for the first member of each pair, retaining the first name for the member less frequently referred to. Because the public careers of Virginia and Vanessa Stephen take place under their married names (nearly all of Virginia Woolf's writing before her marriage consists of anonymous reviews) I have referred throughout to 'VW' and 'VB'; this also avoids confusion in the early years, when they were both 'VS'.

The ten individuals listed below appear very often, and are referred to by initials throughout.

CB Arthur Clive Heward Bell (1881–1964), art critic, educated at Cambridge, where he became a member of the Cambridge Conversazione Society (the 'Apostles'), which included Roger Fry, E. M. Forster, John Maynard Keynes, Desmond MacCarthy, Thoby Stephen, Saxon Sydney-Turner, Leonard Woolf, and others who came to be associated with the Bloomsbury Group. Husband of Vanessa Stephen, and father of Julian and Quentin Bell, he became, after the marriage was dissolved, the companion of Mary Hutchinson.

VB Vanessa Bell, *née* Stephen (1879–1961), painter, VW's elder sister, wife of Clive Bell, but from about 1914 until her death companion of Duncan Grant. See Richard Shone's *Bloomsbury Portraits* (1976), Frances Spalding's *Vanessa Bell* (1983), and Angelica Garnett's *Deceived with Kindness: A Bloomsbury Childhood* (1985).

TSE Thomas Stearns Eliot (1888–1965), American-born poet and critic. An employee of Lloyds Bank 1917–25, in 1917 he became assistant editor of *The Egoist*, in 1922 founded *The Criterion*, and in 1925 he joined publishers Faber and Faber. See Peter Ackroyd's *T. S. Eliot* (1984).

EMF Edward Morgan Forster (1879–1970), novelist and essayist; the last of his novels published during his lifetime was *A Passage to India* (1924), but he continued to publish literary criticism and essays on liberal-humanist themes. His opinion of VW's work held great weight with her. See P. N. Furbank's *E. M. Forster* (1977), and *Selected Letters*, 2 vols, ed. P. N. Furbank and Mary Lago (1983, 1985).

RF Roger Eliot Fry (1866–1934), painter and art critic, introduced London to the work of the Post-Impressionists. He and Vanessa Bell were for a time in love, and remained close friends. After his wife was consigned to a mental institution, Helen Anrep, *née* Maitland, wife of artist Boris Anrep, became his companion. See VW's *Roger Fry* (1940), and *Letters of Roger Fry*, 2 vols, ed. Denys Sutton (1972).

DG Duncan James Corrowr Grant (1885–1978), artist, son of Major Bartle Grant, brother of Lady Strachey, with whose family he spent much of his youth while his father was serving in India; companion of Vanessa Bell and father of Angelica Bell. They lived at Charleston, a farm near Firle, Sussex, and from 1927 onwards spent their winters at Cassis-sur-mer, near Marseille; Clive Bell was a frequent member of both establishments.

JMK John Maynard Keynes (1883–1946), economist, Treasury official, author of a number of influential works on economics, chairman of the board of the *Nation and Athenaeum*, founder of the Cambridge Arts Theatre, and husband of ballerina Lydia Lopokova, who had come to London with the Diaghilev Company. He leased 46 Gordon Square in London, taking over from the Bells in 1916, and after his marriage leased Tilton, the farm next to Charleston. See Robert Skidelsky's *John Maynard Keynes* (1985).

LS Giles Lytton Strachey (1880–1932), biographer and critic, friend of Thoby Stephen and Leonard Woolf at Cambridge, brother of Dorothy, Philippa (suffragist), Oliver (civil servant, husband of author Ray Costelloe), Pernel (Principal of Newnham College, Cambridge), Marjorie (teacher and writer) and James (translator of Freud, husband of Alix Sargant-Florence), and uncle of Julia (author, wife of sculptor Stephen Tomlin). From 1917 he lived with Dora Carrington, and in 1924 after her marriage to Ralph Partridge all three lived at Ham Spray House, near Hungerford, Berkshire. See Michael Holroyd's *Lytton Strachey: A Critical Biography* (1967, 1968).

VSW Victoria (Vita) Mary Sackville-West (1892–1962), poet, novelist, biographer, gardener, wife of diplomat and writer Harold Nicolson. She and her husband lived at Long Barn, Sevenoaks, near Knole (the ancestral mansion she was prevented from inheriting because she was a woman), from 1914 until 1930, when they bought Sissinghurst Castle. Her love affair with VW issued in *Orlando* (1928). See Victoria Glendinning's *Vita: The Life of V. Sackville-West* (1983), and *The Letters of Vita Sackville-West to Virginia Woolf*, ed. Louise A. DeSalvo and Mitchell A. Leaska (1985).

LW Leonard Sidney Woolf (1880–1969), political theorist, critic, editor, publisher, novelist, husband of Virginia Stephen.

Works frequently referred to

The standard abbreviations for the titles of VW's published works have been used throughout, even though in many cases the work took shape under one or more working titles. First publication of VW's works is by the Hogarth Press, except for *The Voyage Out* and *Night and Day*, published originally by Duckworth.

VO	*The Voyage Out* (1915)
N&D	*Night and Day* (1919)
JR	*Jacob's Room* (1922)
CR	*The Common Reader* (1925)
MD	*Mrs Dalloway* (1925)
TL	*To the Lighthouse* (1927)
O	*Orlando* (1928)
Room	*A Room of One's Own* (1929)
W	*The Waves* (1931)
CR II	*The Common Reader*, 2nd ser. (1932)
F	*Flush* (1933)
Y	*The Years* (1937)
3G	*Three Guineas* (1938)
RF	*Roger Fry* (1940)
BA	*Between the Acts* (1941)
DM	*The Death of the Moth and Other Essays* (1942)
HH	*A Haunted House and Other Stories* (1943)
M	*The Moment and Other Essays* (1947)

CDB — *The Captain's Death Bed and Other Essays* (1950)
MDP — *Mrs Dalloway's Party: A Short Story Sequence*, ed. Stella McNichol (1973)
MOB — *Moments of Being: Unpublished Autobiographical Writings of Virginia Woolf*, 2nd edn, ed. Jeanne Schulkind (1985)
CSF — *The Complete Shorter Fiction*, ed. Susan Dick (1985)
L — *The Letters of Virginia Woolf*, 6 vols, ed. Nigel Nicolson and Joanne Trautmann (1975–80)
D — *The Diary of Virginia Woolf*, 5 vols, ed. Anne Olivier Bell and Andrew McNeillie (1977–84)
M&M — Majumdar, Robin, and Allen McLaurin (eds), *Virginia Woolf: The Critical Heritage* (London: Routledge and Kegan Paul, 1975)
LW — Woolf, Leonard, *Autobiography . . .*, 5 vols (London: Hogarth Press, 1960–9)
QB — Bell, Quentin, *Virginia Woolf: A Biography*, 2 vols (London: Hogarth Press, 1972)

Periodicals

N&A — *Nation and Athenaeum*
NS — *New Statesman*
NS&N — *New Statesman and Nation*
TLS — *The Times Literary Supplement*

Other works cited

[Citations by name(s) of author(s)/editors(s), with short title if needed]

Bradbury, Malcolm and James McFarlane (eds), *Modernism 1890–1930* (Harmondsworth: Penguin, 1983).

DeSalvo, Louise A., *Virginia Woolf's First Voyage: A Novel in the Making* (London: Macmillan, 1980).

—— (ed.), *'Melymbrosia' by Virginia Woolf: An Early Version of 'The Voyage Out'* (New York: New York Public Library, 1982).

Dick, Susan (ed.), *'To the Lighthouse': The Holograph Draft* (Toronto: University of Toronto Press, 1982).

Graham, J. W. (ed.), *'The Waves': The Two Holograph Drafts* (Toronto: University of Toronto Press, 1976).

Grun, Bernard, *The Timetables of History: A Horizontal Linkage of People and Events* (New York: Simon and Schuster, 1975).

Hawkes, Ellen (ed.), 'Friendships Gallery', *Twentieth Century Literature*, 25 (Fall–Winter 1979) 270–302.

Kennedy, Richard, *A Boy at the Hogarth Press* (London: Whittington Press, 1972).

Kirkpatrick, B. J., *A Bibliography of Virginia Woolf*, 3rd edn (Oxford: Clarendon Press, 1980).

Leaska, Mitchell A. (ed.), *'The Pargiters' by Virginia Woolf: The Novel–Essay Portion of 'The Years'* (London: Hogarth Press, 1978).

——, *'Pointz Hall': The Earlier and Later Typescripts of 'Between the Acts'* (New York: University Publications, 1983).

Lehmann, John, *Thrown to the Woolfs* (London: Weidenfeld and Nicolson, 1978).

Moore, Madeline (ed.), '*Orlando*: An Edition of the Manuscript', *Twentieth Century Literature*, 25 (Fall–Winter 1979) 303–55.

Poole, Roger, *The Unknown Virginia Woolf* (Cambridge: Cambridge University Press, 1978).

Radin, Grace, *Virginia Woolf's 'The Years': The Evolution of a Novel* (Knoxville: University of Tennessee Press, 1981).

Rose, Phyllis, *Woman of Letters: A Life of Virginia Woolf* (London: Routledge and Kegan Paul, 1978).

Rosenbaum, S. P. (ed.), *The Bloomsbury Group: A Collection of Memoirs, Commentary and Criticism* (Toronto: University of Toronto Press, 1975).

Ruotolo, Lucio (ed.), *Freshwater: A Comedy* (New York: Harcourt Brace Jovanovich, 1976).

Silver, Brenda R. (ed.), '"Anon" and "The Reader": Virginia Woolf's Last Essays', *Twentieth Century Literature*, 25 (Fall–Winter, 1979) 356–441.

——, *Virginia Woolf's Reading Notebooks* (Princeton, NJ: Princeton University Press, 1983).

Spater, George, and Ian Parsons, *A Marriage of True Minds: An Intimate Portrait of Leonard and Virginia Woolf* (London: Jonathan Cape, 1977).

Stansky, Peter, and William Abrahams, *Journey to the Frontier: A Biography of Julian Bell and John Cornford* (London: Constable, 1966).

Trombley, Stephen, *'All that summer she was mad': Virginia Woolf and her Doctors* (London: Junction Books, 1981).

Woolmer, J. Howard, *A Checklist of the Hogarth Press, 1917–1938*, with a short history of the Press by Mary E. Gaither (New York: Woolmer/Brotherson, 1976).

Collections of manuscript material

Berg	The Henry W. and Albert A. Berg Collection of English and American Literature of the New York Public Library, Astor, Lenox and Tilden Foundations.
MHP	Monk's House Papers, University of Sussex.

A Virginia Woolf Chronology

Early Years (1882–1904)

1882 (25 Jan) Adeline Virginia Stephen is born, the third of four children (Vanessa, b. 1879; Thoby, b. 1880; Adrian b. 1883) of Leslie and Julia Stephen. Other members of the family include three children from Julia's first marriage to Herbert Duckworth, George, Gerald, and Stella, and one child from Leslie's first marriage to Harriet Thackeray (daughter of the novelist), the mentally deficient Laura.

(Summer) The Stephen family spends each summer until 1894 at Talland House, St Ives, Cornwall, and the area remains central to VW's art.

(Nov) Leslie Stephen begins work as editor of the *Dictionary of National Biography*.

1889 VW begins to learn Latin, history and French from her mother, mathematics from her father; formal education continues with governesses; Gerald Duckworth has begun to show sexual interest in her (c. 1888).

1891 (Feb) The *Hyde Park Gate News*, issued from the Stephen nursery, begins publication, appearing weekly until April 1895.

(Apr) L. Stephen gives up the editorship of the *Dictionary of National Biography*.

1895 (5 May) Julia Stephen dies, age 49.

(Summer) Stephen family at Freshwater, Isle of Wight; VW has her first breakdown.

(Nov) The lease of Talland House, St Ives, is sold.

1897 (Jan) VW begins to keep a regular diary, and reads extensively in her father's library: between 1 January and 30 June reads *Three Generations of English Women*, ed. T. F. Unwin (1893), vols II and III; James Anthony Froude's *Carlyle* (1882); Mandell Creighton's

Queen Elizabeth (1896), John Lockhart's *Life of Sir Walter Scott* (1837–8), a birthday present from her father; William Thackeray's *The Newcomes* (1853–5); Thomas Carlyle's *Reminiscences* (1881), *French Revolution* (1837), *Cromwell* (1845), *Life of John Sterling* (1851); Charles Dickens' *The Old Curiosity Shop* (1846), *A Tale of Two Cities* (1859); Sir James Stephen's *Essays in Ecclesiastical Biography* (1849); George Eliot's *Felix Holt* (1866), *Silas Marner* (1861); Dinah Mulock Craik's *John Halifax, Gentleman* (1857); James Russell Lowell (her godfather)'s *Among my Books* (1870 and 1876), *My Study Windows* (1871); James Dykes Campbell's *The Life of Coleridge* (1894); Anthony Hope's *The Heart of Princess Osra* (1897); Thomas Babington Macaulay's *History* (1849–61); Anthony Trollope's *Barchester Towers* (1857); Thomas Arnold's *History of Rome* (1838–42); W. E. Norris's *A Deplorable Affair*; Charlotte Brontë's *Shirley* (1849); three volumes of Pepys's diary, a novel by Henry James, and a work by Lady Barlow (*QB* I).

(8 Feb) Travels to Bognor with VB, Stella Duckworth and Jack Hills.

(15 Feb) Allowed to start lessons again.

(24 Feb) L. Stephen receives a thesaurus from the editor of the *Cornhill Magazine*; insulted, he gives it to VW.

(10 Apr) S. Duckworth and J. Hills marry.

(28 Apr) S. Duckworth ill with peritonitis.

(May) VW reads her 'beloved Macaulay'; Dr Seton has advised against her doing any lessons this term (to T. Stephen).

(22 June) VW, VB and T. Stephen watch the procession of Queen Victoria's Diamond Jubilee.

(19 July) S. Duckworth dies, age 28 (see 'A Sketch of the Past', *MOB*).

(Oct) VW begins Greek and history classes at King's College, London.

1898 (Jan) VW concludes her diary.

(Apr) Meets Kitty Maxse, who later becomes the inspiration for Mrs Dalloway.

(Oct) Attends classes at King's College in Greek with Dr Warr, and in Latin with Clara Pater, sister of Walter Pater, and the original of Miss Craye in '"Slater's Pins Have No Points"' (Jan 1928).

Also this year, George Duckworth founds his publishing house.

1899 (Oct) T. Stephen enters Trinity College, Cambridge, together with CB, LS, Saxon Sydney-Turner and LW.

1900 (June) VB and VW visit Cambridge, attend Trinity College Ball.

(Oct) VW attends classes at King's College, London.

1901 (22 Jan) Queen Victoria dies; Edward VII succeeds.

(July) VW reads Sophocles' *Antigone*, *Oedipus Coloneus* and the *Trachiniae*.

(Sep) VB enters the Royal Academy Schools.

(Oct) VW takes up bookbinding.

(Nov) Reads Marlowe, Shakespeare and Jonson; accompanies L. Stephen to Oxford, where he receives an honorary D. Litt. degree.

1902 (Jan) *TLS* begins publishing under the editorship of Bruce Richmond, VW starts private lessons in Greek with Janet Case; for her twentieth birthday T. Stephen gives her J. W. MacKail's *Select Epigrams from the Greek Anthology* (1890).

(June) L. Stephen created Knight Commander of the Bath (KCB) in the Coronation Honours.

(July) Stephen family at Fritham House, Lyndhurst, Hampshire, guests include Emma Vaughan, Margery Snowden, CB and Violet Dickinson, who becomes VW's most intimate friend and the recipient of most of her letters until late in the decade.

(Oct) A. Stephen enters Trinity College, Cambridge.

(Oct/Nov) VW plans to write a play with J. Hills.

1903 (Jan) Reads Montaigne and Bacon (given to her by T. Stephen for her twenty-first birthday), as well as Holinshed, Plato and Euripides.

(Apr) Studies Aeschylus with J. Case.

(May) Reads Jane Carlyle's letters, Sidney Lee's *Life* of Shakespeare (1898).

(June) Meets Lady Robert Cecil, who becomes a friend and frequent correspondent.

(June–Aug) Sends a series of her literary exercises, descriptions of people and events in her life (composed standing at a tall desk, to compete with VB, who stands at her easel) to V. Dickinson.

(Sep) L. Stephen slowly dying; George Duckworth offers consolation to VW in the form of sexual attention.

(Oct) VW resumes Greek lessons with J. Case; VB studies at the Royal Academy Schools; T. Stephen reads for the Bar; L. Stephen finishes *Hobbes*.

(Dec) House-hunting in Bloomsbury; letters to V. Dickinson become primarily medical bulletins.

1904 (22 Feb) L. Stephen dies, age 71; his *English Literature and Society in the Eighteenth Century* is published.

(27 Feb) To Manorbier, Pembrokeshire, for a month with VB, T. Stephen, A. Stephen and Gerald Duckworth. VW continues writing: 'That vision [of what book to write] came to me more clearly at Manorbier aged 21 [22], walking the down on the edge of the sea' (*D*, 3 Sep 1922; see also 28 Nov 1928).

(Apr) To Italy with VB, T. and A. Stephen, Gerald Duckworth; joined in Florence by V. Dickinson.

(May) Entertained in Paris by CB and artist Gerald Kelly; visits Kelly's and Rodin's studios; returns to Hyde Park Gate.

(10 May) Beginning of VW's second, and much more serious, breakdown; at first under the care of Dr Savage and three nurses, later with Nurse Traill, spends nearly three months at V. Dickinson's home, where she attempts suicide.

(Aug) With Nurse Traill, VW rejoins her family in Nottinghamshire for summer vacation.

(Oct) The Stephens return to London and begin move from Hyde Park Gate to 46 Gordon Square, Bloomsbury; George and Gerald Duckworth leave the household. VW goes to Cambridge to stay with her aunt Caroline Stephen; helps F. W. Maitland with his *Life* of L. Stephen, reading through and transcribing from her parents' letters.

(8–18 Nov) At Gordon Square, anxious to make money, begins sending articles to the *Guardian*.

(17 Nov) LW dines before sailing for Ceylon.

(18–29 Nov) On Dr Savage's advice VW travels to Yorkshire to stay with Will and Madge Vaughan (daughter of John Addington Symonds, adored by VW, the original of Sally in *MD*); visits Haworth Parsonage, home of the Brontë sisters, and writes an account for the *Guardian* (21 Dec).

(6 Dec) At Cambridge, lunches with A. Stephen and Walter Headlam, lecturer in classics at King's College, with whom VW develops a mildly flirtatious friendship. Writes a comic life of Aunt Mary Fisher.

(14 Dec) VW's first publication: review of W. D. Howells's *The Son of Royal Langbrith*, in the *Guardian*, where her work henceforth appears frequently.

(21 Dec) To Lyndhurst for Christmas. VW works on a contribution to Maitland's *Life* of her father, reads a biography of Burne-Jones, practises drawing every evening, 'Haworth, November, 1904' in the *Guardian*.

1905

EVENTS AND LETTERS. Beginning of Fauvism in art, led by Henri Matisse; first motor buses in London; Albert Einstein formulates *Special Theory of Relativity*. EMF publishes *Where Angels Fear to Tread*; George Bernard Shaw, *Major Barbara*; John Millington Synge, *The Shadow of the Glen, Riders to the Sea*; H. G. Wells, *A Modern Utopia, Kipps*; Edith Wharton, *The House of Mirth*; Oscar Wilde, *De Profundis* (posth.).

January

4 (Wed) Review of W. Pett Ridge's *Next-Door Neighbours* in the *Guardian*.

14 VW 'discharged cured' by Dr Savage; begins giving weekly classes at Morley College, an evening institute for working men and women, where she continues to work until the end of 1907 (see her report, *QB* I, Appendix B).

18 'On a Faithful Friend', on 'Shag', a dog, in the *Guardian*.

25 VW's twenty-third birthday.

February

8 (Wed) *'A Belle of the Fifties'*, review of *A Belle of the Fifties: Memoirs of Mrs Clay of Alabama*, in the *Guardian*.

16 T. Stephen starts 'Thursday Evenings' at 46 Gordon Square, inviting his university friends: CB, Ralph Hawtrey, Walter Lamb, Robin Mayor, D. MacCarthy, Jack Pollock, LS, S. Sydney-Turner, LW and Hilton Young – beginning of the 'Bloomsbury Group'.

22 'Mr Henry James's Latest Novel', review of James's *The Golden Bowl*, in the *Guardian*.

25 'The Decay of Essay-writing' in *Academy and Literature*.

March

10 (Fri) 'Literary Geography', review of Lewis Melville's *The Thackeray Country*, and Frederick Kitton's *The Dickens Country*, in *TLS*.

17 Review of W. E. Norris's *Barham of Beltana* in *TLS*.

22 Review of Jane Barlow's *By Beach and Bogland* in the *Guardian*.

29 VW and A. Stephen set sail from Liverpool to Oporto. In the weeks following, they visit Lisbon in Portugal, Seville and Granada in Spain. On 'the voyage out' VW enjoys the sensation of being cut off, although bored by most of her fellow-passengers (to V. Dickinson, 10 Apr; cf. early chapters of *VO*).

31 Review of A. J. Dawson's *The Fortunes of Farthings* in *TLS*.

April

24 (Mon) Returns from Portugal to Gordon Square. Review of Elizabeth Robins' *A Dark Lantern* in the *Guardian*

Late this month, B. Richmond rejects VW's review of Edith Sichel's *Catherine de Medici and the French Reformation* because the *TLS* treats books 'in the academic spirit' and VW does not. Preparing English-history lectures for women at Morley College, reads Edward Freeman's *History of the Norman Conquest of England* (1867–79), A. S. Green's *Town Life in the Fifteenth Century* (1893), and A. V. Dicey's *Lectures on the Relations between Law and Public Opinion During the Nineteenth Century* (1905).

May

10 (Wed) Review of Elinor Lane's *Nancy Stair* in the *Guardian*.

26 'Journeys in Spain', review of Rowland Thirlmere's *Letters from Catalonia*, and Somerset Maugham's *The Land of the Blessed Virgin*, in *TLS*.

June

(Mid-month) Attends Trinity College Ball; visits W. Headlam and F. W. Maitland; lunches with CB.

July

19 (Wed) 'An Andalusian Inn', review of Eleanor Hayden's *Rose of Lone Farm*, in the *Guardian*.

26 'A Priory Church' in the *Guardian*.

August

Early this month, *Euphrosyne* published, an anonymous collection of poems, predominantly by S. Sydney-Turner and CB, but including work by LS, LW, W. Lamb, and others; VW sends a copy with a gently mocking cover letter to Lady Cecil, later gives the muse's name to the ship in *VO*, and in *O* to Orlando's lover, Lady Euphrosyne (see *QB* I, Appendix C).

2 (Wed) 'The Letters of Jane Welsh Carlyle' in the *Guardian*.
10 To Carbis Bay, near St Ives, for the summer holidays.
16 'The Value of Laughter' in the *Guardian*.
26 'Their Passing Hour', review of John Fyvie's *Some Famous Women of Wit and Beauty*, in *Academy*.

October

Early this month, VB initiates 'The Friday Club', a society which meets weekly and is concerned with the fine arts. T. and A. Stephen study law; VW continues work at Morley College.

27 (Sat) Review of A. C. Inchbold's *The Letter Killeth* in *TLS*.

November

1 (Wed) Reviews of G. B. Burgin's *The Devil's Due*, and W. E. Norris's *Lone Marie*, in the *Guardian*.
15 Review of E. Wharton's *The House of Mirth* in the *Guardian*.
17 Reviews of Mary Wilkins' *The Debtor*, Mary Debenham's *A Flood Tide*, and Mrs Fred Reynolds' *The Making of Michael*, in *TLS*.

December

6 (Wed) 'A Description of the Desert', review of Gilbert Watson's *The Voice of the South*, and review of Margaret Booth's *The Brown House and Cordelia*, in the *Guardian*.
13 '"Delta"', review of D. M. Moir's *The Life of Mansie Wauch*, in the *Guardian*.
15 'Two Irish Novels', review of Shan Bullock's *Dan the Dollar*, and Louise Kenny's *The Red Haired Woman: Her Autobiography*, in *TLS*.
20 Review of Mrs Henry Graham's *The Tower of Siloam* in the *Guardian*.'Street Music' in the *National Review*.

1906

EVENTS AND LETTERS. Paul Cézanne and Henrik Ibsen die; 'Everyman's Library' begins. Joseph Conrad publishes *Mirror of the Sea*; John Galsworthy, *The Man of Property*; Rudyard Kipling, *Puck of Pook's Hill*.

January

VW continues working at Morley College.

6 (Sat) 'A Nineteenth-century Critic', review of Canon Ainger's *Lectures and Essays*, in the *Speaker*.

10 Review of M. Sturge Henderson's *After his Kind* in the *Guardian*.

13 'The Sister of Frederic the Great', review of Edith Cuthell's *Wilhelmina Margravine of Baireuth*, in *Academy*.

15 Attends a dance; sits in a corner and reads Tennyson's *In Memoriam* (to V. Dickinson).

25 VW's twenty-fourth birthday.

February

16 (Fri) Reviews of Beatrice Harraden's *The Scholar's Daughter*, and Mrs Hamilton Synge's *A Supreme Moment*, in *TLS*.

March

9 (Fri) Review of Reginald Farrer's *The House of Shadows* in *TLS*.

23 Review of Mrs Fuller Maitland's *Blanche Esmead* in *TLS*.

April

12 (Thurs) To Giggleswick, Yorkshire, until the 25th; stays near M. and W. Vaughan. Reads W. S. Landor's *Pericles and Aspasia* (1836).

13 Review of Horace Vachell's *The Face of Clay* in *TLS*.

18 'The Poetic Drama', review of Arthur Dillon's *King William I*, Spencer Moore's *Aurelian*, Archibald Fox's *Sir Thomas More*, Alexandra von Herder's *The Little Mermaid*, Arthur Upson's *The City*, Paul Hookham's *Plays and Poems*, and Rosalind Travers' *Two Arcadias*, in the *Guardian*.

21 'Poets' Letters', review of Percy Lubbock's *Elizabeth Barrett Browning in her Letters*, and *Robert Browning and Alfred Domett*, ed. Frederic Kenyon, in the *Speaker*.

27 VW sends her description of Giggleswick, another of her

literary exercises, to M. Vaughan (Berg). T. Stephen reads a paper to the Friday Club on the Decadence of Modern Art.

May

3 (Thurs) Sends review of Mrs Humphry Ward's *Fenwick's Career* to the *Speaker*, but finds they have already published one, 'longer, and even more vindictive than mine' (to V. Dickinson).

June

Early this month, replies to M. Vaughan's criticism of her sketches: 'This vague and dream like world, without love, or heart, or passion, or sex, is the world I really care about, and find interesting' (to M. Vaughan).

15 (Fri) Review of Dorothea Gerard's *The Compromise*, and 'Wordsworth and the Lakes', review of *Wordsworth's Guide to the Lakes*, intro. Ernest de Selincourt, and Rev. H. D. Rawnsley's *Months at the Lakes*, in *TLS*.

20–3 Writes a story about two young women, 'Phyllis and Rosamond' (*CSF*).

22 Review of Vincent Brown's *Mrs Grundy's Crucifix* in *TLS*.

27 Writes 'A Vision of Greece' (MHP).

July

Early this month, reads Flaubert's correspondence with George Sand (to M. Vaughan).

10 (Tues) Attends wedding of Desmond MacCarthy and Mary Warre-Cornish at Eton.

11 'The Bluest of the Blue', review of Alice Gaussen's *A Woman of Wit and Wisdom*, in the *Guardian*.

13 Review of Winston Churchill's *Coniston* in *TLS*.

22 T. Stephen sells a manuscript of the ballad *Lord Bateman*, written out and illustrated by W. Thackeray, to Pierpoint Morgan for £1000 to pay for Bar expenses and the forthcoming trip to Greece.

25 Review of Adam Lorimer's *The Author's Progress* in *TLS*.

28 'Sweetness – Long Drawn Out', review of Marie Hay's *A German Pompadour*, in *TLS*.

August

2 (Thurs) To Blo' Norton Hall, an Elizabethan manor house in Norfolk, until the end of August; writes 'The Journal of

Mistress Joan Martyn' and 'The Mysterious Case of Miss V.' (*CSF*).

11 'Trafficks and Discoveries', review of Walter Raleigh's *English Voyages of the Sixteenth Century*, in *TLS*.

September

8 (Sat) VW, VB and V. Dickinson leave for Greece, meeting T. and A. Stephen in Olympia on the 13th; they travel to Athens via Corinth, then visit Epidavrus, Tiryns and Mycenae. VW reads Prosper Mérimée's *Lettres à une inconnue* (1873).

October

Early this month, VB is ill for two weeks, stays with V. Dickinson in Athens.

21 (Sun) T. Stephen returns to England; the others go to Constantinople, where VB is again ill; they leave for England on the Orient Express (29th).

November

1 (Thurs) Arrives in London to discover T. Stephen in bed with fever. For the next three weeks VW helps care for both VB and her brother, writes cheerful letters to V. Dickinson – herself ill with typhoid – concealing the fact that T. Stephen is seriously ill.

20 T. Stephen dies of typhoid fever, age 26; for the next month VW continues to write to V. Dickinson, sustaining the pretence that he is alive, so as not to prejudice her recovery.

22 VB agrees to marry CB.

Late this month, reads Christina Rossetti.

December

Early this month, reads Shelley and Swift.

10 (Mon) Plans to send her unpublished manuscripts to W. Headlam, who wants to dedicate his translation of Aeschylus's *Agamemnon* to her.

23 Reads Oliver Elton's *Life* of Frederick York Powell (1906). Learns of death of F. W. Maitland (19th).

25 Reads Ernest Renan's *Cahiers de jeunesse* (1906), Rossetti and Keats.

31 VW and A. Stephen join VB and CB at Cleeve House, the Bells' home near Devizes, Wiltshire; VW begins to accept the

loss of her sister and to appreciate CB (to V. Dickinson, 2 Jan 1907).

1907

EVENTS AND LETTERS. First Cubist exhibition in Paris; Pablo Picasso paints *Les Demoiselles d'Avignon*; R. Kipling awarded Nobel Prize. J. Conrad publishes *The Secret Agent*; EMF, *The Longest Journey*; Edmund Gosse, *Father and Son*; William James, *Pragmatism*; G. B. Shaw, *John Bull's Other Island*; August Strindberg, *The Ghost Sonata*; J. M. Synge, *Playboy of the Western World*; W. B. Yeats, *Deirdre*.

January

Early this month, reads the *Choephori* of Aeschylus.

25 (Fri) VW's twenty-fifth birthday.

February

7 (Thurs) Attends marriage of Clive Bell and Vanessa Stephen at St Pancras Registry Office.

13 '*The Private Papers of Henry Ryecroft* by George Gissing' in the *Guardian*.

(Mid-month) Reads Lucretius's *De Rerum Natura*, and Balzac. House-hunting, finds a house in Fitzroy Square in which G. B. Shaw had lived.

22 Review of Roger Bagot's *Temptation* in *TLS*.

March

23 (Sat) Stays with V. Dickinson while move to 29 Fitzroy Square takes place; CB and VB take over 46 Gordon Square.

28 To Paris with A. Stephen, VB and CB; meets DG.

April

10 (Wed) Returns from Paris to Fitzroy Square.

May

10 (Fri) Review of *Fraulein Schmidt and Mr Anstruther*, by the author of *Elizabeth and her German Garden* (Mary Annette, Countess von Arnim, later Countess Russell), in *TLS*.

24 Review of Marjorie Bowen's *The Glen o'Weeping* in *TLS*.

31 'Philip Sidney', review of *Sir Fulke Greville's Life of Sir Philip Sidney*, intro. Nowell Smith, in *TLS*.

June

3 (Mon) Francis Dodd asks to paint VW; she sits several times between October 1907 and July 1908 (drawing in the National Portrait Gallery).

A. Stephen called to the Bar.

July

26 (Fri) 'Lady Fanshawe's Memoirs', review of *The Memoirs of Ann Lady Fanshawe*, in *TLS*.

August

8 (Thurs) With A. Stephen to Rye, Sussex, until the end of September.

(Mid-month) Continues her literary exercises, including a comic life of V. Dickinson – 'Friendships Gallery' – for Dickinson and Lady Cecil, who figures prominently in the piece (see Hawkes); reads Gustave Flaubert's letters and Thomas Browne's *Christian Morals* (1716); is 'embalmed' in H. James's *The American Scene* (1906) (to Lady Cecil, 16 Aug).

25 Takes tea at the golf club with H. James and George Prothero, historian at King's College, Cambridge, and his wife (see letter to V. Dickinson for a sample of James's notoriously circuitous speech).

September

6 (Fri) Review of Maarten Maartens' *The New Religion* in *TLS*.

27 Returns from Rye to Fitzroy Square.

30 Lectures on Keats at Morley College; '"The poet Keats died when he was 25: and he wrote all his works before that"' (to V. Dickinson, 1 Oct).

October

Early this month, works on her first novel, 'Melymbrosia' (eventually *The Voyage Out*; see *Melymbrosia*, ed. DeSalvo, and DeSalvo, *First Voyage*).

November

Writes frequently to Lady Robert Cecil, discussing plans to write a review section for the *Cornhill* with her.

14 (Thurs) Review of E. V. Lucas's *A Swan and her Friends* in *TLS*.

December

(Mid-month) Visits H. A. L. and Lettice Fisher at Oxford.

19 (Thurs) 'William Allingham', review of *William Allingham: A Diary*, ed. H. Allingham, in *TLS*.

21 'Play Reading Society' formed at 46 Gordon Square, with CB, VB, VW, A. Stephen, LS and S. Sydney-Turner; continues until 24 May 1908.

Late this month, VW resigns from Morley College.

1908

Events and Letters. Ford Madox Hueffer (later Ford) founds the *English Review*. Arnold Bennett publishes *The Old Wives' Tale*; EMF, *A Room with a View*; G. K. Chesterton, *The Man who was Thursday*; Gertrude Stein, *Three Lives*.

January

9 (Thurs) Review of Vernon Lee's *The Sentimental Traveller* in *TLS*.

25 VW's twenty-sixth birthday.

30 'Thomas Hood', review of Walter Jerrold's *Thomas Hood: His Life and Times*, in *TLS*.

February

4 (Tues) Julian Bell is born.

(Mid-month) VW and A. Stephen begin taking German lessons with Miss Daniel.

27 '*The Inward Light*', review of H. Fielding Hall's *The Inward Light*, in *TLS*.

March

5 (Thurs) 'Shelley and Elizabeth Hitchener', review of *Letters from Percy Bysshe Shelley to Elizabeth Hitchener*, intro. Bertram Dobell, in *TLS*.

April

Early this month, reads poems by Mary Coleridge in the *National Review*; thinks them 'slight' (to Lady Cecil, Apr, 14 Aug). Works on review of *The Life and Letters of John Thaddeus Delane*, editor of *The Times*, 1841–77 (Dec), and of William DeMorgan's *Somehow Good* (1908); considers reviewing Lascelles Abercrombie's *Interludes and Poems* (1908).

2 (Thurs) 'Wordsworth Letters', review of *Letters of the Wordsworth Family from 1787 to 1855*, ed. William Knight, in *TLS*.

15 Dreams of her father scorning *VO*.

17 Travels to Cornwall, where she reads Pascal and writes. Begins flirtation with CB when he, VB and the baby arrive on the 24th (cf. Rachel Vinrace and Terence Hewet in *VO*).

May

5 (Tue) Attends performance of Wagner's *Götterdämmerung* with S. Sydney-Turner; has been reading Lamb and Landor, comparing her own prose unfavourably with theirs. Throughout the month VW attends the opera 'almost nightly', writes in the morning, and studies German in the afternoon (by late July she is able, with some assistance, to review a German book).

13 Struggles with her work of 'the Fancy and the Affections', *VO* (to V. Dickinson); receives a copy of her aunt Caroline Stephen's new book, *Light Arising: Thoughts on the Central Radiance* (1908).

June

20 (Sat) W. Headlam dies, age 42; his translation of *The Agamemnon of Aeschylus* is published in 1910.

July

Sits to F. Dodd for her portrait; works on review of *A Week in the White House with Theodore Roosevelt* (Dec); corresponds with George Prothero, editor of the *Quarterly Review*, on the possibility of her writing about Lady Mary Wortley Montagu.

23 (Fri) Review of Lady Charlotte Bury's *The Diary of a Lady in Waiting* in *TLS*.

30 'The Stranger in London', review of Von. A. Rutari's *Londoner Skizzenbuch*, and *Londres comme je l'ai vu, texte et dessins de Ch. Huard*, in *TLS*.

August

1 (Sat) To Wells, Somerset until 17 August. Works on *VO*, now a 100-page manuscript in which there is 'something of a structure', but which she hides when anyone comes into the room (to VB, 7, 12 Aug); searches in graveyards for names for her characters – Rachel is at this point Cynthia, and Clarissa Dalloway, based 'almost verbatim' on Kitty Maxse, is Lettice (to VB, 10 Aug). Reads St Simon, René Bazin's *Les Oberlé* (1901) and LS's poems; proposes articles for the *Cornhill* on *Louise de la Vallière* (Dec) and on E. Raikes's *Dorothea Beale of Cheltenham* (1908), but wonders whether they will call a prostitute a prostitute; determinedly works through G. E. Moore's *Principia Ethica* (1903) at the rate of ten pages nightly. Visits Glastonbury, Cheddar and Bath.

18 To Manorbier, Pembrokeshire. Works on reviews and *VO*; defines her task as an artist: 'I think a great deal of my future, and settle what book I am to write – now I shall re-form the novel and capture multitudes of things at present fugitive, enclose the whole, and shape infinite strange shapes' (to CB, 19 Aug).

28 Orders *Introduction to Astrology* by William Lilly, seventeenth-century astrologer, from the London Library.

29 Finishes Moore's *Principia Ethica*: 'I am not so dumb foundered as I was. . . . He is so humane in spite of his desire to know the truth' (to VB).

September

3 (Thurs) To Italy with the Bells; visits Milan, Pavia, Perugia and Assisi. The static beauty of a Perugino fresco prompts a reflection on her own art: 'He saw it sealed as it were. . . . I attain a different kind of beauty, achieve a symmetry by means of infinite discords . . . some kind of whole made of shivering fragments; to me this seems the natural process; the flight of the mind' (*QB* I). 'Scottish Women', review of Harry Graham's *A Group of Scottish Women*, in *TLS*.

24 To Paris for a week.

October

1 (Thurs) Returns to London. 'Thursday Evenings' begin again; CB comments on *VO* (*QB* I, Appendix D).

22 Review of EMF's *A Room with a View* in *TLS*.

27 Play Reading Society resumes its meetings after a five-month break.
29 'Château and Country Life', review of Mary King Waddington's *Château and Country Life in France*, in *TLS*.

November
12 (Thurs) 'Letters of Christina Rossetti', review of William Rossetti's *The Family Letters of Christina Rossetti*, in *TLS*.
(Mid-month) VW and A. Stephen spend a few days with LS in the Lizard peninsula, Cornwall.
19 Review of Lady Ritchie's *Blackstick Papers* in *TLS*.
20 Reads *Romeo and Juliet*.
24 Struggles with *VO*; pays a brief visit to Lady ('Aunt') Stephen at Godmanchester, Huntingdonshire.

December
3 (Thurs) Review of Mrs Warrenne Blake's *A Vanished Generation* in *TLS*.
(Mid-month) Asks V. Dickinson to give her the *Oxford Book of French Verse*, ed. St John Lucas (1907), for Christmas.
25 Spends Christmas at Fitzroy Square; from CB receives an edition of Byron, 'a poet I have never read, for lack of an edition to read him in' (to CB).
'The Memoirs of Sarah Bernhardt', 'The Memoirs of Lady Dorothy Nevill', '"John Delane"' (review of Arthur Dasent's *The Life and Letters of John Thadeus Delane*) in *Cornhill Magazine* (new ser. 24); reviews of William Hale's *A Week in the White House with Theodore Roosevelt*, J. Lair's *Louise de la Vallière: The Journal of Elizabeth Lady Holland*, ed. the Earl of Ilchester, and Lloyd Sanders' *The Holland House Circle*, in *Cornhill Magazine* (new ser. 25).

1909

Events and Letters. Louis Blériot flies the English Channel; J. M. Synge, Algernon Swinburne, and George Meredith die; André Gide and others found the *Nouvelle revue française*. Harley Granville-Barker publishes *The Voysey Inheritance*; H. G. Wells, *Tono-Bungay*.

January
4 (Mon) Finishes Sophocles' *Ajax*: 'The ancients puzzle me –

they are either so profound or so elementary, and when one has to spell out every word one can't tell which' (to LS). Turns 'hot and cold' on *VO*: 'and all my friends tell me its no good for *me* to write a novel. They say my creatures are all cold blooded' (to V. Dickinson).

7 Review of Pompeo Molmenti's *Venice*, parts 2 and 3, tr. Horatio Brown, in *TLS*.

15 Last meeting of Play Reading Society until its revival, 29 October 1914.

21 'The Genius of Boswell', review of *Letters of James Boswell to the Rev. W. J. Temple*, in *TLS*.

25 VW's twenty-seventh birthday.

From late this month until mid March, takes part in an abortive attempt at creating a novel through imaginary correspondence, with CB, VB, LS, W. Lamb, and Ottoline and Philip Morrell.

February

4 (Thurs) Review of H. Fielding Hall's *One Immortality* in *TLS*.

5 CB comments on seven chapters of *VO*: feels some of the magical quality of the first draft has been sacrificed to give more 'humanity'; praises the writing, but reminds VW the artist should 'create without coming to conclusions'. VW agrees one should not preach, but suggests 'a man, in the present state of the world, is not a very good judge of his sex; and a "creation" may seem to him "didactic"' (*QB* I, Appendix D; to CB, 7 Feb; see also DeSalvo's *First Voyage*).

17 LS proposes marriage, then hastily retracts.

March

2 (Tues) To Cornwall with the Bells for a week.

30 Dines for the first time with Lady O. Morrell, 'who has the head of a Medusa; but she is very simple and innocent in spite of it, and worships the arts' (to M. Vaughan).

April

1 (Thurs) 'More Carlyle Letters', review of *The Love Letters of Thomas Carlyle and Jane Welsh*, ed. Alexander Carlyle, in *TLS*.

7 'The Quaker', aunt Caroline Stephen, dies.

15 Review of Mrs Henry Cust's *Gentleman Errant* in *TLS*.

21 'Caroline Emilia Stephen', obituary, in the *Guardian*.

23 Travels with CB and VB to Florence.

24 '"The Opera"' in *The Times*.

May

9 (Sun) Returns from Italy to Fitzroy Square.

15–17 To Cambridge. H. Young proposes; VW declines, saying she can only marry LS.

18 G. Meredith dies – 'How I wish the Quarterly would ask me to explain him, once and for all!' (to VB). VW attends performance of S. Maugham's *The Explorer*.

June

4 (Fri) 'Absorbed in Michelet' (to LS).

25 Asks LS to lend her Madame de la Fayette's *La Princesse de Clèves* (1678).

July

29 (Thurs) 'A Friend of Johnson', review of Lacy Collison-Morley's *Giuseppe Baretti and his Friends*, in *TLS*.

August

5 (Thurs) To Bayreuth with A. Stephen and S. Sydney-Turner, who are more enthusiastic about opera than VW, then on the 22nd to Dresden; they return on 3 September (to VB, 7–25 Aug). 'Art and Life', review of Vernon Lee's *Laurus Nobilis*, in *TLS*.

12 'Sterne', review of Wilbur Cross's *The Life and Times of Laurence Sterne*, in *TLS*.

21 'Impressions at Bayreuth' in *The Times*.

26 Review of Lewis Townsend's *Oliver Wendell Holmes* in *TLS*.

September

(Mid-month) To Studland, Dorset; rents a cottage near the Bells.

October

2 (Sat) Returns from Studland to Fitzroy Square.

November

10 (Wed) The *Cornhill* rejects 'Memoirs of a Novelist' (*CSF*), VW's review of an imaginary memoir, her first attempt to combine criticism and fiction.

25 'A Cookery Book', review of *The Cookery Book of Lady Clark of Tillypronie*, ed. Catherine Frere, in *TLS*.
27 Spends the weekend with the Darwins at Cambridge; attends performance of Aristophanes' *The Wasps*.

December
2 (Thurs) 'Sheridan', review of Walter Sichel's *The Life of Richard Brinsley Sheridan*, in *TLS*.
9 'Maria Edgeworth and her Circle', review of Constance Hill's *Maria Edgeworth and her Circle in the Days of Buonaparte and Bourbon*, in *TLS*.
24–8 Spends Christmas alone at Lelant, Cornwall; reads R. Bazin's *La Terre qui meurt* (1899).
30 Review of Frank Mumby's *The Girlhood of Queen Elizabeth* in *TLS*.

1910

Events and Letters. Edward VII dies, George V succeeds; Mark Twain, Leo Tolstoy and Florence Nightingale die; RF organises London's first Post-Impressionist exhibition. A. Bennett publishes *Clayhanger*; EMF, *Howard's End*; Bertrand Russell and Alfred North Whitehead, *Principia Mathematica* I; Rainer Maria Rilke, *The Notebook of Malte Laurids Brigge*.

January
1 (Sat) VW volunteers to work for Women's Suffrage (to J. Case).
20 Review of Mrs Charles Roundell's *Lady Hester Stanhope* in *TLS*.
25 VW's twenty-eighth birthday.

February
10 (Thurs) Participates in 'The Dreadnought Hoax', organised by Horace Cole: VW, A. Stephen, DG, Guy Ridley and Anthony Buxton tour HMS *Dreadnought* disguised as the Emperor of Abyssinia and his entourage. The story is subsequently leaked by Cole to the press, and the issue raised in Parliament (see A. Stephen, *The Dreadnought Hoax* [Hogarth, Nov 1936], and VW's 'A Society', *MT*).
24 Review of *Modes and Manners of the Nineteenth Century*, tr. M. Edwardes, intro. Grace Rhys, in *TLS*.

March

3 (Thurs) 'Emerson's Journals', review of *Journals of Ralph Waldo Emerson*, ed. E. W. Emerson and W. Emerson Forbes, in *TLS*.

5–10 To Cornwall with the Bells. VW falls ill on her return.

26 To Studland for three weeks' rest.

April

16 (Sat) Returns to Fitzroy Square. Her health remains uncertain for the rest of the summer.

May

1 (Sun) Olive Ilbert, H. Young's sister-in-law, visits; thinks VW's interest in Adult Suffrage indicates she is reconsidering Young's proposal.

June

14 (Tues) On Dr George Savage's advice VW joins the Bells at Blean, near Canterbury, for a holiday.

28 VW's depression continues; on Dr Savage's recommendation she undergoes a rest cure at Miss Jean Thomas's private nursing home, Twickenham, Middlesex, until mid August.

July

28 (Thurs) Writes VB a long letter on life at the nursing home, concluding, 'I feel my brains, like a pear, to see if its ripe; it will be exquisite by September.'

August

16 (Tues) Takes a two-week walking tour in Cornwall with Miss Thomas.

19 Quentin Bell is born.

September

6 (Tues) Returns to Fitzroy Square.

10 Travels to Studland with S. Sydney-Turner to join CB, VB and their children; visitors include the MacCarthys, Sydney and Alice Waterlow, Marjorie Strachey and H. T. J. Norton.

29 'Mrs Gaskell', review of Mrs Ellis Chadwick's *Mrs Gaskell: Haunts, Homes and Stories*, in *TLS*.

October

10 (Mon) Returns to Fitzroy Square.

15–18 Stays at Court Place, Iffley, Oxford, with the Pearsall Smiths and the Costelloes.

November

8 (Tues) First Post-Impressionist exhibition, 'Manet and the Post-Impressionists', organised by RF, opens at the Grafton Galleries to great public indignation (to V. Dickinson, 27 Nov).

(Mid-month) Visits the Cornishes at Eton, resumes work on *VO* and, less enthusiastically, on Women's Suffrage (to V. Dickinson, 14 Nov).

27 'Seething with fragments of love, morals, ethics, comedy tragedy, and so on' that she pours every morning into a manuscript book (to V. Dickinson).

December

24 (Sat) To Lewes, Sussex, for a week. Finds a house to rent in Firle, near Lewes, which she names Little Talland House in memory of her summers at St Ives.

29 Reads *The Letters of Edward John Trelawny*, ed. H. B. Forman; finds his imagination 'very watery' and his strength that of 'a man of action, whose brain is a simple machine divorced from his body' (to CB).

1911

EVENTS AND LETTERS. Ernest Rutherford introduces revolutionary model of the atom; Winston Churchill appointed First Lord of the Admiralty; copyright in England extended to fifty years from author's death. Max Beerbohm publishes *Zuleika Dobson*; Rupert Brooke, *Poems*; J. Conrad, *Under Western Eyes*; D. H. Lawrence, *The White Peacock*; Katherine Mansfield, *In a German Pension*; Ezra Pound, *Canzoni*; J. M. Synge, *Deirdre of the Sorrows* (posth.); Sidney and Beatrice Webb, *Poverty*.

January

1 (Sun) Returns to London from Lewes. During January begins to furnish Little Talland House.

19–23 Stays at Court Place, Iffley, and Bagley Wood, near Oxford, with Rachel and Karin Costelloe and M. Strachey; meets Katherine Cox.

25 VW's twenty-ninth birthday.

February

2 (Thurs) 'The Duke and Duchess of Newcastle-upon-Tyne', review of *The First Duke and Duchess of Newcastle-upon Tyne*, by the author of *A Life of Sir Kenelm Digby* (Thomas Longueville), in *TLS*.

4–6 VW and VB complete the furnishing of Little Talland House.

March

Reads George Santayana; attends Post-Impressionist Ball as a savage *à la* Gauguin; meets French painter Jacques Raverat.

April

8 (Sat) At Firle; reads Pierre Choderlos de Laclos's *Les Liaisons dangereuses* (1782) and Wordsworth's *Prelude* (1850). Guests this month include Rachel Costelloe (later Strachey), K. Cox (later Arnold-Forster) and Elinor Darwin.

18 Revising *VO*: 'Yesterday I finished the 8th Chapter of Mel[ym-brosia]: which brings them within sight of the South American shore' (to CB; DeSalvo suggests this is the third draft).

20 'Rachel', review of Francis Gribble's *Rachel: Her Stage Life and her Real Life*, in *TLS*.

22 Sets out for Broussa, Turkey, where VB, travelling with CB, RF and H. T. J. Norton, has fallen ill.

29 With the Bells and RF returns to London on the Orient Express.

May

27 (Sat) Travels to Cambridge for the wedding of Jacques Raverat and Gwen Darwin.

June

8 (Thurs) Depressed: 'To be 29 and unmarried – to be a failure – childless – insane too, no writer' (to VB).

July

3 (Mon) LW, on leave from Ceylon, dines with the Bells; VW, DG, and W. Lamb come afterwards.

20 W. Lamb proposes marriage; VW suggests friendship (to VB, 21 July).
29 Thanks Sidney Lee for his *Principles of Biography* (1911) (to S. Lee).

August
12 (Sat) Spends the weekend with P. and O. Morrell at Peppard Common, Oxfordshire.
14–19 Stays at the Old Vicarage, Grantchester, Cambridgeshire, with R. Brooke.
27 With K. Cox camps in Devon with JMK, R. Brooke and other 'Neo-Pagans'.

September
16 (Sat) LW and M. Strachey spend the weekend with VW at Firle.
19–27 At Studland with the Bells, LS and RF.

October
(Mid) Engages in negotiations over two new houses: Asham House, Beddingham, near Firle, and 38 Brunswick Square, London. Her friendship with V. Dickinson, who disapproves of VW's plan to live with DG and JMK, as well as with A. Stephen, has become more distant, and VW sees LW often.
21 (Sat) Attends performance of the *Ring* cycle at Covent Garden.

November
6 (Mon) Visits Francis Cornford and wife Frances (*née* Darwin).
7 Attends performance of the Diaghilev ballet.
20 Moves into 38 Brunswick Square, with A. Stephen, JMK and DG.

December
4 (Mon) LW moves into 38 Brunswick Square (see letter to LW, 2 Dec, for a list of house rules and dining hours).
9 Writes to S. Waterlow, emphasising her refusal of his offer of marriage.
23 Asks S. Sydney-Turner for Alfred Zimmern's *The Greek Commonwealth* (1911).

1912

Events and Letters. The *Titanic* sinks; A. Strindberg dies; *Poetry: A Magazine of Verse* founded in Chicago; *Georgian Poetry*, ed. Edward Marsh, begins publication, J. Conrad publishes *'Twixt Land and Sea*; Carl Jung, *The Theory of Psychoanalysis*; Walter de la Mare, *The Listeners and Other Poems*; J. M. Synge, *The Playboy of the Western World* (posth.).

January

11 (Thurs) LW proposes; VW hesitates. 'The Novels of George Gissing', review of G. Gissing's *The Odd Women, Eve's Ransom, The Whirlpool, The Unclassed, The Emancipated, In the Year of Jubilee, Denzil Quarrier* and *Human Odds and Ends*, in *TLS*.

16–19 To Isle of Wight to stay with VB; on return to London VW suffers another attack of mental illness and is forced to spend several days in bed.

25 VW's thirtieth birthday.

February

3 (Sat) Gives housewarming party at Asham, with A. Stephen, M. Strachey and LW.

9–12 Attends Bell's housewarming party at Asham, with VW, A. Stephen, DG, RF and LW.

14 LW, who must resign or return to Ceylon, and hoping to convince VW to marry him, asks the Colonial Office to extend his leave for four months.

16 On the advice of Dr Savage, VW enters J. Thomas's nursing home for a third time.

28 To Asham for further rest.

March

9 (Sat) Sees Dr Maurice Wright, a psychologist, whom LW had himself consulted regarding his trembling hands.

Spends three weekends at Asham, one with VB, one with K. Cox, and one with VB, A. Stephen, LW, RF and M. Strachey.

April

15 (Mon) Sinking of the *Titanic*.

VW spends most of her time at Asham. Visitors include R. Brooke,

Brynhild Olivier (daughter of Sir Sidney Olivier, Governor of Jamaica), W. Lamb, LW and K. Cox.

May

1 (Wed) Writes to LW explaining her ambivalent feelings for him; he finds the letter sufficiently encouraging for him to resign from the Colonial Service.

2 VW returns to Brunswick Square.

3 With LW attends inquiry into the sinking of the *Titanic*.

(Mid-month) Every morning writes 500 words of *VO* and has five chapters left (to V. Dickinson, 22 May). Exchanges visits with D. MacCarthy, O. Morrell, EMF, H. O. Meredith, and Norwegian novelist Johan Bojer, among others.

29 Agrees to marry LW.

June

4 (Tues) Feels *VO* is 'just upon finished' (to V. Dickinson, but see 21 Dec); spends the rest of June and July introducing LW to her family and friends, and meeting his family.

August

10 (Sat) Leonard Woolf and Virginia Stephen marry at St Pancras Registry Office; both have finished writing their first novels, *The Village in the Jungle* and *VO* (although VW will make extensive revisions to hers).

18 The Woolfs leave on their honeymoon for six weeks in Provence, Spain and Italy. In Tarragona, Spain (1 Sep), reading Dostoevsky's *Crime and Punishment* (1866), VW is convinced he is the greatest author ever born (to LS); LW reads A. Bennett's *Old Wives' Tale* (1908). In Saragossa (4 Sep) VW continues *Crime and Punishment*, and has already read Sir Walter Scott's *The Antiquary* (1816), Charlotte Yonge's *The Heir of Redclyffe* (1853) and two new novels – D. H. Lawrence's *The Trespassers* and Emily Hilda Young's *Yonder*; LW works on his second novel, *The Wise Virgins* (pub. 1914). In Pisa, Italy (17 Sep) VW presses on with *Crime and Punishment* and reads Stendhal's *Le Rouge et le Noir* (1830), finding the latter a little heavy; by Venice (28 Sep) VW has finished Thackeray's *Pendennis* (1849–50). (*L*, 1–28 Sep.)

October

3 (Thurs) The Woolfs return to Brunswick Square.

8 LW starts work as secretary to the second Post-Impressionist exhibition at the Grafton Galleries.

Late this month, the Woolfs move to rooms at Clifford's Inn.

November

28 (Thurs) 'Frances Willard', review of Ray (Rachel) Strachey's *Frances Willard: Her Life and Work*, in *TLS*.

December

VW unwell with headaches, LW with malaria.

21 (Sat) Begins rewriting the middle section of *VO*, the chapters leading up to Rachel's death.

24 Spends Christmas at Asham; reads Thomas Hardy's *The Return of the Native* (1878).

1913

Events and Letters. Suffragette demonstrations in London; S. and B. Webb found the *New Statesman*; Igor Stravinsky outrages Paris with *Le Sacre du printemps*; Niels Bohr revises Max Planck's quantum theory of energy. Sigmund Freud publishes *Totem and Taboo*; Edmund Husserl, *Phenomenology*; B. Russell and A. N. Whitehead, *Principia Mathematica*; D. H. Lawrence, *Sons and Lovers*; Thomas Mann, *Death in Venice*; Marcel Proust, *Du côté de chez Swann*.

January

VW sleeping badly, suffering from headache; LW consults doctors as to the wisdom of VW having a child, and on the 13th begins to keep a daily record of her health.

25 (Sat) VW's thirty-first birthday; travels to Studland for her health.

February

1 (Sat) Returns to London.

March

9 (Sun) *VO* delivered to Gerald Duckworth. VW goes to Liver-

pool, Manchester, Leeds, York, Carlisle and Leicester with LW, who is studying the Co-operative movement.

19 Returns to London, then travels to Asham for Easter with A. Stephen and S. Sydney-Turner.

April

1 (Tues) At Asham with M. Strachey and S. Sydney-Turner for ten days.

12 *VO* accepted for publication by Duckworth; LW works on *The Wise Virgins* and a history of the Co-operative movement (*Co-operation and the Future of Industry*, pub. 1919).

25 VW notes the Morrells have bought a new house: Garsington Manor, Oxfordshire, which becomes noted for its gatherings of artists and intellectuals.

May

1 (Thurs) 'Chinese Stories', review of *Strange Stories from the Lodge of Leisures*, tr. George Soulié, in *TLS*.

16 To Asham until 2 June; visitors include D. MacCarthy, LS and J. Case.

June

9 (Mon) To Newcastle-upon-Tyne to attend Women's Co-operative Congress, returning to London with Margaret Llewelyn Davies, who has become a good friend of LW's; VW is unwell.

19 At Asham until 7 July; guests include Olivier and Ray Strachey, H. T. J. Norton, EMF, LS and M. MacCarthy.

July

12 (Sat) Lunches with B. and S. Webb.

16–21 At Asham, increasingly unwell; LS visits.

22 To Keswick for Fabian Society Congress; VW very ill.

24 After consultation with Dr Savage, enters the nursing home at Twickenham.

August

11 (Mon) Leaves nursing home for Asham.

22 LW takes VW to London to see Drs Savage and Henry Head (on the subject of VW's mental illness, see Poole, Spater and Parsons, and Trombley, as well as *QB*).

23 To Holford, VW's delusions and resistance to food increase.

September

2 (Tues) In response to LW's telegram, K. Cox joins them at Holford.

8 All return to London.

9 VW sees Drs Wright and Head, in the evening attempts suicide by taking an overdose of veronal; Dr Head is called, but Dr Geoffrey Keynes (JMK's brother), happening by first, races to the hospital for a stomach pump, and spends the rest of the night washing out the drug. Next day VW remains unconscious but out of danger.

20 Taken to Dalingridge Place, Sussex, where she remains until mid November under the care of LW and two nurses.

November

18 (Tues) Judged well enough to be moved to Asham, still under the care of the nurses.

December

3 (Wed) LW arranges to vacate their rooms at Clifford's Inn. The Woolfs spend until next August at Asham, VW slowly recovering.

1914

Events and Letters. The First World War begins; Wyndham Lewis founds Vorticist movement, *Blast* begins publication; the *Egoist* under E. Pound begins publication. J. Conrad publishes *Chance*; James Joyce, *Dubliners*; *Des Imagistes*, ed. E. Pound; LW, *The Wise Virgins*.

January

VW able to see friends, walk on the Downs, and to type LS's story 'Ermyntrude and Esmeralda'.

25 (Sun) VW's thirty-second birthday.

February

16 (Mon) VW's last nurse leaves.

March

7 (Sat) K. Cox, J. Case and VB take turns until the 18th at staying

with VW at Asham while LW, suffering from severe headaches, takes a holiday. VW makes notes on manuals on the Co-operative movement for LW, and reads CB's *Art* (1914), in which he articulates his theory of 'significant form'; thinks it 'good – anyhow very clear and brisk' (to LW).

April

6 (Mon) The Woolfs travel to London to consult Dr Maurice Craig, who agrees that VW is well enough for a vacation.

8–30 Holidays in the St Ives district of Cornwall.

May

1 (Fri) Returns to Asham, where she and LW remain all summer. LW reads S. Freud's *Interpretation of Dreams* (1900), preparing to review his *Psychopathology of Everyday Life* (1904).

June

16 (Tues) LW attends Women's Co-operative Guild meeting for two days in Birmingham; draws up a treaty which VW signs, agreeing to take proper care of herself.

28 Archduke Ferdinand assassinated in Sarajevo.

August

4 (Tues) Britain declares war on Germany. Asham is 'practically under martial law', with soldiers digging trenches, and all the civilians expecting an invasion (to K. Cox, 12 Aug).

6 The Woolfs go to Northumberland until 15 September; VW is impressed by the country, and by the people, who 'discuss Thompson's poetry, and post impressionism, and have read everything' (to K. Cox, 12 Aug).

September

(Mid-month) House-hunting in London.

October

The Woolfs move into lodgings in Twickenham and then in Richmond, at 17 The Green, and look for a house in the same area; LW's *The Wise Virgins: A Story of Words, Opinions, and a Few Emotions* is published by Edward Arnold, but VW does not read it until January 1915. By the middle of the month, VW has improved sufficiently for LW to discontinue his daily record of her condition.

29 (Thurs) Play Reading Society revived (see Jan 1909).

November
Visits friends and attends cookery classes.

December
9 (Wed) Asks CB to lend her Jules Michlet's *L'Histoire de France* (1833–43); advises M. L. Davies to publish *Maternity: Letters from Working Women* (to CB, and to M. K. Davies).
10 Reads T. Hardy's new volume of poems, *Satires of Circumstance* ('They're quite the most beautiful things I've read since . . . Meredith') and A. Bennett's new novel, *Price of Love* (to J. Case; see also to T. Hardy, 17 Jan 1915).
25 Spends Christmas near Marlborough, Wiltshire, with LS.
Late this month, the Woolfs discover Hogarth House.

1915

EVENTS AND LETTERS. First Zeppelin attack on London; R. Brooke dies. A. Einstein publishes *General Theory of Relativity*; R. Brooke, *1914 and Other Poems*; J. Conrad, *Victory*; Ford Madox Ford, *The Good Soldier*; D. H. Lawrence, *The Rainbow*; S. Maugham, *Of Human Bondage*; G. Stein, *Tender Buttons*; VW, *The Voyage Out*.

January
1 (Fri) VW begins to keep a diary.
Early this month, reads LS's 'Cardinal Manning'; is enthusiastic and commands him to complete 'a whole series' (to LS; he is already at work on 'Florence Nightingale', essays on Dr Arnold and General Gordon follow, and in 1918 the four are published as *Eminent Victorians*).
2 Works on 'poor Effie's story' (*D*).
6 Reading J. Michlet's *Histoire* (see 9 Dec 1914), and Dostoevsky's *The Idiot*, tr. Constance Garnett (1913); finds a likeness between Dostoevsky and W. Scott, but 'Scott merely made superb ordinary people, & D. creates wonders, with very subtle brains, & fearful sufferings' (*D*, 19 Jan).
7 Attends lecture by John Atkinson Hobson, supporter of Women's Suffrage.
18–21 Reads Alexander Pope's *The Rape of the Lock* (1714) –

'supreme' – the *Essay on Criticism* (1711) and the *Epistle to Dr Arbuthnot* (1735), as well as a life of Victorian actress Fanny Kemble and 'Gilbert Murray on Immortality' (*D*; possibly *Four Stages of Greek Religion*, 1912).

20 JMK, now working in the Treasury, dines; predicts Britain and its allies will win the war, '& in great style too' (*D*).

22 Attends meeting of Fabian Society; 'the idea that these frail webspinners can affect the destiny of nations seems to me fantastic' but 'I have now declared myself a Fabian' (*D*, 23 Jan).

25 VW's thirty-third birthday; reads her father on Pope (the biography, 1880, or the essay 'Pope as a Moralist', 1892); LW gives her a 3-vol. first edition of W. Scott's *The Abbot* (1820). They decide to take Hogarth House and to buy a printing press.

27 Visits J. Case; talks about her novel, which she predicts everyone will privately condemn (*D*).

31 Reads LW's *The Wise Virgins* (1914): 'a remarkable book; very bad in parts; first rate in others' (*D*).

February

14 (Sun) Reading 'a later volume' of Michlet's *Histoire*.

15 Writes in diary for the last time until August 1917.

18 Suffering from headaches and sleeping badly, the early stages of another breakdown.

22 Writes to M. L. Davies to ask for W. Morris's essay 'The Pilgrims of Hope' (1885).

23 Becomes incoherent; attack lasts two days.

March

4 (Thurs) Becomes violent; nurses called in.

25 Taken to nursing home while LW organises the move to Hogarth House. The next day VW's first novel, *The Voyage Out*, already postponed from 1913 because of her mental illness, is published to appreciative reviews: the *TLS* finds the sudden death of Rachel illogical, but 'so intense that one is desolated by a sense of the futility of life and forgets the failure of design' (*M&M*).

April

1 (Thurs) Brought to Hogarth House with four nurses. April and May are the most violent months.

23 R. Brooke dies of blood poisoning in Scyros, Greece, age 27 (see to K. Cox, 12 Jan 1916).

June

VW's condition gradually improves.

August

31 (Tues) Allowed only to write postcards, to M. L. Davies notes EMF has visited, and that he cannot get on with his novel (*A Passage to India*, probably begun summer 1913; abandoned for *Maurice*, Sep 1913–June 1914; pub. 1924).

September

11 (Sat) Moves to Asham with LW and one nurse.

30 Reading Latin and French.

October

14 (Thurs) Reads J. Conrad's *Victory*, 'with distant admiration'; bored by Mrs Gaskell's *Sylvia's Lovers* (1863): 'What I object to in the mid Victorians is their instinctive fluency – as if Mrs G. sat down to her writing with the cat on her knee' (to Lady Cecil).

22 Reading H. James, finding nothing but 'faintly tinged rose water', unlike Dostoevsky's *The Insulted and the Injured* (1861), which sweeps her away (to LS).

November

2 (Tues) Gerald Shove and wife Fredegond (*née* Maitland, VW's cousin) visit; he is editor of *War and Peace*, she is writing poetry. VW finds them both 'very young and incompetent' and cannot persuade her to join the Co-op stores (to M. Davies).

4 Returns to Hogarth House.

14 Recovering, weighs '12 stones' (168 lbs); becomes conscious of the war, worries about Zeppelin attacks on London because of VB and friends in Bloomsbury, though she and LW feel safe in Richmond (nevertheless, on 14 Feb 1916 an explosion

knocks two trees over onto their house; see letter to S. Sydney-Turner).

December

22 (Wed) Spends Christmas at Asham; J. Strachey and N. Olivier are guests. VW reads and criticises RF's translations of poems by Pierre-Jean Jouve (from *Vous êtes hommes,* pub. Omega as *Men of Europe,* Feb 1916); LW reads aloud from D. H. Lawrence's *Love Poems and Others* (1913) (to RF, 26 Dec).

1916

EVENTS AND LETTERS. Dada launched in Zurich with Cabaret Voltaire; H. James dies. J. Joyce publishes *Portrait of the Artist as a Young Man;* G. B. Shaw, *Androcles and the Lion, Pygmalion;* H. G. Wells, *Mr Britling Sees It Through.*

January

13 (Thurs) 'Queen Adelaide', review of Mary Sandars' *The Life and Times of Queen Adelaide,* in *TLS.*

23 Reads Thomas Carlyle's *Past and Present* (1843); questions whether 'all his rant has made a scrap of difference practically'. Notes she is becoming 'steadily more feminist', wonders how 'this preposterous masculine fiction [the war] keeps going a day longer – without some vigorous young woman pulling us together and marching through it' (to M. L. Davies).

25 VW's thirty-fourth birthday.

February

1 (Tues) Nelly Boxall and Lottie Hope, servants who remain with the Woolfs for many years, arrive.

(Mid-month) Studies Italian, makes occasional trips into London, sees Lady Cecil, R. C. Trevelyan, S. Sydney-Turner, the Waterlows and others. RF stays with the Woolfs while restoring the Mantegna paintings, *Triumphs of Caesar,* at Hampton Court.

17 '"A Scribbling Dame"', review of George Whicher's *The Life and Romances of Mrs Eliza Haywood,* in *TLS.*

18 Reads W. M. Strutt's *The Reminiscences of a Musical Amateur,* ed. by his mother, Lady Raleigh (1915); A. Bennett (possibly *These Twain,* 1916); Viola Meynell (either *Columbine,* 1915, or

Narcissus, 1916); and C. K. Shorter's *The Brontës: Lives and Letters* (1908) for the article she is writing on Charlotte Brontë (13 Apr).

28 H. James dies (to K. Cox, 19 Mar).

March

VB travels to Suffolk and DG and David Garnett (son of translator Constance Garnett, and publisher's reader Edward Garnett) who take up fruit-farming in order to strengthen their case for exemption from military service; VW notes 'Bloomsbury is vanished like the morning mist' (to K. Cox, 19 Mar).

26 (Sun) LS visits, jubilant at having been exempted from military service on medical grounds.

April

13 (Thurs) 'Charlotte Brontë' in *TLS*.

18 To Asham; LS and lawyer Charles Sanger are guests for Easter.

21 LS visits; reads his essay on Florence Nightingale (which becomes part of *Eminent Victorians*, 1918).

May

Early this month, DG and D. Garnett appear before a local tribunal in Suffolk to try to obtain military exemption as conscientious objectors; VW writes on behalf of DG to Lord Salisbury of the Central Tribunal, and writes to VB trying to persuade her to move to Charleston, a farm near Asham. Mary MacCarthy visits, works on her novel, *A Pier and a Band* (pub. 1918).

26 (Fri) Asks V. Dickinson for a copy of *Miss Eden's Letters* (the letters of her great aunt, pub. 1919).

30 LW exempted from military service because of his trembling hands.

June

17 (Sat) Spends the weekend with S. and B. Webb in Sussex; G. B. Shaw, a fellow guest, tells 'interminable stories about himself' (to K. Cox, 25 June; to VB, 28 June).

29 Review of Canon Rawnsley's *Past and Present at the English Lakes* in *TLS*.

Late this month, meets Alix Sargant-Florence, later wife of J. Strachey (and for one day in Oct 1917 assistant at the Hogarth Press), for the first time.

July

7 (Fri) To Asham until mid September.

20 'A Man with a View', review of John Harris's *Samuel Butler: Author of 'Erewhon', the Man and his Work*, in *TLS*.

21–4 Visits VB and DG in Suffolk, begins thinking of a new novel: *N&D*, in which VB is the model for Katharine Hilbery (to VB, 30 July).

25 Asks LS to arrange a meeting with Katherine Mansfield, whom he has just met at Garsington and who praised *VO* (Mansfield and John Middleton Murry dine with the Woolfs 17 Jan 1917; the first meeting probably takes place toward the end of 1916).

August

10 (Thurs) Reads eighteenth-century Italian dramatist Carlo Gozzi in Italian.

15 'Heard on the Downs: The Genesis of Myth' in *The Times*.

15–19 Pernel Strachey and G. E. Moore visit at Asham; Moore sings to them every night, and strikes VW as 'much more human than his followers' (to VB, 25 Aug; to S. Sydney-Turner, 30 Sep). Subsequent guests include A. and K. Stephen, A. Sargant-Florence, J. Strachey, R. C. Trevelyan, the Waterlows, and RF.

31 Review of Elinor Mordaunt's *The Park Wall* in *TLS*.

September

10 (Sun) Supports RF's plans for a club, which comes into being in early 1917, meeting once a week at the Omega Workshops.

16 Returns to Richmond.

18 To Cornwall for two weeks, with M. L. Davies and her friend Lilian Harris, assistant-secretary (Davies is general secretary) of the Women's Co-operative Guild.

October

2 (Mon) Returns to Richmond.

12 '"The Fighting Nineties"', review of Elizabeth Robins Pennell's *Nights*, in *TLS*.

17 Lectures to Richmond branch of Women's Co-operative Guild; for the next four years VW organises speakers and holds monthly meetings at Hogarth House.

19 Dora Carrington, who has been working on the Mantegna paintings at Hampton Court with RF, to dinner; explains why

she, Barbara Hiles and D. Garnett broke into Asham earlier in the month; Garnett sends poems in apology.

20–4 At Asham; VB and DG have moved to Charleston.

November

2 (Thurs) 'Among the Poets', review of the Hon. Stephen Coleridge's *An Evening in my Library among English Poets*, in *TLS*.

9 Review of E. V. Lucas's *London Revisited* in *TLS*.

23 'In a Library', review of W. H. Hudson's *A Quiet Corner in a Library*, in *TLS*.

24 Invites B. Hiles, whom Nicholas Bagenal and S. Sydney-Turner are both hoping to marry, to dinner; VW becomes involved in the latter's courtship (see letters to B. Hiles, S. Sydney-Turner and DG through Nov and Dec).

27 Reading G. Cannan's new novel, *Mendel*, in which the main character is based on painter Mark Gertler, who is in love with D. Carrington.

30 'Hours in a Library' in *TLS*.

December

5 (Tues) Prime Minister Asquith resigns; Lloyd George succeeds.

14 'Old and Young', review of Stephen Paget's *I Sometimes Think: Essays for the Young People*, in *TLS*.

21 To Asham for Christmas; on Dr Craig's orders VW rests and tries to put on weight. 'Social Life in England', review of F. J. Foakes Jackson's *Social Life in England, 1750–1850*, and 'Mr Symons's Essays', review of Arthur Symons' *Figures of Several Centuries*, in *TLS*.

24–9 K. Cox visits; DG and JMK drop in ('Maynard thinks that we may be on the verge of ruin, and thus of peace'). VW finishes B. Russell's *Principles of Social Reconstruction* – 'this sort of lecturing does me no good' (to M. L. Davies, 29 Dec).

1917

Events and Letters. Bolshevik Revolution in Russia; T. E. Hulme and Edward Thomas die. S. Freud publishes *Introduction to Psychology*; Carl Jung, *Psychology of the Unconscious*; Norman Douglas, *South Wind*; TSE, *Prufrock and Other Observations*; Siegfried Sassoon,

The Old Huntsman; E. Thomas, *Poems*; W. B. Yeats, *The Wild Swans at Coole*.

January

16 (Tues) Attends Beethoven concert at the Wigmore Hall.
18 'Romance', review of Sir W. Raleigh's *Romance: Two Lectures*, in *TLS*.
23 Holds meeting of Women's Co-operative Guild; is astonished that her audience is outraged by her speaker, who lectures on venereal diseases (to M. L. Davies, 24 and 26 Jan).
25 VW's thirty-fifth birthday.

February

1 (Thurs) 'Tolstoy's *The Cossacks*', review of Tolstoy's *The Cossacks and Other Tales of the Caucasus*, tr. Louise and Aylmer Maude, in *TLS*.
3 Excited by reading Aeschylus in French (finds it better than in English), wakes LW in the night to look for Zeppelins; 'He then applied the Freud system to my mind, and analysed it down to Clytemnestra and the watch fires, which so pleased him that he forgave me' (to S. Sydney-Turner).
8 'Melodius Meditations', review of Henry Sedgwick's *An Apology for Old Maids*, in *TLS*.
22 'More Dostoevsky', review of Dostoevsky's *The Eternal Husband and Other Stories*, tr. C. Garnett, in *TLS*.

March

1 (Thurs) Review of E. Mordaunt's *Before Midnight* in *TLS*.
6 Works on *N&D*; VB has become a 'Shakespeare character' in her mind (to DG).
8 'Parodies', review of J. C. Squire's *Tricks of the Trade*, in *TLS*.
15 'Sir Walter Raleigh', review of *Sir Walter Raleigh: Selections from his 'Historie of the World', his Letters & c.*, ed. G. E. Hadow, in *TLS*.
23 The Woolfs order a printing press.
29 'The House of Lyme', review of Lady Newton's *The House of Lyme from its Foundation to the End of the Eighteenth Century*, in *TLS*.

April

3 (Tues) To Asham for Easter; C. P. Sanger and M. Strachey

visit. Reads J. Conrad's *The Shadow-Line* (1917): 'very beautiful and very calm. I wish I knew how he gets his effect of space' (to Lady Cecil, 14 Apr).

5 Review of Caroline Ticknor's *Poe's Helen* in *TLS*.

12 Review of Coulson Kernahan's *In Good Company*, and 'A Talker', review of Edgar Lee Masters' *The Great Valley*, in *TLS*.

24 Printing press delivered to Hogarth House: 'I see that real printing will devour one's entire life' (to VB, 26 Apr).

May

10 (Thurs) 'A Cambridge V. A. D.', review of E. M. Spearing's *From Cambridge to Camiers under the Red Cross*, in *TLS*.

22 Begins printing LW's story 'Three Jews' (see July).

24 'The Perfect Language', review of *The Greek Anthology*, tr. W. R. Paton, vol. II, in *TLS*.

31 'Mr Sassoon's Poems', review of Siegfried Sassoon's *The Old Huntsman and Other Poems*, in *TLS*.

June

5 (Tues) At O. Morrell's urging reads Aldous Huxley's story 'The Wheel', in the *Palatine Review*, a literary magazine founded by him while he was at Oxford.

7 'Creative Criticism', review of J. E. Spingarn's *Creative Criticism: Essays on the Unity of Genius and Taste*, in *TLS*.

14 Review of N. Douglas's *South Wind* in *TLS*.

26 Talks with K. Mansfield: 'She seems to have gone every sort of hog since she was 17', and she 'has a much better idea of writing than most' (to VB, 27 June).

July

5 (Thurs) Review of A. Bennett's *Books and Persons* in *TLS*.

12 'Thoreau' in *TLS*.

24 Reading J. Joyce's *A Portrait of the Artist as a Young Man* (1916), 'beaten by the unutterable boredom' (to CB).

26 Review of J. Conrad's *Lord Jim* in *TLS*.

29 K. Mansfield to dinner.

First publication of the Hogarth Press: *Two Stories* ('The Mark on the Wall' by VW and 'Three Jews' by LW), with woodcuts by D. Carrington.

August

3 (Fri) To Asham for two months. VW begins to keep a brief diary, notes German prisoners working in the fields and aeroplanes passing overhead; guests include Goldsworthy Lowes Dickinson, LS, B. Hiles and H. Bagenal, P. Morrell, S. Waterlow, D. MacCarthy, K. Mansfield, D. Garnett and his father Edward, the reader for Duckworth's who had recommended *VO* for publication.

16 'John Davidson', review of Hayim Fineman's *John Davidson: A Study of the Relation of his Ideas to his Poetry*, in *TLS*.

30 'Mr Galsworthy's Novel', review of John Galsworthy's *Beyond*, in *TLS*.

September

4 (Thurs) 'To Read or not to Read', review of Viscount Harberton's *How to Lengthen our Ears*, in *TLS*.

18 Resists S. Sydney-Turner's advice to read H. James's *The Sense of the Past* (1917): 'My old image must still hold good . . . the laborious striking of whole boxfulls of damp matches' (to S. Sydney-Turner).

20 'Mr Conrad's *Youth*', review of J. Conrad's *Youth*, in *TLS*.

October

5 (Fri) Returns to Richmond from Asham. Air raids become frequent between now and the end of the year, depending on the weather and the phase of the moon.

8 VW begins regularly keeping a diary; E. Vaughan gives bookbinding equipment to VW.

9 Works on setting type for K. Mansfield's story *Prelude*.

10 K. Mansfield to dinner; VW is shocked by her commonness (she stinks like a 'civet cat that had taken to street walking') but impressed by her illuminating remarks on H. James (*D*, 11 Oct). 1917 Club founded by Ramsay MacDonald and others, including LW; named after the February Revolution in Russia, and located in Soho, it consists partly of left-wing politicians, partly of Bloomsbury intellectuals.

11 'Flumina Amen Silvasque', review of Edward Thomas's *A Literary Pilgrim in England*, and 'A Minor Dostoevsky', review of *The Gambler and Other Stories*, tr. C. Garnett, in *TLS*.

17 Attends 'An Exhibition of Works Representative of the New Movement in Art', organised by RF; meets O. Morrell and A.

Huxley, with whom she talks about his aunt, Mrs Humphry Ward.

18 'The Old Order', review of H. James's *The Middle Years*, in *TLS*.

21 G. L. Dickinson and LS to lunch, the latter in high spirits because he has finished *Eminent Victorians*.

25 Review of Alice Meynell's *Hearts of Controversy* in *TLS*.

29 VW to Asham with S. Sydney-Turner, while LW goes to Bolton, Manchester and Liverpool.

November

7 (Wed) Attends show at the Omega Workshops; chiefly impressed by the Gertlers' and VB's work, less so by DG's.

8 Review of Serge Aksakoff's *A Russian Schoolboy* in *TLS*.

11 Lunches with the Webbs. Afterward K. Cox, Rosalind and Arnold Toynbee visits; VW talks with R. Toynbee about *King Lear* and the 'proper' relation of cooks & governesses', finds her husband 'conventional' and difficult to talk to (*D*).

12 Reads *The Leading Note* by Rosalind Murry (Toynbee) (1910), 'which does not seem a very masterly performance after Turgenev' (*D*).

13 Anxious to get on with her novel (first reference in *D* to *N&D*, about which VW records very little).

15 The Woolfs buy a larger second-hand press, continue printing K. Mansfield's *Prelude*.

17–19 Visits Garsington Manor, home of P. and O. Morrell, for the first time; fellow guests include LS, A. Huxley, Thomas Earp (who with Huxley had started the *Palantine Review*), Dorothy Brett, who had been a fellow student of D. Carrington at the Slade School, and poet Evan Morgan (*D*; to VB, 27 Nov).

21 B. Hiles starts work as part-time assistant in the Hogarth Press; before long the Woolfs begin to find her presence an irritant (as they eventually do with anyone who comes to work for the press). VW dines with CB and RF, discusses literature and aesthetics. (*D*.)

29 'Stopford Brooke', review of L. P. Jacks's *Life and Letters of Stopford Brooke*, in *TLS*.

December

5 (Wed) Reading Dante's *Purgatorio*, finding it 'stiff' (*D*).

6 'Mr Gladstone's Daughter', review of *Some Hawarden Letters*,

1878–1913, chosen by L. March-Phillipps and Bertram Christian, in *TLS*.

9 LS to tea, to drop off 'General Gordon', the last essay in *Eminent Victorians*, and to discuss his relations with D. Carrington (who comes to live with him at Mill House, Tidmarsh, Berkshire, and devotes herself to him for the rest of his life).

10 Reads E. Pound's *Gaudier-Brzeska: A Memoir* (1917).

13 'Charlotte Brontë', review of *Charlotte Brontë: A Centenary Memorial*, ed. Butler Wood, in *TLS*.

19 Attends first general meeting and dinner of the 1917 Club; Josiah Wedgwood gives the inaugural speech to approximately 120 members.

20 To Asham for Christmas, with K. Cox. Review of Arthur and Dorothea Ponsonby's *Rebels and Reformers*, and 'Sunset Reflections', review of E. M. Martin's *The Happy Fields*, in *TLS*.

22 Thanks CB for his book of privately printed poems, *Ad Familiares*, which she had read in the coal cellar during a bombardment a few nights previously (to CB).

27 '"The New Crusade"', review of John Drinkwater's *Prose Papers*, in *TLS*.

28 Reads 'The End of General Gordon'; thinks it 'masterly' but is not altogether convinced by the character of Gordon (to LS).

1918

Events and Letters. Women over 30 gain the right to vote in Britain; E. Rutherford splits the atom; Wilfred Owen dies; the First World War ends. R. Brooke's *Collected Poems*, ed. Edward Marsh, published; Gerard Manley Hopkins' *Poems*, ed. Robert Bridges, published; J. Joyce, *Exiles*; M. Proust, *A l'ombre des jeunes filles en fleurs*; LS, *Eminent Victorians*.

January

3 (Thurs) Returns to Hogarth House; air raids continue, as do rumours of peace. 'Visits to Walt Whitman', review of J. Johnston and J. W. Wallace's *Visits to Walt Whitman in 1890–91*, in *TLS*.

9 Visits 1917 Club (as she often does in her daily rounds); meets F. Shove, Faith Henderson, LS, and Lancelot Hogben, just

down from Cambridge, who later becomes an eminent social biologist.

10 'Philosophy in Fiction', review of *Writings by L. P. Jacks: Mad Shepherds; The Country Air; Philosophers in Trouble; All Men are Ghosts; Among the Idolmakers; From the Human End*, in *TLS*.

11 Notes the House of Lords has passed the Suffrage Bill (the Representation of the People Act, which gives women over 30 the right to vote) – 'I don't feel much more important'. Reads Sidney Colvin's *John Keats, his Life and Poetry, his Friends, Critics, and After Fame* (1917). (*D.*)

13 CB and the Shoves to tea; they discuss the fascination Bloomsbury exerts upon the younger generation, the 'Bloomsbury Bunnies' or 'Cropheads' (including D. Carrington, A. Sargant-Florence, Dorothy Brett, B. Hiles and F. Henderson).

15 Visits Lady Strachey, who reads to her from Ben Jonson's masques.

17 'A Book of Essays', review of Robert Lynd's *If the Germans Conquered England and Other Essays*, in *TLS*.

21 LS visits; amazes the Woolfs with an account of a meeting of the British Society for the Study of Sex and Psychology.

24 Review of Hugh Walpole's *The Green Mirror* in *TLS*.

25 VW's thirty-sixth birthday.

27 D. MacCarthy visits, discusses Thackeray, Enid Bagnold's first book, *Diary without Dates* (1918), and the development of psychology since Shakespeare's time.

31 'Across the Border', review of Dorothy Scarborough's *The Supernatural in Modern English Fiction*, in *TLS*.

February

6 (Wed) Visits Dr Craig, who advises her that her weight is too low.

8 In bed with influenza for a week.

7 'Coleridge as Critic', review of *The Table Talk and Omniana of Samuel Taylor Coleridge*, with a note on Coleridge by Coventry Patmore, in *TLS*.

19 To Asham until 2 March.

March

2 (Sat) For the next two weeks has no books to review and

makes great headway with *N&D*, reaching a total of well over 100,000 words.

14 'Mr Conrad's Crisis', review of J. Conrad's *Nonstromo: A Tale of the Seaboard*, in *TLS*.

21 To Asham for Easter; LS visits. 'Swinburne Letters', review of *The Letters of Algernon Charles Swinburne, with some Personal Recollections by Thomas Hake and Arthur Compton Rickett*, in *TLS*.

April

4 (Thurs) 'Papers on Pepys', review of *Occasional Papers Read by Members at Meetings of the Samuel Pepys Club*, vol. I, ed. H. B. Wheatley, in *TLS*.

8 Meets RF, who persuades her to buy Jean-Richard Bloch's *Et Cie* (1918).

14 Harriet Weaver, who had published J. Joyce's *Portrait of the Artist as a Young Man*, comes to tea with the manuscript of *Ulysses*; VW is not impressed: 'First there's a dog that p's – then there's a man that forths . . . moreover, I don't believe that his method, which is highly developed, means much more than cutting out the explanations and putting in the thoughts between dashes' (to LS, 23 Apr); in any case it is beyond the capacity of the Hogarth Press (to H. Weaver, 17 May; *Ulysses* is finally published in Paris, 1922).

15 Visits RF, who reads from a book by Proust, 'whose name I've forgotten' (*Du côte de chez Swann*; *D*, 18 Apr).

18 Receives D. MacCarthy's new book, *Remnants*.

22 Works on *N&D*, making VB (Katharine) 'mysterious and romantic' (to VB).

25 Review of Viola Meynell's *Second Marriage* in *TLS*.

May

2 (Thurs) 'Two Irish Poets', review of Francis Ledwidge's *Last Songs*, and James Stephens' *Reincarnations*, to *TLS*.

9 K. Mansfield, newly married to J. M. Murry, visits looking 'ghastly ill' (she has tuberculosis). CB's *Potboilers* is published, in which he refers to VW along with Hardy and Conrad as 'our three best living novelists'; VW judges the book 'stout morality & not very good criticism' (*D*, 28 May).

16 'Tchehov's Questions', review of Anton Chekhov's *The Wife and Other Stories* and *The Witch and Other Stories*, tr. C. Garnett, in *TLS*.

23 'Imitative Essays', review of J. C. Squire's *The Gold Tree*, and 'Moments of Vision', review of Logan Pearsall Smith's *Trivia*, in *TLS*.
24 Thanks LS for the copy of his *Eminent Victorians*, which has just been published; confesses her jealousy of his sudden fame (to LS).
30 'Dreams and Realities', review of W. de la Mare's *Motley and Other Poems*, *TLS*.

June

Early this month, attends performance of Mozart's *The Magic Flute*.
13 (Thurs) Attends performance of Mozart's *Don Giovanni*. 'The Claim of the Living', review of W. L. George's *A Novelist on Novels*, in *TLS*.
14 Attends League of Nations meeting.
15–17 Visits the Waterlows at Oare, Wiltshire.
18 M. Gertler and S. S. Koteliansky to dinner; VW feels that 'the shadow of the underworld' rests on Gertler, as it does on K. Mansfield and J. M. Murry (*D*, 24 June).
20 'Loud Laughter', review of Stephen Leacock's *Frenzied Fiction*, in *TLS*.
24 Finishes setting up type for K. Mansfield's *Prelude*.
27 'A Victorian Socialist', review of Ernest Bax's *Reminiscences and Reflections of a Mid and Late Victorian*, in *TLS*.

July

1 (Mon) Sends VB *Kew Gardens*, asking her to design a title page (to VB).
2 Reads George Trevelyan's *The Life and Letters of Lord Macaulay* (1876).
4 'Mr Merrick's Novels', review of Leonard Merrick's *While Paris Laughed*, and *Conrad in Quest of his Youth*, intro. Sir James Barrie, in *TLS*.
10 Glues, covers and sends out the first copies of K. Mansfield's *Prelude*; reading it for the first time finds it 'watered with some of her cheap realities; but it has the living power, the detached existence of a work of art' (*D*, 12 July).
11 'Two Soldier Poets', review of S. Sassoon's *Counter Attack and Other Poems*, and Geoffrey Dearmer's *Poems*, in *TLS*.
20–2 Visits LS and D. Carrington at Tidmarsh.

25 'On Re-reading Meredith', review of J. H. E. Crees's *George Meredith: A Study of his Works and Personality*, in *TLS*.
27–9 Visits the Morrells at Garsington Manor, where the talk focuses on P. Morrell's attack on J. M. Murry in the *Nation* for the latter's unfavourable review of S. Sassoon's *Counter-attack and Other Poems* (1918).
31 To Asham for the summer.
HOGARTH PRESS: K. Mansfield, *Prelude*.

August
4 (Sun) Buys books by Charles Leconte de Lisle (probably his French translations of classical Greek authors).
7 Reads K. Mansfield's *Bliss*; throws it down 'with the exclamation, "She's done for!"' Turns with relief to Byron; admires the 'elastic shape' of *Don Juan* (*D*, 7–8 Aug).
8 'Rupert Brooke', review of *The Collected Poems of Rupert Brooke, with a Memoir*, in *TLS*.
15 'A Practical Utopia', review of Oliver Onions' *The New Moon*, in *TLS*.
17 D. Carrington visits for the weekend. VW finishes Sophocles' *Electra*: 'The heroic woman is much the same in Greece & England. She is of the type of Emily Brontë' (*D*, 19 Aug).
29 'The "Movie" Novel', review of Compton Mackenzie's *The Early Life and Adventures of Sylvia Scarlett*, and review of Dora Sigerson's *The Sad Years*, in *TLS*.

September
3 (Tues) Buys *Memoirs of the Life of Colonel Hutchinson . . . by his widow Lucy* (1806).
8 LW becomes editor of the *International Review*.
10 Reads Milton's *Paradise Lost*: 'He deals in horror & immensity & squalor & sublimity, but never in the passions of the human heart' (*D*).
12 'War in the Village', review of Maurice Hewlett's *The Village Wife's Lament*, in *TLS*.
14 The Webbs and George Young (eldest brother of Hilton Young), who is working for Admiralty Intelligence, to tea; Mrs Webb, as usual, produces a 'curious discomfort of soul' in VW (*D*, 18 Sep).
19 'The Rights of Youth', review of H. G. Wells's *Joan and Peter*, in *TLS*.

26 'Mr Hudson's Childhood', review of W. H. Hudson's *Far Away and Long Ago*, in *TLS*.

October

3 (Thurs) 'Caution and Criticism', review of Harold Williams' *Modern English Writers*, in *TLS*.
7 Returns to Hogarth House for the winter.
9 Meets Osbert and Sacheverell Sitwell; invited to a party next day where she talks with J. T. Sheppard about Sophocles and meets Edith Sitwell, 'a very tall young woman, wearing a permanently startled expression' (*D*, 12 Oct).
10 'Honest Fiction', review of Frank Swinnerton's *Shops and Houses*, and 'Adventurers All', review of Muriel Stuart's *The Cockpit of Idols*, A. Huxley's *The Defeat of Youth and Other Poems*, E. Sitwell's *Clown's Houses*, and *Songs for Sale: An Anthology of Recent Poetry*, ed. E. B. C. Jones, in *TLS*.
13 VW's cousin H. A. L. Fisher brings the news that Lord Milner, Secretary of State for War, says Britain has won the war.
17 'Women Novelists', review of R. Brimley Johnson's *The Women Novelists*, in *TLS*.
23 Attends Bach concert, reads Edith Sichel's *New and Old*, intro. A. C. Bradley (1917).
24 'Valery Brussof', review of Valery Brussof's *The Republic of the Southern Cross and Other Stories*, in *TLS*.
31 'Abraham Lincoln', review of J. Drinkwater's *Abraham Lincoln: A Play*, and review of *The Candle of Vision* by A. E. (pseud. of George William Russell) in *TLS*.

November

2 (Sat) Talks with J. Case, who seems to VW to hint that she should turn to something other than fiction; the conversation casts a chill on 'the last pages' of *N&D* (*D*, 3–4 Nov).
6 Visits K. Mansfield, who is considering going to Switzerland for a cure.
7 Begins to set type for *Kew Gardens*.
11 Armistice Day; VW notes, 'The rooks wheeled round & were for a moment, the symbolic look of creatures performing some ceremony, partly of thanksgiving, partly of valediction over the grave', but the drunks depress her (*D*).
14 'Mr Howells on Form', review of L. Merrick's *The Actor Manager*, in *TLS*.

15 TSE visits; on this first meeting VW is impressed with his intelligence but regrets that he admires E. Pound, W. Lewis and J. Joyce (*D*).

21 Finishes *N&D*. 'Bad Writers', review of *Books in General*, by Solomon Eagle (pseud. of J. C. Squire) in *TLS*.

28 Attends performance of the Diaghilev Ballet to see Lydia Lopokova.

30 Reads J. M. Murry's poem *The Critic in Judgement or Belshazzar of Baronscourt* (Hogarth, May 1919).

December

9 (Mon) Visits K. Mansfield, whom she has been seeking weekly.

12 'Trafficks and Discoveries', review of J. A. Froude's *English Seamen in the Sixteenth Century* and *The Hakluyts' Voyages, Travels and Discoveries of the English Nation*, and review of Joseph Hergesheimer's *The Three Black Pennys*, in *TLS*.

14 Spends the weekend at Durbins, near Guildford, Surrey, with RF.

19 'A View of the Russian Revolution', review of Meriel Buchanan's *Petrograd: The City of Trouble, 1914–1918*, 'The Russian View', review of *The Village Priest and Other Stories from the Russian of E. Militsina and M. Saltikov*, tr. Beatrix Tollemache, and '*Mummery*', review of G. Cannan's *Mummery*, in *TLS*.

21 Recommends Mrs H. Ward's *A Writer's Recollections* (1918) to VB.

25 Angelica Bell, daughter of DG and VB, is born at Charleston.

26 Review of Joseph Warren Beach's *The Method of Henry James* in *TLS*.

HOGARTH PRESS (month of publication unknown): C. N. Sidney Woolf, *Poems by C. N. Sidney Woolf*.

1919

EVENTS AND LETTERS. German peace treaty signed at Versailles; JMK publishes *The Economic Consequences of the Peace*; André Breton and others found *Littérature*; J. Conrad publishes *The Arrow of Gold*; T. Hardy, *Collected Poems*; G. B. Shaw, *Heartbreak House*; VW, *Night and Day*.

January

1 (Wed) Returns to Hogarth House with J. and Q. Bell.
2 Has a tooth extracted; is bedridden for two weeks.
9 'The War from the Street', review of D. Bridgman Metchim's *Our Own History of the War from a South London View*, in *TLS*.
22 Begins setting up TSE's *Poems* (finishes printing 19 Mar).
25 VW's thirty-seventh birthday.
30 Reads Sophocles' *Antigone*, and Mary Fraser Watts's *George Frederic Watts: The Annals of an Artist's Life* (1912); the latter's description of the Camerons' departure for Ceylon inspires VW's play *Freshwater* (see 8 July 1923).

Late this month, begins reading through the collected works of G. Eliot for a centenary article (20 Nov).

February

13 (Thurs) 'Small Talk About Meredith', review of S. M. Ellis's *George Meredith: His Life and Friends in Relation to his Work*, and 'The Tunnel', review of Dorothy Richardson's *The Tunnel*, in *TLS*.
14 Attends show by W. Sickert, 'the pleasantest, solidest most painter-like show in England' (*D*; cf. 'A Conversation about Art', Sep 1934); meets CB, who has written the preface to the catalogue, and Mary Hutchinson (*née* Barnes; VW has known her since her youth), wife of barrister St John Hutchinson, and the primary focus of CB's affections.
21 Asked to write for the *Athenaeum*, of which J. M. Murry becomes editor in April.
26 Lady Ritchie (Aunt Anny) dies; VW writes obituary (6 Mar).
28 To Asham; given notice to leave the house.

March

6 (Thurs) 'Lady Ritchie' in *TLS*.
7 Making the final corrections to *N&D*.
19 Finishes TSE's poems, their job so far, owing to the quality of the ink. Reads Henrietta Barnett's *Rev. Canon S. A. Barnett: His Life, Work and Friends* (1918); finds its philanthropy repulsive.
20 Review of Compton Mackenzie's *Sylvia and Michael* in *TLS*.
21 At 1917 Club meets Hope Mirrlees, who discourses on Swift's use of words. Visits K. Mansfield for the first time since 17 December 1918; discusses Dorothy Richardson (the previous month VW had reviewed the fourth volume of her thirteen-

volume *Pilgrimage,* the 'stream of consciousness' novel which had begun to appear in 1915). Mansfield tells VW of three cottages for rent near Zennor, Cornwall, one of which D. H. Lawrence had lived in (the Woolfs finally do not take them and never meet Lawrence).

27 LW reads *N&D* (as he will all her books before she sends them to the publisher); likes it but finds the philosophy very melancholy (*D*). *'Within the Rim'*, review of H. James's *Within the Rim,* and 'Dickens by a Disciple', review of Walter Crotch's *The Secret of Dickens,* in *TLS.*

April

1 (Tues) Submits *N&D* to Gerald Duckworth.

3 'Washington Irving', review of *Tales of Washington Irving,* ed. Carl van Doren, in *TLS.*

10 'Submerged' in Daniel Defoe's *Roxana,* trying to read one novel a day for her article (24 Apr). 'Modern Novels' in *TLS.*

11 Reads *Moll Flanders;* meets EMF at the London Library, discovers he has not read Defoe and commands him to do so.

17 Visits K. Mansfield; contrasts the rapport they have with the 'male atmosphere' (*D*). VW continues to visit her on a more or less weekly basis.

23 George Cole and his wife Margaret, socialists who both work in the Labour Research Department, to dinner.

24 'The Novels of Defoe' in *TLS.*

25 To Asham for ten days, house-hunting in the area. 'The Eccentrics' in the *Athenaeum.*

29 Reading W. B. Yeats, *The Wild Swans at Coole* (1917): 'I think – for the first time – that he really is a poet' (to O. Morrell).

May

1 (Thurs) Review of W. E. Norris's *The Obstinate Lady* in *TLS.*

7 Duckworth accepts *N&D.*

9 'The Soul of an Archbishop', review of Ethel Thomson's *The Life and Letters of William Thomson, Archbishop of York,* in the *Athenaeum.*

12 *Kew Gardens* published.

16 'The Anatomy of Fiction', review of Clayton Hamilton's *Materials and Methods of Fiction,* in the *Athenaeum.*

23 LS to tea; VW cautions him against becoming 'a superior dilettante' (*D,* 25 May).

27 To Asham, house-hunting.
29 *TLS* praises the 'vital force' of *Kew Gardens*, and prompts a rush of orders. Review of J. Hergesheimer's *Java Head* in the *Athenaeum*.

HOGARTH PRESS: TSE, *Poems*; H. Mirrlees, *Paris: A Poem*; J. M. Murry, *The Critic in Judgment or Belshazzar of Baronscourt*; VW, *Kew Gardens*.

June

6 (Fri) 'On Some of the Old Actors', review of Joseph Daly's *The Life of Augustin Daly*, in the *Athenaeum*.
13 Begins correcting proofs of *N&D*.
19 'Joseph Addison' in *TLS*.
20 'Is this Poetry?', review by VW and LW of J. M. Murry's *The Critic in Judgment*, and TSE's *Poems* (the former reviewing Murry and the latter TSE) in the *Athenaeum*.
21–3 To Garsington for the weekend; fellow guests include G. L. Dickinson, A. Huxley and M. Gertler. O. Morrell is annoyed because Picasso declines her invitation in order to attend a dinner party organised by CB and JMK.
26 Review of Samuel Butler's *The Way of All Flesh* in *TLS*.
28 Peace Treaty between the Allies and Germany signed at Versailles.

HOGARTH PRESS: VW, *The Mark on the Wall*.

July

1 (Tues) The Woolfs buy Monk's House, in Rodmell, Sussex, which becomes their country home for the rest of their lives (see *D* for a dramatic account of the auction).
4 To tea with K. Mansfield, conscious that she will be leaving soon (in September), to spend the winter by the Mediterranean). 'Forgotten Benefactors', review of *Edward Jerningham and his Friends*, ed. Lewis Bettany, in the *Athenaeum*.
17 'A Positivist', review of Frederick Harrison's *Obiter Scripta* (1918), in *TLS*.
19 Official peace celebrations in Britain.
23 Reads the poetry of G. M. Hopkins with admiration: 'He makes a very strange jumble; so that what is apparently pure nonsense is at the same time very beautiful, and not nonsense at all' (to J. Case).
29 To Asham for all of August; guests include EMF and H.

Mirrlees, and the Woolfs exchange visits frequently with VB, DG and JMK, who are at Charleston, JMK writing his critique of the conditions imposed upon Germany, *The Economic Consequences of the Peace.*

31 'Horace Walpole', review of *Supplement to the Letters of Horace Walpole, Fourth Earl of Oxford*, ed. Paget Toynbee, in *TLS*.

August

1 (Fri) '"These are the Plans"', review of Donald Johnson's *Poems*, and Charles Sorley's *Marlborough and Other Poems*, in the *Athenaeum*.

7 'Herman Melville' in *TLS*.

8 H. Mirrlees visits for the weekend; VW is impressed with her sophistication and her 'very obscure, indecent, and brilliant poem' *Paris* (to M. L. Davies, 17 Aug).

14 'The Russian Background', review of A. Chekhov's *The Bishop and Other Stories*. tr. C. Garnett, in *TLS*.

17 Finishes correcting proofs of *N&D*; LW finishes proofs of *Empire and Commerce in Africa*.

21 'A Real American', review of Theodore Dreiser's *Free and Other Stories* and *Twelve Men*.

22 'The Royal Academy' in the *Athenaeum*.

28 Review of Stephen McKenna's *Sonia Married* in *TLS*.

September

1 (Mon) The Woolfs move to Monk's House.

12 Reads seventeenth-century prose writer Sir Thomas Browne.

19 'Wilcoxiana', review of Ella Wilcox's *The Worlds and I*, in the *Athenaeum*.

25 Review of F. Swinnerton's *September* in *TLS*.

27 National Union of Railwaymen goes on strike, cutting off papers and mail.

October

2 (Thurs) 'Mr Gosse and his friends', review of Edmund Gosse's *Some Diversions of a Man of Letters*, in *TLS*.

6 Railwaymen's strike settled; the Woolfs return to Hogarth House.

9 'Madeleine', review of H. Mirrlees' *Madeleine, One of Love's Jansenists*, in *TLS*.

16 'Landor in Little', review of *A Day-book of Landor*, ed. John Baily, in *TLS*.
20 *N&D* published by Duckworth.
23 'Dostoevsky in Cranford', review of Dostoevsky's *An Honest Thief and Other Stories*, in *TLS*.
30 *TLS* praises *N&D* as a book of 'wisdom' and 'brilliance'; in the *Athenaeum*, K. Mansfield judges it disappointingly traditional, comparing it to an old sailing ship, gliding serenely into harbour – 'In the midst of our admiration it makes us feel old and chill: we had never thought to look upon its like again' (*M&M*). 'Winged Phrases', review of George Moore's *Avowals*, in *TLS*.

November

2 (Sun) Asks RF, who has been in France, to bring back copies of Proust (the second volume of *A la recherche du temps perdu*, *A l'ombre des jeunes filles*, had been published in 1918); tells him the success of *N&D* has earned her an invitation from society hostess Sybil Colefax.
5 S. Sydney-Turner and EMF to dinner; the latter explains why he likes *N&D* less than *VO*, and speaks of his own trouble with *A Passage to India* (pub. 1924).
6 'Real Letters', review of *Miss Eden's Letters*, ed. Violet Dickinson, and 'The Limits of Perfection', review, of M. Beerbohm's *Seven Men*, in *TLS*.
8–10 To Tidmarsh to stay with LS and D. Carrington; S. Sydney-Turner also visits.
20 'George Eliot' in *TLS*.
21 'Maturity and Immaturity', review of Pamela Glenconner's *Edward Wyndham Tennant: A Memoir*, and *Joyce Kilmer*, ed. Robert Holliday, in the *Athenaeum*.
28 Negotiates with American publishers over the rights to *VO* and *N&D*; George H. Doran of New York becomes VW's first American publisher.
30 Reads *Impressions that Remain* (1919), the autobiography of Ethel Smyth, who in the 1930s becomes a close friend.

December

2 (Tues) Lunches at Lord and Lady Robert Cecil's, with Lord Robert's nephew, Lord Cranborne, and Prince Antoine Bibesco and his wife Elizabeth Asquith (wife of the former prime

minister), who have asked to meet her: 'Perhaps this is my first appearance as a small Lioness' (*D*, 6 Dec).

11 'Watts-Dunton's Dilemma', review of C. Kernahan's *Swinburne as I Knew Him*, and 'The Intellectual Imagination', review of W. de la Mare's *Rupert Brooke and the Intellectual Imagination: A Lecture*, in *TLS*.

12 'Behind the Bars', review of Ralph Nevill's *The Life and Letters of Lady Dorothy Neville*, in the *Athenaeum*.

18 Review of Lady Butcher's *Memories of George Meredith* in *TLS*.

25 Review of J. Hergesheimer's *Gold and Iron* in *TLS*.

29 To Monk's House.

1920

EVENTS AND LETTERS. First meeting of League of Nations; Dada festival in Paris. J. Conrad publishes *The Rescue*; TSE, *The Sacred Wood*; RF, *Vision and Design*; J. Galsworthy, *The Skin Game*; Sinclair Lewis, *Main Street*; K. Mansfield, *Bliss*; E. Pound, *Hugh Selwyn Mauberley*; M. Proust, *Le Côté de Guermantes*; Jessie Weston, *From Ritual to Romance*; Edith Wharton, *The Age of Innocence* (Pulitzer Prize); W. B. Yeats, *Michael Robartes and the Dancer*.

January

1 (Thurs) Preparing to review H. James's letters, 'stuck' in *The Ambassadors* (1903) (to K. Arnold-Forster).

2 Notes reactions to *N&D*: K. Maxse thinks it very bad, Sir George Savage 'one of the great novels of the world' (to VB; for other responses to *N&D* see *L* and *D* for Jan).

3 Rereads LW's *Empire and Commerce in Africa* (1920) – 'superb' (to M. Davies).

5 Reads H. B. Adams' *The Education of Henry Adams* (1907), and G. M. Hopkins' poetry: impressed with 'The Wreck of the Deutschland', enchanted with 'Heaven-Haven' (to J. Case).

8 Meets CB, EMF and others at 1917 Club, which she visits regularly.

9 'Pictures and Portraits', review of Edmund X. Kapp's *Personalities: 24 Drawings*, in the *Athenaeum*.

13 Talks with M. Strachey at 1917 Club about her projected novel (*The Counterfeits*, 1927).

17 D. MacCarthy, just appointed literary editor of *NS*, spends the night.
22–4 Visits Lucy Clifford, popular writer, and L. Harris.
24 Prepares second editions of *VO* and *N&D*; purchases Charlotte Mew's *The Farmer's Bride* (1915), and R. C. Trevelyan's translation of Sophocles' *Ajax* (1919).
25 VW's thirty-eighth birthday; attends Mozart and Beethoven concert.
26 Conceives 'a new form for a new novel' – *JR* (*D*).
28 Takes tea with E. Richmond to discuss *TLS* article on L. Clifford.
29 'An American Poet', review of Nicholas Lindsay's *General William Booth Enters into Heaven and Other Poems*, in *TLS*.
30 'English Prose', review of *A Treasury of English Prose*, ed. L. P. Smith, in the *Athenaeum*.

February
1 (Sun) Printing H. Mirrlees' *Paris: A Poem*.
4 Rereads *VO*: a 'harlequinade', but 'a more gallant & inspiriting spectacle' than *N&D* (*D*).
5 'Cleverness and Youth', review of A. Huxley's *Limbo*, in *TLS*.
9 Attends lunch party in Café Royal to celebrate DG's first one-man show, with LS and Philippa Strachey (Secretary of the National Council for Women's Service), A. and Karin Stephen (*née* Costelloe), D. Garnett, JMK and others.
10 Accepts one of DG's watercolours.
13 Attends evening party at O. Morrell's with the Eliots, the Huxleys, EMF, J. C. Squire and critic W. J. Turner.
14 Lunches with the Webbs and Felix Cross of the Foreign Office, A. Stephen, C. P. Sanger, Doris Hussey to dinner.
19 Speaks for first time at 1917 Club, subject unrecorded; RF speaks on modern art.
21 To Rodmell for a week of painting, gardening, and attending auctions.

March
1 (Mon) With D. MacCarthy cheers the return of Asquith to Parliament.
2 Elena Richmond (*née* Rathbone, wife of *TLS* editor Bruce Richmond) to dinner and to speak to Richmond branch of the Women's Co-operative Guild, at Hogarth House.

4 Dines at the MacCarthys': first Memoir Club meeting, with CB, VB, RF, DG, S. Waterlow. 'Mr Norris's Method', review of W. E. Norris, *The Triumphs of Sara*, in *TLS*.

6 'A Talk about Memoirs' – review of *Recollections of Lady Peel*, compiled by her daughter Ethel Peel; John Bridges, *Victorian Recollections;* C. L. H. Dempster, *The Manners of my Time;* Dorothea Conyers, *Sporting Reminiscences; John Porter of Kingsclere: An Autobiography* – written in collaboration with Edward Moorhouse, in *NS*.

7 Attends chamber-music concert at George Booth's; makes notes for 'The String Quartet' (*MT*).

12 'Money and Love', review of Ernest Hartley Coleridge's *The Life of Thomas Coutts, Banker*, in the *Athenaeum*.

14 Lunches at Lord and Lady R. Cecil's with Irene Noel-Baker, the Hon. W. Ormsby-Gore and Lady Beatrice.

15 To VB's for second meeting of Memoir Club. VW regrets her 'egoistic sentimental trash' (*D*).

18 'Men and Women', review of Léonie Villard's *La Femme anglaise au XXIXe siècle et son evolution d'après la roman anglais contemporain*, in *TLS*.

24 Novelist Mrs H. Ward dies (to VB, 2 Apr; *D*, 10 Apr).

25 'Freudian Fiction', review of J. D. Beresford's *An Imperfect Mother* in *TLS*. To Rodmell for two weeks.

HOGARTH PRESS: VW, *Monday or Tuesday*, with woodcuts by VB.

April

8 (Thurs) Review of *The Letters of Henry James*, ed. P. Lubbock, in *TLS*.

10 Plans to begin *JR* next week (first reference in *D*). Winces at praise of K. Mansfield in the *Athenaeum*.

11 Attends performance of M. Young's *The Higher Court* (reviewed 17 Apr).

14 Attends show of African sculpture at Chelsea Book Club; meets Alexander Hannay, art critic of the *London Mercury*, and D. MacCarthy.

15 Review of H. James admired by D. MacCarthy, attacked by Arthur Walkley in *The Times* (14 Apr). VW predicts abuse for 'An Unwritten Novel', is slightly checked from beginning *JR*, but drafts preliminary notes. At the Press, sends out L. P. Smith's *Stories from the Old Testament* and H. Mirrlees' *Paris;* prints EMF's *Story of the Siren* (to VB).

16 Writes opening of *JR*; attends Bach festival.
17 'The Higher Court', drama review of *The Higher Court* by M. E. M. Young, in *NS*.
HOGARTH PRESS: LW, *Stories of the East*.

May
4 (Tues) LS dines, is about to begin on *Queen Victoria* in earnest (pub. 1921).
5 Works with S. S. Koteliansky on translation of Maxim Gorky's *Reminiscences of Leo Nicolayevitch Tolstoi*.
6 'An Imperfect Lady', review of Constance Hill's *Mary Russell Mitford and her Surroundings* in *TLS* (see 26 and 28 May).
11 Working on *JR*, finds that, with the initial ease gone, 'the sense of an impending shape' keeps one at it. J. M. Murry has asked her to write stories for the *Athenaeum*. (*D*.)
17 Attends concert of Bohemian String Quartet with Oliver Strachey (LS's elder brother) and S. Sydney-Turner.
19 Visits VB, who has lost money through JMK's speculation in international currency.
26 'A Good Daughter', review of *Mary Russell Mitford*, in the *Daily Herald*.
27 'An Old Novel', review of *A Lost Love* by Ashford Owen (pseud. of Charlotte Ogle), in *TLS*.
28 Visits K. Mansfield – 'We fell into step' (*D*). 'The Wrong Way of Reading', review of *Mary Russell Mitford*, in the *Athenaeum*.
HOGARTH PRESS: H. Mirrlees, *Paris: A Poem*.

June
2 (Wed) Lunches with K. Mansfield: 'To no one else can I talk in the same disembodied way about writing' (*D*).
5 'Body and Brain', review of William Thayer's *Theodore Roosevelt: An Intimate Biography*, in *NS*.
7 Riding home from VB's, sights a defiant beggar woman singing to herself (cf. *JR*, ch. 6, and the street singer in *MD*).
13 Attends RF's exhibition, which fills '3 rooms garishly, as with coloured sheets of tin', and does not sell (*D*).
26 Memoir Club to dinner.
18 G. E. Moore visits; VW cannot follow his explanation of Berkeley. Review of E. Robins' *The Mills of the Gods* in *TLS*.
28 Dines with VB, hears of a young man who fell off the roof and died at Mrs Russell's party (*D*; cf. Septimus in *MD*).

July

1 (Thurs) 'A Disillusioned Romantic', review of J. Conrad's *The Rescue*, in *TLS*; K. Mansfield praises the book at an *Athenaeum* lunch, VW demurs. VW's 'An Unwritten Novel' has appeared in the *London Mercury*, praised by Violet and Sydney Schiff (pseud. of Stephen Hudson, novelist, later a translator of Proust, taking over after Scott-Moncrieff's death).

8 'The Pursuit of Beauty', review of J. Hergesheimer's *Linda Condon*, in *TLS*.

13 Busy with the Press and reviews, has not worked on *JR* for three weeks.

15 'Pure English', review of *Gammer Gurton's Nedle*, by Mr S. . . ., ed. H. Brett-Smith, in *TLS*.

16 'Mr Kipling's Notebook', review of R. Kipling's *Letter of Travel, 1892–1913*, in the *Athenaeum*.

21 Sends note to D. Garnett asking him to send Chekhov's plays and a Greek grammar to Rodmell.

22 To Rodmell for the summer.

23 'The Plumage Bill' in *Woman's Leader*.

24 'The Cherry Orchard', dramatic review of A. Chekhov's *The Cherry Orchard*, in *NS*.

25 On RF's advice begins Albert Adès and Albert Josipovici's *Le Livre de Goha le simple* (1919); recommends K. Mansfield's stories to him, confesses jealousy, discusses translation of Mallarmé (to RF).

26 Returns to London to say goodbye to K. Mansfield; declines to review her book.

28 Works on ch. 4 of *JR* (Mrs Pascoe, the Cornish peasant).

29 'A Born Writer', review of G. Moore's *Esther Waters*, in *TLS*.

HOGARTH PRESS: EMF, *The Story of the Siren*; M. Gorky, *Reminiscences of Leo Nicolayevitch Tolstoi* tr. S. S. Koteliansky and LW.

August

2 (Mon) Reading *Don Quixote* (1615), and *Goha le simple* – 'interesting, yet so arid & spick & span. With Cervantes everythings . . . deep, atmosphere, living people casting shadows solid, tinted as in life' (*D*).

7 'Gorky on Tolstoi', review of M. Gorky's *Reminiscences of Leo Nicolayevitch Tolstoi*, in *NS*.

10 Reads *Don Quixote* ('rather sinking in the sand'), R. Macaulay's *Potterism: A Tragi-farcical Tract* (1920) ('a don's book'), and *An*

Irish Peer on the Continent, 1801–1803 (1920), ed. T. U. Sadleir (*D*).

13 Reads RF's translations of Mallarmé; asks for notes and introduction for the edition (finally published in 1936). 'A Character Sketch', review of *Frederick Locker-Lampson: A Character Sketch*, ed. Augustine Birrell, in the *Athenaeum*.

14 To Charleston. Talks with CB about approaching American publishers; meets Arthur Clutton-Brock, art critic of *The Times*.

15 Begins ch. 5 of *JR* (London).

19 Refuses book reviews. Work on *JR* interrupted by Lady Cecil, who discusses the *Autobiography* (1920) of Margot Asquith, Lady Oxford.

23 To London for farewell visit with K. Mansfield; plans to review *Bliss* (though she does not); feels 'the blankness of not having her to talk to' (*D*).

25 Forging ahead with *JR*, hopes to finish by Christmas. Feels abandoned as a reviewer for *The Times*.

28–9 Ralph Partridge and D. Carrington visit at Rodmell, he to become partner in and she to become secretary for the Press; all watch J. C. Squire and S. Sassoon play cricket.

HOGARTH PRESS: Frank Prewett, *Poems*.

September

7 (Tues) CB, M. Hutchinson and LS visit, talk of 'immortality' – of whether their group has justified its promise (*D*).

8 Dictates terms to *The Times*: no reviews, only leading articles or those she suggests herself.

10 Works on *JR*, ch. 6 (Jacob and Florinda in Soho).

10–13 LS visits; praises *VO* and *N&D*, reads opening chapters of *Queen Victoria*, which strikes VW as lively but not at all 'meditative or profound' (*D*).

17 Works on *JR*, ch. 7 (Mrs Durrant's party).

18–19 TSE visits at Rodmell; discusses his proposed verse dramas, W. Lewis, Pound and Joyce. VW taxes him with 'wilfully concealing his transitions' (*D*). VW and LW consider trying to publish *Ulysses* (see 14 Apr 1918).

22 Spends the evening at Charleston in the confusion of JMK's 'Charleston time', one hour earlier than summer time.

26 Intimidated by TSE more than she thought, finds *JR* halted, after two months steady writing, in the middle of the party scene: 'I reflected how what I'm doing is probably being better

done by Mr Joyce' (*D*). Turns to essay on John Evelyn (28 Oct); begins composing a 'counterblast' to A. Bennett's essay on women (9 Oct.).

October

1 (Fri) Returns to London for the winter. Has not read or written since 27 September because of headache; concludes that it was this, not TSE, that broke off *JR*.
6 R. Patridge begins part-time work at the Press.
9 'The Intellectual Status of Women', letter to the editor, in *NS*.
22 'Solid Objects' in the *Athenaeum*.
25 Attends performance of John Gay's *Beggar's Opera*.
28 'John Evelyn', review of *The Early Life and Education of John Evelyn, 1620–1641,* with commentary by H. Maynard Smith, and 'Jane Austen and the Geese', review of Mary Austen-Leigh's *Personal Aspects of Jane Austen*, in *TLS*.

November

4 (Thurs) Reads Plato's *Symposium*.
10 Has been doing no work on *JR*, preparing to do a chapter for the Memoir Club. With LW and R. Patridge sets up LW's *Stories of the Orient*.
11 'John Evelyn', reply to H. Maynard Smith's criticism of VW's review (28 Oct), admitting chronological errors, in *TLS*.
13 Translates Chekhov.
17 Reads paper to the Memoir Club, probably '22 Hyde Park Gate' (*MOB*).
20–1 H. Mirrlees, 'scented, extravagant', visits for the weekend. VW works on review of D. H. Lawrence's *The Lost Girl* (2 Dec).
22 R. C. Trevelyan comes to tea; discusses poetic drama.
24 Works on *JR*, ch. 8 (Jacob leaving the house).
26 Continues with ch. 8 (Mrs Flanders' letter).

December

1 (Wed) TSE and G. L. Dickinson to dinner.
2 'Postscript or Prelude', review of D. H. Lawrence's *The Lost Girl*, in *TLS*.
5 Reads Coleridge, prompted by TSE's *The Sacred Wood*, which LW is reviewing.
12 Notes 'Everyone's book is out' – TSE's *The Sacred Wood*, RF's

Vision and Design, K. Mansfield's *Bliss*, J. M. Murry's *Aspects of Literature* – and that she has read none of them yet (*D*).

16 'Pleasant Stories', review of J. Hergesheimer's *The Happy End*, in *TLS*.

19 Writes a note to K. Mansfield on the publication of *Bliss*, 'an insincere–sincere letter'. Reads RF's *Vision and Design* (1920) – 'rudimentary compared with Coleridge'. (*D*.)

22 To Rodmell for Christmas.

23 'A Flying Lesson', review of M. Beerbohm's *And Even Now*, in *TLS*.

Hogarth Press: L. P. Smith, *Stories From the Old Testament Retold by Logan Pearsall Smith* (month of publication unknown, but see 15 Apr 1920).

1921

Events and Letters. Anatole France awarded Nobel Prize. A. Huxley publishes *Crome Yellow*; D. H. Lawrence, *Women in Love*; P. Lubbock, *The Craft of Fiction*; Eugene O'Neill, *The Emperor Jones*; G. B. Shaw, *Back to Methuselah*, *Heartbreak House*; Luigi Pirandello, *Six Characters in Search of an Author*; M. Proust, *Sodome et Gomorrhe* (4 vols, 1921–3); LS, *Queen Victoria*; VW, *Monday or Tuesday*.

January

2 (Sun) Returns to Richmond.

3 Works on *JR*, ch. 9 (Jacob at Lady Rocksbier's).

6 Lunches with the Webbs.

7 Dislikes G. Raverat's woodbuts. 'Not in the least jealous' of K. Mansfield's laudatory reviews (to VB). Writer Richard Hughes (*A High Wind in Jamaica*, 1929) to dinner.

21 Continues with *JR*, ch. 9 (Jacob walking home from Hammersmith).

25 VW's thirty-ninth birthday. At a 'crisis' in *JR*, wants 'to finish in 20,000 words, written straight off in a frenzy' (*D*).

26 Initiaties the 'Cock Club': dines at the Cock Tavern, Fleet Street, with C. P. Sangar, S. Waterlow, Philippa Strachey, and editor's assistant Mary Hamilton (see *D*, 17 Feb 1922).

27 Review of J. D. Beresford's *Revolution* in *TLS*.

28 To Philip Woolf's farm, near Tidmarsh.

29 To Tidmarsh to visit LS, D. Carrington and R. Partridge. Talks

of going to Italy, but is 'settling in' to the Press; considers learning Russian (*D*).

February

2 (Wed) Memoir Club to dine; CB and JMK read, 'both elaborate and polished' (*D*).

5 Has first Russian lesson with S. S. Koteliansky. Books arrive for review, a welcome relief from *JR* – 'a sprint towards the end, difficult to keep up' (*D*).

10 'Mr Norris's Standard', review of W. E. Norris's *Tony the Exceptional*, in *TLS*.

11 Attends farewell dinner at CB's for J. M. Murry, who is joining K. Mansfield in Italy.

16 Has been neglecting diary to keep up with LW in Russian: 'I feel myself attached to an express train'. Reads Dorothy Wordsworth. (*D*.)

18 Records 'the return of peace', noting the sales and the few wounded soldiers about (though 'empty sleeves are common enough'), but feels it will all be recorded more accurately in Mrs Gosse's diary or Mrs Webb's (*D*).

21 Asked by H. Massingham to review D. Richardson's *Deadlock*, refuses. S. Sydney-Turner and Louise Matthaei, LW's assistant on the *International Review*, to dinner.

22 Attends performance of Gordon Bottomley's *King Lear's Wife*, Oscar Wilde's *A Florentine Tragedy*, and Henry's Fielding's The Virgin Unmasked.

24 'Henley's Criticism', review of *Essays by William Ernest Henley*, in *TLS*.

Late this month, attends tea party at Rodmell Rectory; meets Edward Shanks, assistant editor of the *London Mercury*, Sylvia Lynd, novelist and poet, and others.

March

1 (Tues) Works on *JR*, ch. 11 (Mrs Flanders waiting for the post). Melancholy because EMF is leaving for India.

3 'A Prince of Prose', review of J. Conrad's *Notes on Life and Letters*, in *TLS*.

4 Apprehensive about forthcoming reviews of *MT*. Dines at the Cock Tavern with B. Trevelyan, M. Strachey, Beatrice Mayor, Elizabeth Meinertzhagen (pseud. of Betty Potter, Goneril in *King Lear's Wife*).

9 'George Eliot' in 'Great Names' series in the *Daily Herald*.
13 Planning trip to Manchester; reviews the Labour Party programme. Cannot begin D. Wordsworth or start 'Jacob's travels to the East' (*JR*, ch. 11). TSE to dinner; VW wonders, 'Will he become "Tom"? . . . Not that Tom admires my writing, damn him' (*D*).
16 To Manchester for two days, LW to be adopted as Labour candidate for the Combined Universities.
17 Spends the morning at the Manchester art gallery, the afternoon at the zoo; in the evening dines at the university refectory: '"Are you a politician?" they asked me. . . . I said I listened. Mrs Findlay shook her head' (*D*).
20 TSE to dinner, then to a performance of Congreve's *Love for Love* (reviewed 2 Apr).
23–30 To Zennor, Cornwall. Reads Voltaire's *Candide* (1759) and E. Smyth's *Streaks of Life* (see 23 Apr), and practises Russian – boasts she can 'read one page of Aksakov in 45 minutes' (to S. Sydney-Turner). Discusses literature with a man who lives in a cottage with the entire Everyman's Library.

April

2 (Sat) 'Congreve', review of *Love for Love*, in *NS*.
5 Works on *JR*, ch. 11 (Jacob at Versailles).
7 *MT* published; VW despondent because review in *TLS* is complimentary but unintelligent and short, and LS's *Queen Victoria* receives three columns of praise (*M&M*).
8 Depressed by reviews, unable to work on *JR*.
8–12 RF stays at Hogarth House while restoring Mantegna canvases at Hampton Court.
12 Delighted because LS and RF, whose opinions matter much more to her than the reviews, approve *MT*. Notes responses to the coal strike (*D*).
15 Reads Carlyle and Macaulay and compares them with *Queen Victoria*, which has sold 5000 copies in a week where *MT* has sold 300 total. Has put off going to Rodmell because of threat of a General Strike (which does not occur).
17 Works on *JR*, ch. 12 (Jacob on Italian trains). Tells LS *Queen Victoria* is 'magnificent'; her only reservation that 'one is a little conscious of being entertained' (to LS).
18 Lunches with H. A. L. Fisher; discusses Ireland, disarmament,

painting, Southey's letters, mentions Joyce as a 'promising litterateur'.
23 'Ethel Smyth', review of E. Smyth's *Streaks of Life*, in *NS*.
28 'Scott's Character', review of Archibald Stalker's *The Intimate Life of Sir Walter Scott*, in *TLS*.
25–9 Attends Beethoven Festival.
Late this month, sees LS often, discusses his 'place': '"Yes, Macaulay" he said. "A little better than Macaulay"' (*D*, 29 Apr).

May
2 (Mon) Buys the *Chapbook* for TSE's 'Prose and Verse', and Romer Wilson's *The Death of Society* (1921).
3 'Momentarily' jealous of positive review of LW's *Stories*. Hopes Romer Wilson will get the Hawthornden Prize instead of K. Mansfield (she does). Reads TSE: 'shocked as usual, when I read Eliot, to find how wrong I am, and how right he is'. At a 'full stop' in *JR*. (To S. Waterlow; *D*.)
5 'Gothic Romance', review of Edith Birkhead's *Tale of Terror: A Study of the Gothic Romance*, in *TLS*.
6 Continues *JR*, ch. 12 (Jacob on the Acropolis).
9 Judges R. Wilson's book 'a perfect example of the faux bon' (*D*); attends lecture on prison reform with M. Fry.
(Mid-month) Attends the 'Nameless Exhibitions', organised by RF, at the Alpine Art Gallery.
18 Hosts dinner party for RF and the MacCarthys to capture D. MacCarthy's brilliant conversation – Minna Green, LW's secretary, records surreptitiously in shorthand but the result is utterly dull.
21 R. Patridge and D. Carrington marry; VW, who 'gave motherly advice', feels the marriage 'more risky than most' (to VB).
23 Wonders how to shape her 'Reading book' (*D*; first reference to *CR*).
25 Talks with JMK in Gordon Square about praise, her memoir ('22 Hyde Park Gate') and *N&D* – 'a dull book', but 'you must put it all in before you can leave out' (*D*).
26 'Patmore's Criticism', review of Coventry Patmore's *Courage in Politics and Other Essays*, in *TLS*.
27 M. Vaughan visits, disappoints: 'And this was the woman I adored! I see myself now standing in the night nursery at Hyde Park Gate . . . & saying to myself "At this moment she is actually under this roof"' (*D*, 2 June; cf. Sally Seton in *MD*).

June

2 (Thurs) Attends party at Miss Royde Smith's to discuss Ireland; meets Margaret Haig Thomas, Lady Rhondda (feminist and founder of *Time and Tide*), Arthur Duncan-Jones (a clergyman), Robert Lynd, Rose Macaulay and others.

4 J. M. Murry reviews *The Notebooks of Anton Tchekhov* in *N&A*, decries the tendency to approach authors by the backstairs. 'Trousers', review of A. Trystan Edwards' *The Things which are Seen*, in *NS*.

5 TSE visits; discusses Murry's black character, praises *MT*, says *Ulysses* is 'prodigious' (*D*).

10 Attends concert; afterward cannot sleep, begins two months of ill health.

17 To Rodmell.

20 Reads W. Scott's *The Bride of Lammermoor* (1819) and D. H. Lawrence's *Women in Love* (1921), 'lured on by the portrait of Ottoline' (to M. MacCarthy).

25 Judges *Women in Love* better than *The Lost Girl*; thinks the *Times* reviewer 'stupid and unfair' (to S. S. Koteliansky).

Late this month, reads Scott's Waverley novels; notes that the Ritchies are 'furious' with her for Mrs Hilbery in *N&D*, based on Lady Ritchie (to VB).

July

1 (Fri) Returns to Richmond; cannot sleep without medication.

18 To Rodmell until October; able now to dispense with medication.

Late this month, has visitors, 'one every day': VB, DG, RF, LS, writer Dorothy Bussy (*née* Strachey, one of LS's older sisters), Philippa Strachey, D. Carrington, J. and A. Strachey.

August

8 (Mon) Writes for the first time in 60 days, records compensations of illness: 'I can take stock of things in a leisurely way. Then the dark underworld has its fascinations as well as its terrors' (*D*).

9–10 Reads E. Gosse's *Books on the Table* (1921) and T. Hardy's works for posthumous article (14 Jan 1928).

13 Reads *The Autobiography of Leigh Hunt* (1850) – 'our spiritual grandfather, a free man'; notes death of Lady Carlisle (*D*).

29 Reads H. James's *The Wings of the Dove* (1902), impressed but

'vaguely annoyed by the feeling that – well, that I am in a museum' (to RF).

31 Orders J. C. Squire's *Selections from Modern Poets* (1921).

Late this month, reads memoirs from Lewes library. Visited by J. and A. Strachey, 'fresh from Freud' (to J. Case, 2 Sep).

September

10 (Sat) Works on 'Lives of the Obscure'; interrupted by LS, with whom she discusses writing (*D*).

12 Finishes *The Wings of the Dove*: 'Very highly American, I conjecture, in the determination to be highly bred, & the slight obtuseness as to what high breeding is' (*D*).

15 'I have been dabbling in K M[ansfield]'s stories, & have to rinse my mind – in Dryden?' (*D*).

24–5 TSE visits; VW disappointed to find she is no longer afraid of him.

October

6 (Thurs) Returns to Richmond for the winter.

17 Reads J. M. Murry's 'clay-cold castrated costive comatose' *Poems: 1916–20*; notes TSE says *Ulysses* is the 'greatest work of the age' (to RF).

24 Has purchased a press for £70; turns the basement into a printing shop.

25 Reads EMF's letters to his mother from India.

November

2 (Wed) Reads Anatole France and T. Hardy; concludes, 'I feel a profound distrust of the Gallic genius in literature' (to RF).

4 Finishes *JR*.

15 Struggles with H. James's ghost stories for *The Times*; must do Hardy, and Paston letters for *CR*.

16 Takes the *Westminster Gazette*: 'Politics are beginning to interest me, as I suppose they interest City men – like a football match'; is annoyed that Britain has accepted the principle of equal naval strength with the United States (*D*).

19–20 Visits LS, R. Partridge, and D. Carrington at Tidmarsh.

25 Finishes stitching the last of 150 copies of RF's woodcuts.

26 'Cross examines' S. S. Koteliansky on the quarrel between Dostoevsky and Turgenev for her review (8 Dec).

December

Early this month, attends performance of G. B. Shaw's *Heartbreak House* with LS, R. Patridge and D. Carrington.

8 (Thurs) 'A Glance at Turgenev', review of I. Turgenev's *The Two Friends and Other Stories*, tr. C. Garnett, in *TLS*.

15 Dines with D. Brett and M. Gertler in Hampstead. 'Fantasy', review of L. P. Jacks's *Legends of Smokeover*, in *TLS*.

17 R. Toynbee brings manuscript of her new novel. RF to tea and dinner, discusses Julien Benda (author of *Le Bergsonisme ou une philosophie de la mobilité*, 1912) and Proust.

19 B. Richmond (editor of *TLS*) objects to use of 'lewd' in review of James; VW, annoyed, substitutes 'obscene'.

22 'Henry James' Ghost Stories' in *TLS*.

24–30 To Rodmell for Christmas, works on Hardy article.

Hogarth Press: CB, *Poems*; RF, *Twelve Original Woodcuts*; M. Gorky, *The Note-books of Anton Tchekhov together with Reminiscences of Tchekhov*, tr. S. S. Koteliansky and LW.

1922

Events and Letters. M. Proust dies. TSE publishes *The Waste Land*; J. Galsworthy, *The Forsyte Saga*; J. Joyce, *Ulysses*; K. Mansfield, *The Garden Party*; D. H. Lawrence, *Aaron's Rod*, *Fantasia of the Unconscious*; S. Lewis, *Babbitt*; W. B. Yeats, *Later Poems*; Henri Bergson, *Dureé et simultanéité*; Hermann Hesse, *Siddhartha*; Ludwig Wittgenstein, *Tractatus Logico-Philosophicus*; VW, *Jacob's Room*.

January

3 (Tues) Resolves to give up reviewing, 'now that Richmond re-writes my sentences to suit the mealy mouths of Belgravia' (*D*).

5 Suffers from influenza for the next six weeks.

12 'Dostoyevsky the Father', review of Aimée Dostoyevsky's *Fyodor Dostoyevsky: A Study*, in *TLS*.

22 Gordon Luce to dinner to discuss publishing his poems (Hogarth, Feb 1924).

25 VW's fortieth birthday.

Hogarth Press: Leonid Andreev, *The Dark*, tr. L. A. Magnus and K. Walter.

February

3 (Fri) VW and LW, disgruntled with R. Partridge, consider parting company with him.

4 Still bedridden with 'flu; has had few visitors, except VB, who makes her defensive about her settled life.

6 Impressed with CB's 'sprightly' journalism (attack on Shaw in the *New Republic*); unable to get through W. de la Mare's memoirs. Dr D. J. Fergusson, general practitioner at Richmond, pronounces VW's pulse 'insane'; orders her to stay in bed for two to three weeks.

11 Reads Lady G. Cecil's *Life of Robert, Marquess of Salisbury* (1922). Complains to LS about A. B. Walkley on Molière, A. Meynell on Austen, Sterne and Milton; expresses admiration for Thomas Love Peacock's *Crotchet Castle* (1831) (to LS).

14 Concerned that K. Mansfield 'bursts upon the world in glory next week' (with *The Garden Party and Other Stories*), and that by the time *JR* appears it will seem 'stale acrobatics'. Reads Madame de La Fayette's *La Princesse de Clèves* (1678), Herman Melville's *Moby Dick* (1851), W. Scott's *Old Mortality* (1816), Cecil Torr's *Small Talk at Wreyland* (2 vols, 1918, 1922). LS visits, discusses P. Lubbock's *The Craft of Fiction* (1921). (*D*.)

15 Finds Peacock's *Nightmare Abbey* (1818) and *Crotchet Castle* (1831) much better than she remembered.

18 Finds her interest as a writer lies 'in some queer individuality', the quality she respects in Peacock, Donne, G. Borrow, N. Douglas's *Alone* (1921) and E. Fitzgerald's *Letters*; notes that reviews have come to seem frivolous, while criticism absorbs her more and more (*D*).

27 Consults Dr Harrington Sainsbury, heart specialist, who advises against going abroad; reads *Lord Byron's Correspondence*, ed. John Murray (1922).

March

6 (Mon) Begins work on *JR* again.

8 CB visits regularly on Wednesdays – 'enough of my old friend, & enough of my old lover, to make the afternoons hum' (*D*).

(Mid-month) Visited by V. Dickinson, by EMF, just back from India, and by TSE, who is starting a magazine (the *Criterion*) and has written a poem of 40 pages, to be printed in the autumn (see 18 June).

12 Works on a preface to *CR* ('Byron and Mr Briggs'); notes that

K. Mansfield 'soars in the newspapers. . . . The more she is praised, the more I am convinced she is bad' (*D*).

15 Lunches with RF and J. H. Mason, typographer and printer.

20 Has been asked to copy out passages from her novels for the Queen's doll house, but LW will not allow it. Attends performance of John Dryden's *All for Love*.

24 Works on the first chapter of *CR* with 'the usual fabulous zest' of beginnings; plans to finish in under a year.

30 Helps S. S. Koteliansky with translation of Dostoevsky's *Stavrogin's Confession*.

April

2 (Sun) S. Sydney-Turner and M. Green to tea, the latter to pick up the manuscript of *JR* for typing. VW dines at the MacCarthys'; attends B. Mayor's plays *The Girl in the City* and *Thirty Minutes in a Street*.

4 Attends meeting of Memoir Club.

9 Asks CB to let B. Potter produce his comedy *Love and Liberty*; asks D. Garnett to send *Ulysses*, and to sell her privately printed edition of Lord Lovelace's *Astarte* (1905).

14 TSE invites her to submit work to *Criterion*. Works on 'Mrs Dalloway in Bond Street' and Dostoevsky translations (one chapter in April *Criterion*).

27 Attends *The Cockatoo's Holiday*, ballet with L. Lopokova.

May

Early this month, ill, bedridden for several days.

5 (Fri) Begins vol. II of Proust, *A l'ombre des jeunes filles eu fleurs*: 'Scarcely anyone so stimulates the nerves of language in me: it becomes an obsession' (to RF).

(Mid-month) Meets writer Gerald Brenan at Tidmarsh.

21 Argues with LW about the influence of G. B. Shaw; contends 'the Edwardians, from 1895 to 1914, made a pretty poor show' (to J. Case).

Hogarth Press: I. A. Bunin, *The Gentleman from San Francisco and Other Stories*, tr. S. S. Koteliansky and LW; Ruth Manning-Sanders, *Karn*; Fredegond Shove, *Daybreak*.

June

1 (Thurs) Plans article on P. Lubbock's *Craft of Fiction* ('On Re-reading Novels').

5 To Brighton to hear M. L. Davies address the Women's Co-operative Guild.
11 Works on 'On Re-reading Novels'; copies out *JR* for M. Green.
18 TSE dines, reads his poem: 'He sang it & chanted it rhythmed it. It has great beauty & force of phrase: symmetry; & tensity. . . . The Waste Land, it is called' (*D*; to D. Garnett, 20 Oct).
19 Dines at CB's for meeting of the Memoir Club; LS and EMF read.
21 Attends RF's lecture on Rembrandt at Mortimer Hall.
23 Still copying *JR*, to be sent to American publishers 14 July. Guards herself against forthcoming reviews with 'Mrs Dalloway in Bond Street' and 'Miss Ormerod'.
26 Sees Dr Philip Hamill, who suspects tuberculosis; Dr Fergusson disagrees.

HOGARTH PRESS: Countess Tolstoi, *The Autobiography of Countess Sophie Tolstoi*, preface by Vasilii Spiridonov, tr. S. S. Koteliansky.

July
15 (Sat) 'Jane Austen Practising', review of Austen's *Love and Friendship*, with preface by G. K. Chesterton, in *NS*.
15–17 Spends weekend at Garsington with the Morrells; discusses proposal to provide TSE with an income to free him to write.
17 Finishing *JR*; notes 1917 Club has extended premises, where she is accosted by D. Hussey, who wants to talk about her new book, *A Lady of the Salons: The Story of Louise Colet* (1922) by D. E. Enfield (her married name).
18 Reads J. M. Murry's novel *The Things We Are* (1922), 'half paralysed with disgust and boredom' (to O. Morrell).
21 CB to tea, discusses LS's proposal to take over the *English Review*.
22 Dr Hamill maintains VW's right lung is infected; Dr Fergusson finds nothing. 'On Re-reading Novels' – review of *The Novels of Jane Austen*, with illustrations by G. E. Brock; *The Novels of Charlotte, Emily and Anne Brontë; The Works of George Meredith*; and P. Lubbock's *The Craft of Fiction* – in *TLS*.
23 Encouraged by LW's judgement that *JR* is a work of genius; 'There's no doubt in my mind that I have found out how to begin (at 40) to say something in my own voice' (*D*).

August

1 (Tues) To Rodmell for the summer.

3 Records the 'true' beginning of *CR*; notes that she and LW are becoming celebrities; surprised to hear that VSW thinks her the best woman writer (*D*).

6 Proposes to O. Morrell that subscribers to the Eliot fund give something down rather than be asked to guarantee a yearly amount; respects Rebecca West, having just begun reading *The Judge* (1922) (to O. Morrell).

9 Dr Sainsbury discovers pneumonia germs.

10 Asks VB to alter dustjacket for *JR* and to send a copy of VSW's *The Heir* (1922).

18 Works on 'Mrs Dalloway in Bond Street', feels she is writing too quickly. Has given up on West's *The Judge* – an 'over stuffed sausage' (to O. Morrell) – and is 200 pages into *Ulysses*: 'an illiterate, underbred book. . . . When one can have the cooked flesh, why have the raw?' (*D*, 16 Aug; to LS, 24 Aug).

22 Stalled on 'Mrs Dalloway in Bond Street', the mood broken by S. Waterlow's visit: 'One must get out of life. . . . Sydney comes and I'm Virginia; when I write I'm merely a sensibility' (*D*).

23 Advises K. Arnold-Forster to subscribe to the *Criterion*, for it will have a story by her ('In the Orchard', Apr 1923).

24 Considers poetry by Robert Graves (Hogarth, July 1923).

26 Thinks *Ulysses* 'more & more unimportant; & dont even trouble conscientiously to make out its meanings' (*D*).

September

6 (Wed) Corrects proofs of *JR*, which 'now reads thin & pointless'; finishes *Ulysses*: 'Genius it has I think; but of the inferior water' (*D*).

7 LS visits; gives VW a review of *Ulysses* in the New York *Nation* which makes it 'very much more impressive than I judged' (*D*).

11 Edward Shanks visits; has just resigned as assistant editor of the *London Mercury* because J. C. Squire refused to review *Ulysses*.

12 LS visits; talks about Gibbon, Boswell, Mrs Thrale, the English prison system, and above all R. Partridge (whom he loves) and D. Carrington (who is loved by Partridge but in love with LS).

21 Reads the *Odyssey*.
22 EMF visits; works on article for the *Nation* on the Graeco-Turkish war.
23 TSE visits; talks of Joyce, Dostoevsky, S. Sitwell, J. M. Synge, D. H. Lawrence, and of how there is not great poet in the present age.
25 Writes to TSE to confirm his position with regard to the Fellowship Fund: that £500 a year is the minimum sum he will accept, and that pledges of yearly contributions are not sufficient security to warrant giving up his position (to TSE).

October

4 (Wed) Harcourt Brace accepts *JR*. VW has finished 'Mrs Dalloway in Bond Street' and the chapter on Chaucer, read five books of the *Odyssey* is reading Proust, Chaucer and the Pastons, and plans to read Greek, and the lives of classical scholars R. Bentley and R. Jebb.
5 Returns to Richmond for the winter.
6 Drafts plan for 'a book to be called, perhaps, At Home: or The Party'; begins 'The Prime Minister' (*MDP*).
8 Saddened by death – perhaps suicide – of K. Maxse (4 Oct), on whom Clarissa Dalloway is modelled in part (*D*, 8 and 14 Oct).
14 Finds 'Mrs Dalloway' has branched into a book: 'I adumbrate here a study of insanity & suicide: the world seen by the sane & the insane side by side – something like that'. Continues to read for the Greek chapter – finishing J. H. Monk's *The Life of Richard Bentley* (1833), beginning A. Zimmern's *The Greek Commonwealth: Politics and Economics in Fifth Century Athens* (1911), and Aeschylus. (*D*.)
16 Drafts 'a possible revision' of *MD*; sits for portrait for *John O'London's Weekly* (pub. 11 Nov).
20 Thanks D. Garnett for his praise of *JR*, but wonders 'how far can one convey character without realism?' (to D. Garnett).
21 EMF and Herbert Read, art historian and critic, to dinner.
26 *JR* reviewed in *TLS*: the real interest 'is not Jacob's history simply, nor anyone else's, but the queer simultaneousness of life. . . . But it might still be questioned whether her . . . method does not condemn [the characters] to be external' (*M&M*).
27 *JR* published; VW annoyed that the *Daily News* calls her an

'elderly sensualist' and *Pall Mall* declares the 'originality' of the book 'only doubtfully worth while' (*M&M*).

29 Admires D. Garnett's *Lady into Fox* (1922), but advises him to 'drop the 18th Century' (to D. Garnett). Mary Butts, author of *Speed the Plough and Other Stories* (1923) to tea.

Late this month, at L. P. Smith's, meets, among others, P. Lubbock for the first time since the evening LS proposed to her (17 Feb 1909).

HOGARTH PRESS: F. M. Dostoevsky, *Stavrogin's Confession and The Plan of the Life of a Great Sinner*, tr. S. S. Koteliansky and VW; S. Freud, *Beyond the Pleasure Principle*, tr. C. J. M. Hubback; VW, *Jacob's Room*.

November

4 (Sat) A 'stormy' weekend at Tidmarsh: it is settled that R. Partridge must leave the Press.

7 V. Dickinson to tea. A. Stephen speaks to Women's Co-operative Guild on psychoanalysis; LW campaigns in Liverpool as Labour candidate for the Combined English Universities.

8 Finishing 'Modern Essays', wants to sketch out *MD* and write the 'aeroplane chapter'.

11 Reads the Book of Job – 'I don't think God comes well out of it' (to Lady R. Cecil).

13 Reads Aeschylus.

16 Relieved that LW not elected.

(Mid-month) Considers offer by Heinemann to enter into partnership with Hogarth.

26 Marjorie Thomson and Cyril Joad to tea to discuss her working for the Press.

30 'Modern Essays', review of *Modern English Essays*, ed. Ernest Rhys, in *TLS*.

December

1 (Fri) The Woolfs decline Heinemann's offer, and reject R. Partridge's proposal to have Noel Carrington become London manager.

3 Works on an edition of Aeschylus (text, translation and notes of her own); reads Stephen Reynolds' *Letters* and Emily Hobhouse's translation of *Tant Alie of Transvall: Her Diary, 1880–1902,* for the Press. Sends JMK and LS the printed proposal for the Eliot Fellowship Fund (to JMK).

14 Dines at CB's; meets 'the lovely gifted aristocratic' VSW. 'Eliza and Sterne', review of Arnold Wright and William Sclater's *Sterne's Eliza*, in *TLS*.
19 Dines at VSW's London house, with CB and D. MacCarthy.
20 To Rodmell for Christmas.
25 Writes to G. Brenan (who is in Spain, struggling to write) urging him not to renounce his writing, however difficult the effort: 'Though I try sometimes to limit myself to the thing I do well, I am always drawn on and on, by human beings, I think, out of the little circle of safety, on and on, to the whirlpools; when I go under.'
28 Asks VSW for *Knole and the Sackvilles* (1922).
29 Likes VSW's poetry, in *Georgian Poetry*, ed. E. Marsh (1922), but 'bored to death with apple trees and acorns' in the rest of the volume. Finishes P. Lubbock's memoir *Earlham* (1922); thinks it 'thoroughly bad'. (To R. C. Trevelyan.)

HOGARTH PRESS: S. Freud, *Group Psychology and the Analysis of the Ego*.

1923

EVENTS AND LETTERS. Hitler's *coup d'état* ('Beer Hall Putsch') fails; W. B. Yeats awarded Nobel Prize. J. Conrad publishes *The Rover*; EMF, *Pharos and Pharillon*; A. Huxley, *Antic Hay*; D. H. Lawrence, *Kangaroo, Studies in Classic American Literature*; M. Proust, *La Prisonnière* (posth.); R. M. Rilke, *Duino Elegies, Sonnets to Orpheus*.

January

2 (Tues) Compares her position with VB's, envies her children and unsettled ways, yet feels she must be unencumbered in order to write (*D*).
7 Plans to work at *MD*, dash off 'Lives of the Obscure', finish the memoirs of Laetitia Pilkington (30 June), master the *Agamemnon*, read Greek regularly, perhaps tackle another volume of Proust, and 'write to the new apparition Vita, who gives me a book every other day' – most recently James Flecker's play *Hassan* (1922) (*D*).
9 K. Mansfield dies; VW feels she has 'lost some spur to write' (*D*, 16 Jan), and her melancholy persists: 'Go on writing of course: but into emptiness. There's no competitor' (*D*, 28 Jan).

(Mid-month) Plagued with colds and temperatures, occasionally bedridden in the coming weeks, finally vaccinated with pneumonia germs (15 Feb).

21 TSE visits to discuss the fund; VW writes to Richard Aldington suggesting their committee be amalgamated with E. Pound's.

25 VW's forty-first birthday.

28 Notes *N&A* has been sold to JMK and associates; is uncertain about LW's position.

29 M. Thomson begins work full-time at the Press; her drawl offends but her seriousness impresses VW.

February

Early in the month, VW asks CB for the *Journal intime* of Benjamin Constant (1767–1830); 'boasts' that Scott-Moncrieff 'pesters for a few words' – presumably for his *M. Proust: An English Tribute* (1923), which RF seems to have been instrumental in organising, but to which neither he nor VW contribute (to CB).

3 (Sat) To King's College, Cambridge. Dines with JMK, H. Norton, his sister Jane Norton, and J. T. Sheppard; attends Marlowe Society production of Sheppard's version of Sophocles' *Oedipus Tyrannus*. Next day, lunches with the Shoves and meets classicist Francis Cornford, visits G. E. Moore and family, dines at JMK's room (decorated by VB and DG), meets undergraduates Frank Ramsay and W. ('Sebastian') Sprott, and the Hon. Vera Benedicta (Mrs Frank Birch).

7 With S. Sydney-Turner attends concert by the Bohemian String Quartet.

8 Resumes work on *MD*; wonders 'if this next lap will be influenced by Proust' (*D*, 10 Jan).

10 Sets type for H. Read's *Mutations of the Phoenix*; prints EMF's *Pharos and Pharillon*.

12 Writes to JMK, asking him to hire TSE as literary editor of *N&A*.

23 Writes to LS asking him to support TSE's appointment to *N&A*; wishes TSE had 'more spunk' (*D*).

March

2 (Fri) Types of K. Mansfield's letters to her for J. M. Murry (for his edition of Mansfield's letters, 1927–8).

6 Gloomy over her and LW's uncertain status with *N&A*.

Impatient with TSE's cautiousness, agrees with B. Richmond he is not the man for the job.

9 Corrects S. S. Koteliansky's translation of *Tolstoy's Love Letters* and A. Goldenveizer's *Talks with Tolstoi* (May, June).

13 Writes to JMK asking him to guarantee TSE a minimum of two years on *N&A*.

14 R. Partridge leaves the Press.

17 Reads B. Jonson's *Epicoene, or the Silent Woman* (1609) for reading at JMK's. J. C. Squire accepts 'Lives of the Obscure' at £13, declines it at £15, finally publishes it January 1924.

18 Begins 'How it Strikes a Contemporary'; must make money and so has shelved her fiction and *CR*.

23 TSE declines literary editorship of *N&A*; LW accepts.

26 Receives letter from VSW inviting her to join PEN, the international authors' society; she declines (to VSW, 15 Apr).

27 The Woolfs depart on a month-long holiday to Spain, stopping at Madrid (30 Mar), and Granada (1 Apr), where they stay with a former Governor of Northern Nigeria, Charles Temple, and his wife, before travelling by mule to G. Brenan's cottage in Yegen, in the Sierra Madre (3 Apr); there VW reads a life of Cézanne, as well as Rimbaud, and other French authors. In Paris on the way home finishes 'To Spain', begins review of May Yates's *George Gissing: An Impression* (30 June), visits the Louvre (likes only the Poussins), Notre Dame and Galéries Lafayette, visits H. Mirrlees and classicist Jane Harrison, and meets Spanish painter Maria Blanchard and others (22–6 Apr). Returns to London 27 April. (See *L*, 30 Mar–28 Apr.)

April

5 (Thurs) 'How it Strikes a Contemporary' in *TLS*.

18, 25 'Talks with Tolstoi: Revealing Diary about the Life of the Great Russian' in *Cassell's Weekly*.

'In the Orchard' in the *Criterion*.

May

5 (Sat) 'To Spain' in *N&A*.

11 At 'the Greek chapter' in *CR*, feels she can only 'sketch' it and 'must perpetually enrich it from time to time', shelving it and *MD* to make way for paying journalism.

13 Attends performance of Charles Perrault's *Puss in Boots*, by the Marionette Players of Teatro di Piccoli.

17 Invites T. Hardy to contribute to *N&A* (he does eventually: 'Coming up Oxford Street – Evening', 13 June 1925). TSE dines – 'I feel that he has taken the veil, or whatever monks do' (to RF, 18 May).
18 Attends Spring Show of London Group of artists, and Richmond Dog Show.
19 'Romance and the Heart', review of R. Wilson's *The Grand Tour* and D. Richardson's *Revolving Lights*, in *N&A*.
21 Attends polo match at Hurlingham.

HOGARTH PRESS: EMF, *Pharos and Pharillon*; H. Read, *Mutations of the Phoenix*; S. Renolds, *Letters*, ed. Harold Wright; *Tolstoi's Love Letters, with a Study of the Autobiographical Elements in Tolstoi's Work, by Paul Biryukov*, tr. S. S. Koteliansky and VW.

June

2 (Sat) Travels to Garsington for the weekend. Talks with LS about literature in the train, takes tea with '37 undergraduates', including writers Lord David Gascoyne-Cecil and Edward Sackville-West (VSW's cousin), and future film director Anthony Asquith, as well as a 'shabby embroideress, to whom Ott. is being kind' (cf. Ellie Henderson in *MD*). The visit inspires a determination to bring out 'the slipperiness of the soul' of such people as O. Morrell in *MD*. (*D*.)
4 Sends 'Mrs Dalloway in Bond Street' and another story to the *Criterion*: 'Mrs Dalloway doesn't seem to me complete as she is – but judge for yourself' (to TSE; he publishes neither); works on T. Browne's *Urn Burial* (28 June).
12 Attends performances of *Façade*, a combination of E. Sitwell's poetry and William Walton's music.
19 Works on *MD* – 'the mad part . . . makes my mind squint'; wants to move from Richmond into London but must convert LW (*D*).
24 Sets type for *The Waste Land*.
28 'Sir Thomas Browne', review of *Urn Burial*, *The Garden of Cyrus*, *Religio Medici*, in *TLS*.
30 'An Impression of Gissing', review of M. Yates's *George Gissing: An Impression*, and *The Private Life of Henry Maitland*, ed. Morley Roberts, in *NS*; 'Laetitia Pilkington' in *N&A*.

HOGARTH PRESS: A. B. Goldenveizer, *Talks with Tolstoi*.

July

1 (Sun) Begins *Freshwater: A Comedy* (first conceived 30 Jan 1919, finally completed and performed Jan 1935; see Ruotolo).

8 Wishes she could write *MD* as freely as *Freshwater*; plans to finish next day, reluctant to return to the novel. Finishes setting up *The Waste Land*.

(Mid-month) A. Birrell visits; gives VW a copy of James Boswell's *An Account of Corsica. The Journal of a Tour to that Island; and Memoirs of Pascal Paoli* (1768), ed. S. C. Roberts (1923).

15 A nervous Vivien and T. S. Eliot to tea (conversation recorded in *D*).

20 Dines with critic Raymond Mortimer and Schofield Thayer, editor of the *Dial*, before party at M. Hutchinson's; meets George Rylands, who later works for the Press.

23/26 Attends performance of *Tancred*, adapted from Benjamin Disraeli's novel by E. Millbank.

28 Has 'pulled through' her chapter on Chaucer and continues to work on *MD*.

29 Asks CB to bring Conrad's *Notes on Life and Letters* to Charleston.

'Mrs Dalloway in Bond Street' in the *Dial*, New York.

Hogarth Press: R. Graves, *The Feather Bed*.

August

2 (Thurs) To Rodmell for the summer.

3 Reads H. Nicolson's *Tennyson: Aspects of his Life, Character, and Poetry* – 'a sprawling floundering book' (to P. Strachey), and the works of Conrad.

10 Reading Chekhov – 'There is a perpetual unexpectedness in his mind' – and Marlowe (to G. Brenan).

17 Conceives idea of giving her essays a conversational frame to unify the collection.

30 In *MD* digs out 'caves' behind her characters: 'The idea is that the caves shall connect, & each comes to daylight at the present moment' (*D*). Reads a chapter of Elizabeth Gaskell's *Wives and Daughters* (1866), thinks it better than A. Bennett's *Old Wives' Tale*.

September

Early this month, reads *Freshwater* at Charleston.

1 (Sat) 'Mr Conrad: A Conversation', review of *Almayer's Folly*

and Tales of Unrest, An Outcast of the Islands, The Nigger of the Narcissus and Typhoon, Lord Jim, Youth, Romance, in *N&A*.

5 Begins again what is now to be called *The Common Reader*.

7–10 With R. Mortimer and G. Rylands visits JMK and L. Lopokova in Studland; observes Lopokova as a type for Rezia in *MD*, reads some of JMK's forthcoming *Tract on Monetary Reform* (1923), visits Bindon Abbey and Woolbridge Manor (setting for Hardy's *Tess*). G. Rylands offers to join the Press.

11 Reads CB's essay on VW (*Dial*, Dec 1924); judges it the 'best', and not merely the most complimentary, criticism of her work (to CB).

15 EMF visits for the weekend, discusses his preference for Lawrence over Proust.

29 'The Compromise', review of *The Life of Mrs Humphry Ward*, by her daughter Janet Penrose Trevelyan.

30 Returns to Richmond for the winter.

HOGARTH PRESS: TSE, *The Waste Land*.

October

6 (Sat) Writes to VB, and next day to D. MacCarthy, organising reading of *Freshwater*; later decides it is too thin to warrant getting people together (it is rewritten and produced Jan 1935).

(Mid-month) Begins house-hunting in London.

15 In *MD* works on the mad scene in Regent's Park, writing 'perhaps 50 words a morning'; doubtful of Clarissa, feels her perhaps too 'glittering & tinsely' (*D*).

HOGARTH PRESS: Ernest Jones, *Essays in Applied Psycho-analysis*.

November

3 (Sat) Reads Sophocles for *CR*.

17 First version of 'Mr Bennett and Mrs Brown' in *Literary Review of the New York Evening Post* (repr. *N&A*, 1 Dec; see 4 Feb, 17 May 1924); 'The Chinese Shoe', review of Kathleen Fitzpatrick's *Lady Henry Somerset*, in *N&A*.

HOGARTH PRESS: Alice Lowther, *When it was June*.

December

1 (Sat) To Rodmell; reads Greek, and manuscripts for the Press, including Theodora Bosanquet's *Henry James at Work*.

15 'Jane Austen at Sixty', review of *The Works of Jane Austen*, in *N&A*.

17 Dines with CB, M. Hutchinson and VB before party at TSE's at which they discuss the personal element in literature and TSE becomes sickly drunk.

21–30 To Rodmell for Christmas; VW dictates 'Scenes in the Life of Mrs Bell' to Q. Bell for inclusion in the Charleston Bulletin.

HOGARTH PRESS: CB, *The Legend of Monte della Sibilla*.

1924

EVENTS AND LETTERS. J. Conrad, Franz Kafka, and Nikolai Lenin die; *La Révolution surréaliste* review founded in France. EMF publishes *A Passage to India*; Ernest Hemingway, *In our Time*; Thomas Mann, *The Magic Mountain*; G. B. Shaw, *St Joan*.

January

1 (Tues) Returns to Richmond.

3 Works on the scene of the streetsinger in *MD*.

8 Attends performance of Charles Méré's *The Flame*.

9 Purchases ten-year lease of 52 Tavistock Square, London.

19 Review of *The Poems, English and Latin of Edward, Lord Herbert of Cherburg*, ed. G. C. Moore Smith, in *N&A*.

20 Lord Berners, S. Sassoon and VSW to dinner: 'Ever hear of Moore?' 'George Moore the novelist?' 'My dear Vita, we start at different ends' (to CB).

21 Fidgets through C. K. Munro's four-and-a-half-hour play, *Progress*.

23 Content, in spite of strike by locomotive engineers and firemen, because the *Dial* has paid £22 for 'Lives of the Obscure' (see 17 Mar 1923), and the *New Republic* has accepted 'Jane Austen at Sixty'. EMF writes to announce he has finished *A Passage to India*.

25 VW's forty-second birthday.

28 Works on the streetsinger's chant in *MD*.

31 'Montaigne', review of *Essays of Montaigne*, tr. C. Cotton, in *TLS*.

Late this month, dines at E. Sands's with RF, L. P. Smith; meets Prince and Princess Bibesco and A. Bennett – 'a lovable sea lion, with chocolate eyes, drooping lids, & a protruding tusk' (*D*).

'The Lives of the Obscure' in the *London Mercury*.

February

3 (Sun) Reads Elizabethans for *CR*.

8 EMF visits, consults LW on publisher's terms for *Passage to India*.

9 Review of Caroline Ticknor's *Glimpses of Authors* in *N&A*.

16 Review of *Unpublished Letters of Matthew Arnold*, ed. Arnold Whitridge, and *Arthur Yates: An Autobiography*, written in collaboration with Bruce Blunt, in *N&A*.

(Mid-month) At K. Stephen's party meets B. Russell; does not much like him but would 'like the run of his headpiece' (*D*, 23 Feb). Reads Aristophanes' *The Birds*, and manuscripts of Flora Mayor's *The Rector's Daughter* (Hogarth, May) and T. Bosanquet's essay on James (Hogarth, Nov).

22 Arranges for VB and DG to decorate 52 Tavistock Square.

23 Review of *Letters and Journals of Anne Chalmers*, ed. by her daughter, in *N&A*.

25 Thanks L. P. Smith for his article 'First Catch your Hare' in *N&A*, a response to one on character in fiction by J. D. Beresford, which took issue with 'Mr Bennett and Mrs Brown' (both essays influence 'Character in Fiction', the second version of 'Mr Bennett and Mrs Brown'; see *M&M*).

HOGARTH PRESS: RF, *Duncan Grant*; G. H. Luce, *Poems*.

March

11 (Tues) Attends farewell dinner for poet and critic Edmund Blunden, who is moving to University of Tokyo; argues with J. M. Murry about writing.

15 Moves in to 52 Tavistock Square; works on the portrait of Bradshaw in *MD*. 'The Enchanted Organ', review of *The Letters of Anne Thackeray Ritchie*, ed. by her daughter Hester Ritchie, in *N&A*.

21 Reads Harold Nicolson's *Bryon: The Last Journey* (1924) – 'tawdry and melodramatic', a poor imitation of LS (to LS).

30 With TSE attends Phoenix Society performance of *King Lear*: 'We both jeered & despised; & now he comes out in the Criterion with solemn & stately rebuke of those who jeer & despise' (*D*, 26 May).

31 Speaks on the unity of the arts at a London Group dinner.

April

5 (Sat) Has finished 'the Dr chapter' in *MD*, is furbishing up the

Greeks and working on the Elizabethans, with no principle in her criticism 'except to follow this whimsical brain'; finds London noisy and 'stony hearted', but convenient and exciting after Richmond (*D*). Paragraph commencing 'I was given the opportunity to see a demonstration of a new colour film process . . .' in *N&A*.

12 'The Patron and the Crocus' in *N&A*.

14 Writes to G. Rylands for his opinion of E. Thompson's poetry (Hogarth, Nov 1925). With R. Mortimer attends Brahms recital by singer Elena Gerhardt.

17 To Rodmell for Easter.

18 Begins second manuscript volume of *MD* ('*The Hours* or *Mrs Dalloway*') with Rezia's reflections after leaving Bradshaw's office.

19 Reads D. Garnett's *A Man in the Zoo* (1924); likes it better than *Lady into Fox*, though it is clumsier. Paragraph commencing 'Aesthetically speaking . . .' in *N&A*.

24 Reads André Maurois's biography of Shelley, *Ariel* (1923), and, for 'Character in Fiction', A. Bennett's *Riceyman Steps* (1923) – 'Such dishwater!' (to E. Sands).

May

3 (Sat) Review of James May's *Anatole France, the Man and his Work* in *N&A*.

5 Declines TSE's invitation to publish part of *MD* in the *Criterion*; offers him 'Character in Fiction' (pub. July).

9 To Tidmarsh to visit LS.

10 'Mr Benson's Memories', review of A. C. Benson's *Memories and Friends*, and paragraph commencing 'The private view of the Royal Academy . . .', in *N&A*.

17–19 To Cambridge; reads 'Character in Fiction' (an expanded version of 'Mr Bennett and Mrs Brown') to the Society of Heretics.

20 In *MD* writes Lady Bruton's letter. RF and Philip Ritchie to dinner; VB, DG, LS and TSE ('sinister & pedagogic') join later.

21 Asks TSE for printer's estimate on 1000 copies of 'Character in Fiction' 'to be published as the first of the Hogarth Essays, entitled *Mr Bennett and Mrs Brown*).

26 Finds *MD* 'reeling off' easily in London – 'to see human beings freely & quickly is an infinite gain' (*D*); plans to work at *MD* through September, shift to *CR* until January, revise *MD* from

January to April, in April publish the essays and in May the novel (she does). Dr James Glover of British Psycho-Analytical Society visits to negotiate arrangements for publishing the International Psycho-analytical Library – and thus of the English translation of Freud's complete works.

HOGARTH PRESS: R. Graves, *Mock Beggar Hall*; Coralie Hobson, *In our Town*; F. M. Mayor, *The Rector's Daughter*; L. Stephen, *Some Early Impressions*.

June

5 (Thurs) To Rodmell for Whitsun holiday.
7 Review of *Marie Elizabeth Townley: A Memoir*, preface by the Bishop of Southwark, in *N&A*.
9 In *MD* Clarissa reflects that she gives parties because she 'likes life'; VW notes '4 or 5 scenes more, Kilman & Elizabeth, The Warren Smiths, Peter, London, The Party' (*D*).
21 Reads *Romeo and Juliet*, and EMF's *Passage to India*, which she finds 'too restrained'. Reviews of Cosmo Hamilton's *Unwritten History*, Stephen Graham's *The Life and Last Words of Wilfrid Ewart*, R. S. Surtees and E. D. Cuming's *Robert Smith Surtees (Creator of 'Jorrocks') 1803–1864*, in *N&A*.
28 'Thunder at Wembly' in *N&A*.
28–9 Visits Garsington with TSE, Lord Balniel and others.

July

2 (Wed) G. Rylands begins work at the Press.
3 'The Weekend', review of *The Week End Book*, ed. V. Mendel and Francis Meynell, in *TLS*.
5 Lunches with VSW and Lord Sackville at Knole House ('Ropes fence off half the rooms . . . life has left them'; cf. 17 Jan 1927); meets Geoffrey Scott and Lady D. Wellesley. Manuscripts pour into the Press and M. Thomson (Joad) has pneumonia. 'Stendhal', review of *Stendhal: Journal, Le Rouge et le Noir, Vie de Rossini*, and review of B. de Sales La Terrière's *Days that are Gone*, in *N&A*.
12 Review of Sir Walter Runciman's *Before the Mast – and After* in *N&A*.
19 Review of C. Hawtrey's *The Truth at Last* in *N&A*.
20 Swamped at the Press by the International Psycho-analytical Library.
30 To Rodmell for the summer.

31 Begins third manuscript volume of *MD* ('*Mrs Dalloway* or *The Hours*') with the scene of Rezia decorating the hat.

'Character in Fiction' in the *Criterion*.

HOGARTH PRESS: Ena Limebeer, *To a Proud Phantom*.

August

2 (Sat) Progressing slowly with *MD*, working on the death of Septimus; determined to refute J. M. Murry's prediction that there is no way to go on after *JR* (10 Mar 1923).

3 Talks with LW about Germany and reparations – 'the facts come in, & I can't deal with them. . . . I think my brain & his are of different orders' (*D*). Begins *CR* for 'the 80th' time; resolves to read John Bunyan's *Pilgrim's Progress* (1678–84), Samuel Richardson's *Clarissa* (1748), Euripides' *Medea*, Plato, and the *Memoirs of the Life of Colonel Hutchinson* (1806). J. Conrad dies; *TLS* wires asking VW for leading article.

9 To Charleston; finds Q. Bell has grown fat and RF truculent. Economist Dennis Holme, JMK and L. Lopokova (whom VW calls 'Rezia' by mistake) return to Monk's House for tea.

14 'Joseph Conrad' in *TLS*.

15 Reading Shakespeare's *King John*, wants to read *Richard the Second* and James Thompson's *The Seasons* (1746) – her taste is now for long poems. Busy at the Press getting estimates for Nancy Cunard's *Parallax* (Apr 1925) and issuing circulars for RF's *Living Painters – Duncan Grant*; M. Joad still absent with pneumonia.

17 In *MD* works on the scene of Septimus alone with the screen.

19 Pained by VSW's charge that she looks upon everything as 'copy' (to VSW).

23 'Editions-de-Luxe', review of Shakespeare's *A Midsomer Night's Dreame* and Clifford Bax, *Studio Plays*, in *N&A*.

Late this month, sees H. Mirrlees and reads her novel *The Counterplot* (1924).

September

4 (Thurs) Reads Yeats, Ramond Radiguet's *La Bal du Comte d'Orgel* (1924), Jean Giradoux's *Suzanne et le Pacifique* (1912), Lord Willoughby de Broke's *The Sport of our Ancestors* (1921), Elizabethan plays, and 'mere daily trash': G. B. Shaw's *Saint Joan* (1924).

7 Works on the final party in *MD*, which is to end 'on three notes,

at different stages of the staircase, each saying something to sum up Clarissa' (*D*).

13 VSW brings her story *Seducers in Ecuador*, and spends the night.

15 Admires *Seducers* – 'she has shed the old verbiage' (*D*).

22 Reads RF's pamphlet *The Artist and Psycho-analysis*; is annoyed that CB cribbed from RF for his article 'Dr Freud on Art', which LW published in *N&A*. Reading P. Lubbock on form in literature: 'I say it is emotion put into the right relations; and has nothing to do with form as used of painting' (to RF; cf. 'Modern Fiction' in *CR*).

27 K. and A. Stephen visit, blowing 'to smithereens' the final chapter of *MD*. 'Appreciations', review of J. B. Priestley's *Figures in Modern Literature*, and paragraph commencing 'The cheapening of motor cars . . .', in *N&A*.

October

2 (Thurs) 'The Schoolroom Floor', review of M. MacCarthy's *A Nineteenth Century Childhood*, in *TLS*.

3 Replies to J. Raverat's charge that writing is 'essentially linear': the falsity of Bennett, Galsworthy *et al*. is that 'they adhere to a formal railway line of sentence'; asks him where she can buy Paul Valéry's recently published dialogues *L'Ame et la danse* and *Eupalinos ou l'architecte* (to J. Raverat).

4 In *MD* writes Sally Seton's account of Hugh's kiss. Returns to Tavistock Square for the winter.

8 Visits R. Partridge, D. Carrington and LS at his new house, Ham Spray, near Hungerford, Berkshire.

9 Writes the final lines of *MD*; compares her achievement to what K. Mansfield would have done, and notes, 'I see already The Old Man' – *TL* (*D*, 17 Nov).

11 Reads H. Walpole's *The Old Ladies* (1924).

17 Feels herself moving into the inner circle of London society, which her father had said represents the Apostles on a larger scale: 'To know everyone worth knowing . . . just imagine being in that position – if women can be' (*D*).

18 Paragraphs commencing 'It is strange as one enters the Mansard Gallery . . .' and 'Not the least pitiable victims of the deplorable summer . . .' in *N&A*.

20 Begins second draft of *MD*.

25 Review of Foster Watson's *Richard Hakluyt*, and *Smoke Rings and Roundelays*, compiled by Wilfred Partington, in *N&A*.

25–6 Visits LS, Carrington and Partridge at Ham Spray; meets Roger Senhouse, friend of LS's newest love, P. Ritchie.

HOGARTH PRESS: VW, *Mr Bennett and Mrs Brown*.

November

1 (Sat) Preparing to revise *MD* and *CR*, notes that the diary has 'loosened the ligatures' of her style.

8 Reviews Annie Kenney's *Memories of a Militant*, and Peggy Webling's *Peggy: The Story of One Score Years and Ten*, in *N&A*.

(Mid-month) Exchanges letters with R. Aldington over the disbanding of the Eliot Fund; the money collected is returned to the donors.

17 Packages Freud's works.

18 Revising the mad chapters in *MD*, wonders whether the book would be better without them.

22 'The Antiquary', review of Mona Wilson's *These were Muses*, and paragraph 'From Alpha to Omega', in *N&A*.

29 Finds P. Valéry trite beneath the brilliant surface (to J. Raverat). 'Indiscretions' in *Vogue*.

HOGARTH PRESS: *Avvakum: The Life of the Archpriest Avvakum by Himself*, tr. J. Harrison and H. Mirrlees, with preface by Prince D. S. Mirsky; T. Bosanquet, *Henry James at Work*; TSE, *Homage to John Dryden: Three Essays on Poetry of the Seventeenth Century*; S. Freud, *Collected Papers*, vols I and II; RF, *The Artist and Psycho-analysis*; Norman Leys, *Kenya*; H. Nicolson, *Jeanne de Héaut*; John Crowe Ransom, *Grace after Meat*; VSW, *Seducers in Ecuador*.

December

10 (Wed) At the Press, Angus Davidson replaces G. Rylands, who returns to Cambridge to work on his fellowship dissertation.

13 Has begun retyping *MD* from the beginning, working with a 'wet brush', joining parts composed separately. Jubilant because *Harper's* has offered her 'at least £50' for an article.

19 RF and VSW dine, a 'disastrous' combination.

21 Putting on a spurt to finish *MD* and *CR*, wants to be free to write out 'one or two more stories', though is 'less & less sure that they are stories'. S. Tomlin wants to sculpt her.

24 To Rodmell for Christmas; writes 'The Dunciad', an apocryphal life of DG illustrated by Q. Bell.

'Miss Ormerod', founded upon *Autobiography and Correspondence of Eleanor Ormerod*, ed. Robert Wallace, in the *Dial*, New York.

1925

EVENTS AND LETTERS. G. B. Shaw awarded Nobel Prize. John Dos Passos publishes *Manhattan Transfer*; T. Dreiser, *An American Tragedy*; TSE, *Poems 1905–25*; F. Scott Fitzgerald, *The Great Gatsby*; M. Proust, *Albertine disparue* (posth.); VW, *The Common Reader*, *Mrs Dalloway*; W. B. Yeats, *A Vision*.

January

6 (Tues) Works on 'Notes on an Elizabethan Play'; sets type for N. Cunard's *Parallax*; conceives stories: 'The Old Man (a character of L.S. [Leslie Stephen]). The Professor on Milton – (an attempt at literary criticism) & now The Interruption, women talking alone' (*D*; 'The Old Man' evolves into *TL*; 'The Professor' appears at the party at the end of *MD*, added after the manuscript draft).

24 Wrangles with L. P. Smith, who claims writing for *Vogue* is demeaning. Bedridden with influenza for the next two weeks.

25 VW's forty-third birthday.

February

2 (Mon) Reads J. Austen's *Mansfield Park* (1814).

4 M. Joad leaves the Press and Bernadette Murphy fills in until June.

5 Sends proofs of *MD* to J. Raverat, who is dying, notes that much has been rewritten (the space breaks that mark a change of scene are added after the manuscript draft).

9 Declares Dickens' *Hard Times* (1854) 'mere sentiment and melodrama'; advises M. L. Davies, for a 'modern with a zest, why not try Proust?' – has read three of the ten volumes of 'difficult French' (to M. L. Davies).

March

5 (Thurs) 'Notes on an Elizabethan Play' in *TLS*.

10 Receives letter from J. Raverat on *MD*, and one from G. Raverat announcing his death.

14 'From Alpha to Omega', paragraph commencing 'Coming back to London . . .', in *N&A*.

18 Visits Q. Bell and J. Bell at Leighton Park School. 'Olive Schreiner', review of *The Letters of Olive Schreiner*, ed. Cronwright Schreiner, in the *New Republic*, New York.

26 To Hotel Cendrillon in Cassis, France, for 12 days – sails, discusses books, visits Marseille and Toulon, meets New Zealand novelist Miss Toogood and various 'Bugger-Bloomsbury' young men whose presumptuous familiarity annoys her but cannot spoil her 'perfect happiness' (*D*, 8 Apr).

28 Review of Bernard, Lord Coleridge's *This for Remembrance* in *N&A*.

April

8 (Wed) Reflects on J. Raverat's praise of *MD*; wonders if this time she has achieved something: 'Well, nothing anyhow compared with Proust, in whom I am embedded now. . . . He is as tough as catgut & as evanescent as a butterfly's bloom' (*D*). Begins reading for 'American Fiction' (Aug).

9 To Rodmell for Easter.

11 'The Two Samuel Butlers', review of S. Butler's *The Life and Letters of Dr Samuel Butler*, plus reviews of Una Taylor's *Guests and Memories: Annals of a Seaside Villa* and Stewart Ellis's *Mainly Victorian*, in *N&A*.

18 Attends exhibition of new caricatures by M. Beerbohm at Leicester Galleries. 'John Addington Symonds', review of Margaret Symonds' *Out of the Past*, plus reviews of S. Baring-Gould's *Further Reminiscences 1864–1894* and *The Letters of Mary Russell Mitford*, intro. by R. Brimley Johnson, in *N&A*.

19 Works on new stories and on Ring Lardner for 'American Fiction'; wants to make £300 this summer to build a bath and hot-water range at Rodmell.

20 Has 'at least 6 stories welling up' inside; has a new faith in her writing and wonders if she might not become 'one of the interesting – I will not say great – but interesting novelists' (*D*).

23 *CR* published; a flurried and stammering Robert Graves introduces himself at the Press; VW attends performance of G. B. Shaw's 'strange rhetorical romantic' *Caesar and Cleopatra*.

25 'Pictures', plus review of Sir Johnston Forbes-Robertson's *A Player under Three Reigns*, and paragraph commencing 'What the bloods of the nineties . . .', in *N&A*.

27 Photographed for *Vogue*; wants to investigate 'the party consciousness, the frock consciousness' (*D*).

28 TSE, 'tremulous & excited', announces that he is leaving the bank, but does not say to where.

HOGARTH PRESS: Ferenc Békássy, *Adriactica and Other Poems*; N. Cunard, *Parallax*; Kathleen Innes, *The Story of the League of Nations Told for Young People*; C. H. B. Kitchin, *Streamers Waving*; Edwin Muir, *First Poems*; R. C. Trevelyan, *Poems and Fables*; VW, *The Common Reader*.

May

2 (Sat) To Cambridge, her criticism praised by G. L. Dickinson and John Hayward (student, later bibliophile and editor); dines at Newnham College with P. Strachey while LW dines with the Apostles.

7 *CR* praised soberly in *TLS* and enthusiastically by G. L. Dickinson; a week later the *Manchester Guardian* calls it 'a combination of brilliance and integrity' (*M&M*).

9 Attends performance of J. T. Sheppard's versions of Euripides' *Helen* and *Cyclops* at Chiswick Empire with L. Lopokova and popular novelist Berta Ruck whom VW had first met through lawyers after placing her name on a tombstone in *JR*: see *QB* II). Review of Louis Piérard's *The Tragic Life of Vincent Van Gogh*, tr. Herbert Garland, in *N&A*.

10 Attends performance of Thomas Otway's *The Orphan*.

13 Dr Leys, D. MacCarthy, Lord Sydney Olivier (administrator and author), G. Rylands, J. Strachey visit; VW offers to make a selection of MacCarthy's essays for a collection.

14 Decides *TL* will include 'all the usual things': 'life, death &c. But the centre is father's character'; it is to simmer while VW writes a few stories (*D*; to VSW, 27 May). *MD* published, reviewed unfavourably in *Western Mail* and *The Scotsman*, favourably in the *Saturday Review of Literature* (New York), which likens her 'creative faculty of form' to that of Cézanne (*M&M*).

15 Lunches with D. MacCarthy, has found his essays lack the drive which makes an article whole.

16 'Gypsy or Governess?', review of M. Asquith's *Places and*

Persons, and review of Herman Bernstein's *Celebrities of our Times*, in *N&A*.

17 Notes positive review of *MD* in the *Observer* but anxiously awaits EMF's judgement.

19 Attends dinner party given by O., S. and E. Sitwell; admires their breeding and their grotesque faces. Fellow guests include F. Birrell, R. Mortimer, orientalist Arthur Waley, and American novelist and editor Charles Towne.

20 EMF admires *MD*, thinks it better than *JR*.

26 VSW writes that she prefers *CR*, 'a guide, philosopher, and friend', to *MD*, a 'will-of-the-wisp'.

27 Reads Geoffrey Scott's *Portrait of Zélide*; does not like it. At JMK's meets Sylvia Warner, whose poems, *The Espalier*, have just been published – she has sufficient merit to warrant VW spending 2*s*. 6*d*. (*D*, 1 June).

31 TSE visits; announces his appointment to the editorial board of Faber and Gwyer (later Faber and Faber) – and that his works must go to them; does not mention VW's books. Florence Hardy sends T. Hardy's 'Coming up Oxford Street: Evening'; says he is reading *CR* with 'great pleasure'. Tauchnitz (Leipzig publishers) inquire about European rights.

HOGARTH PRESS: Mrs Eliza Fay, *Original Letters from India (1779–1815)*, notes by EMF; VW, *Mrs Dalloway*.

June

1 (Mon) At the Press, B. Murphy is proving 'temperamental, untidy, sloppy' and 'crusty' (*D*).

13 F. L. Lucas and medieval historian Eileen Power to dinner; O. and R. Strachey come in afterward. 'Harriette Wilson', review of *The Memoirs of Harriette Wilson*, in *N&A*.

14 Has written six stories and thought out, 'perhaps too clearly', *TL*. Reads Lady Murasaki's *The Tale of Genji* (reviewed July). Attends party at O. Morrell's; infuriates her by ignoring the brilliant young men. Replies to G. Brenan, taking up his criticism that Septimus has no function in *MD*.

16 Drafts review of *Genji*; begins '*David Copperfield*' (22 Aug).

18 LS does not like Clarissa Dalloway; VW admits she found her 'tinselly' (*D*).

27 Composes *TL* – 'the sea is to be heard all through it'; wants a name for her books to supplant 'novel', 'But what? Elegy?' (*D*).

Late this month, inspired by Pirandello season at New Oxford Theatre, 'stumbles' through a play in Italian (to J. Case).
'George Moore' in *Vogue*.

July

5 (Sun) Works on 'The New Dress'; attends performance of George Villiers' *The Rehearsal*.
9 Lady Colefax and G. Rylands to tea; TSE visits after dinner, still hedging over whether or not to leave the bank.
12 Attends performance of LS's play *The Son of Heaven*.
(Mid-month) Mrs Cartwright succeeds B. Murphy at the Press; remains until 31 March 1931.
19 JMK brings his pamphlet *The Economic Consequences of Mr Churchill* to the Press; needs 7000 copies to be printed and distributed in a week.
20 Finishes article on Jonathan Swift (24 Sep). Wants to begin *TL* the first day at Monk's House; conceives the book in three parts: '1. at the drawing room window; 2. seven years passed; 3. the voyage' (*D*).
27 Assures P. Morrell that he was not the model for the dull Hugh Whitbread or Richard Dalloway in *MD* (to P. Morrell).
30 With *TL*, vacillating between 'a single & intense character of father; & a far wider slower book' (*D*).
Late this month, *'The Tale of Genji*, review of Lady Murasaki's *The Tale of Genji*, vol. I, tr. A. Waley, in *Vogue*.
Hogarth Press: Conrad Aiken, *Senlin: A Biography*; Bonamy Dobrée, *Histriophone: A Dialogue on Dramatic Diction*; JMK, *The Economic Consequences of Mr Churchill*; Alan Lubbock, *The Character of John Dryden*; LW, *Fear and Politics*.

August

1 (Sat) 'Pattledom', review of Lady Troubridge's *Memoirs and Reflections*, in *N&A*.
5 To Rodmell for the summer.
8 Reviews of Donald Maxwell's *Unknown Essex*, and W. G. Elliot's *In my Anecdotage*, in *N&A*.
15 Review of John Gloag's *Time, Taste and Furniture* in *N&A*.
16 Lunches with the Keyneses: JMK and L. Lopokova, married 4 August.
19 To Charleston for Q. Bell's birthday. VW collapses, spends

the next two weeks in 'that odd amphibious life of headache' (*D*); she continues bedridden off and on until December.

22 *'David Copperfield'*, and review of Dickens' *The Uncommercial Traveller, Reprinted Pieces and Christmas Stories*, in *N&A*.

24 Weighed down by manuscripts for the Press, especially by 'the whole of Gertrude Stein' (her 59-page pamphlet, *Composition as Explanation*): 'I think her dodge is to repeat the same word 100 times over in different connections, until at last you feel the force of it' (to VSW).

'American Fiction' in *Saturday Review of Literature*.

September

1 (Tues) Fumes over VSW's doubting her admiration for the poet Crabbe – 'I bought a copy out of my own pocket money before you were weaned' (to VSW); and over J. Case's assumption that she values technique above thought – 'The better a thing is expressed, the more completely it is thought' (to J. Case).

4 B. and E. Richmond visit; VW, who had admired her, finds them painfully dull.

5 In spite of headaches for the last two weeks, has made a 'quick & flourishing attack on *TL* . . . 22 pages straight off in less than a fortnight', much quicker than the opening of *MD* (*D*). Paragraph commencing 'A brilliant Englishwoman . . .' in *N&A*.

7 TSE invites VW to contribute to the *New Criterion*.

8 Replies to TSE; is 'honoured' to contribute, and notes demand for reprint of Hogarth edition of *The Waste Land*.

10 'Tom has treated us scurvily' (*D*): *TLS* announces Faber and Gwyer is to publish TSE's *Collected Poems*, including *The Waste Land*.

12 *'David Copperfield'*, letter to the editor, in *N&A*.

18 Insists again to J. Case that one cannot separate technique from matter in good writing, and therefore she cannot read R. L. Stevenson but admires W. Lamb; plans to lecture on this to a girl's school (30 Jan 1926). Still suffering from headaches (to J. Case).

20 Disappointed in D. Garnett's *The Sailor's Return* (1925).

22 Reads *Hamlet*.

23 The Keyneses visit, back from honeymoon in Russia; LS visits,

says Garnett's novel is humourless, with nothing of the author in it, 'like a perfectly restored Inn' (*D*).

24 Writes two pages of a story to 'test' herself. 'Swift's Journal to Stella' in *TLS*.

26 Paragraph commencing 'In any family save the Darwins . . .' in *N&A*.

30 Annoyed at TSE's 'poaching': he has asked H. Read to write for Faber.

October

2 (Fri) Returns to London for the winter.

5 Ill again, bedridden for most of October and November.

13 Writes to VSW, disturbed that H. Nicolson has been posted to Persia.

17 'Congreve', review of *Comedies of William Congreve*, and review of Louise Jopling-Rowe's *Twenty Years of my Life*, in *N&A*.

19 VSW to tea.

Hogarth Press: Willa Muir, *Women: An Inquiry*; Herbert Palmer, *Songs of Salvation, Sin and Satire*; H. Read, *In Retreat*; E. Sitwell, *Poetry and Criticism*.

November

7 (Sat) Attends funeral of M. Vaughan, who has ceased to mean anything to her, but who was the first woman to engage VW's love, and the model for Sally Seton in *MD* (*D*, 27 Nov). 'Sterne's Ghost' in *N&A*.

14 'Saint Samuel of Fleet Street', review of James Boswell's *The Life of Samuel Johnson*, ed. Arnold Glover, intro. Arthur Dobson, Boswell's *The Life of Samuel Johnson*, ed. Roger Ingpen, and *Boswell's Life of Johnson*, abridged and ed. F. H. Pritchard, in *N&A*.

27 Wants to write a book of criticism ('Phases of Fiction', which she struggles with over the next three years).

Hogarth Press: Gates Barrington, *Poems*; R. Graves, *Contemporary Techniques of Poetry*; J. Harrison, *Reminiscences of a Student's Life*; Edward Thompson, *The Other Side of the Medal*.

December

2 (Wed) Attends ballet, first night out for two months.

5 'Melba', review of Nellie Melba's *Memories and Melodies*, and

review of Viscountess Wolseley's *Some of the Smaller Manor Houses of Sussex*, in *N&A*.

7 Reads EMF's *A Passage to India*.

17–20 Stays with VSW at Long Barn for the weekend, the beginning of their love affair.

26 Review of W. Lancely's *From Hall-boy to House-steward* in *N&A*.

22–8 Spends Christmas with the Bells and RF at Charleston, while builders work on Monk's House; VSW to lunch on Boxing Day.

HOGARTH PRESS: John Doyle, *The Marmosite's Miscellany*; EMF, *Anonymity: An Enquiry*; JMK, *A Short View of Russia*; G. Rylands, *Russet and Taffeta*.

1926

EVENTS AND LETTERS. General Strike in Britain; R. M. Rilke dies. E. Hemingway publishes *The Sun also Rises*; F. Kafka, *The Castle* (posth.); D. H. Lawrence, *The Plumed Serpent*; T. E. Lawrence, *Seven Pillars of Wisdom*; Sean O'Casey, *The Plough and the Stars*; E. Pound, *Personae*; A. Gide, *Les Faux-monnayeurs*; M. Proust, *Thérèse Desqueyroux* (posth.).

January

7 (Thurs) Reads *The Tempest* to compare with Defoe (for review, 6 Feb).

9 Intends to begin *TL* but is bedridden with German measles.

15 Begins *TL*; works on 'How Should One Read a Book?'

(Mid-month) Visited by actress Hilda Trevelyan, the original 'Wendy' in *Peter Pan* (1904) and Doris Daglish, who asks if she should devote her life to literature (LW advises her to be a cook). Sees R. Mortimer, S. Sassoon, G. Rylands, G. Raverat, as well as CB and M. Hutchinson.

18 Works on ch. 4 of *TL* (Lily and Bankes looking at the bay).

21 *TL*, ch. 5 (Mrs Ramsay knitting).

24 *TL*, ch. 6 (Mr Ramsay chanting, 'Someone had blundered').

25 VW's forty-fourth birthday.

26 Missing VSW, who has departed for four months in Persia, and stung by her charge that she writes 'lovely phrases' that rob things of reality; in *TL* working faster than ever before, but conceded her books always go quickly for the first 50

pages (to VSW, the first of several long letters to her, Jan–Apr).

30 Delivers lecture 'How Should One Read a Book?' to private girls' school at Hayes Court in Kent. Review of *Mary Elizabeth Haldane: A Record of A Hundred Years*, ed. by her daughter, in *N&A*.

Late this month, attends lecture by Tolstoy's daughter on her mother and father; the lecture is dull but the sight of the Countess inspiring.

31 Works on *TL*, ch. 7 (James's hatred of his father).

'On being Ill' in the *New Criterion*.

February

3 (Wed) 'In the thick of' *TL* from 10 a.m. to 1 p.m.; reading manuscripts and setting poetry (Ruth Manning-Sanders' *Martha Wish-You-Ill*) in the afternoon, finding it discordant to shift from the world of the novel to the social world. EMF visits; delights VW with news that Mrs T. Hardy rejects the idea of J. M. Murry writing her husband's biography (in the February *Adelphi* Murry had condemned *JR* and *The Waste Land*, predicting they would be forgotten 50 years hence, unless their authors achieved 'real spontaneity').

5 To Rodmell for the weekend, having two waterclosets made: one paid for by *MD* and one by *CR*.

6 *'Robinson Crusoe'*, review of *The Life and Adventures of Robinson Crusoe, Further Adventures of Robinson Crusoe* and *Serious Reflections of Robinson Crusoe*, and review of Elizabeth Villiers' *Queen Alexandra the Well-Beloved*, in *N&A*.

8 Returns from Rodmell; receives letter of 'hysterical flattery' from Marie Kieffer, who with Claude Dravaine is translating two extracts of *JR*, which appear in *La Revue nouvelle* (Mar 1927) and *Revue politique et littéraire: revue bleue* (6 Aug 1927).

(Mid-month) Lunches with LS; talks about E. Gosse, whose writing she abominates, and LS's work on Queen Elizabeth (*Elizabeth and Essex*, pub. 1928).

18 Works on *TL*, ch. 14 (Nancy and Minta Doyle).

22 Begins *TL*, ch. 11 (Mrs Ramsay watching the lighthouse).

23 F. Birrell and R. Macaulay dine; G. Raverat arrives later, and they talk of L. Stephen's love of lamentation and of his wife's beauty – VW thinks of how much of this is in *TL*.

25 Dines at CB's; meets Lord Berners, says all you need do in

writing is 'float off the contents of your mind', but she wants to do more (*D*).

27 In *TL* begins convention of starting each day on a new page.

28 Visits Herbert Woolf, LW's stockbroker brother, and his wife Freda, and, enchanted by the simplicity of their lives, briefly falls in love with 'being a stockbroker' (to VSW).

March

1 (Mon) Argues with F. L. Lucas about poetry: he condemns TSE, champions Housman and de la Mare; VW dismisses the latter as a 'drawing room singer' (*D*, 3 Mar).

2 Reads VSW's poem *The Land*; advises her to alter the opening. Wonders how to manage the passage of ten years in *TL*; complains that the social demands of London make novel writing an impossibility (to VSW).

4 Attends tea at E. Sands's with Leigh Ashton, of the Victoria and Albert Museum, O. Morrell, P. Lubbock, G. Rylands and others.

5 Works on *TL*, ch. 16 (Mrs Ramsay dressing for dinner).

6 Review of Harry Furniss's *Paradise in Piccadilly* in *N&A*.

5/8 Attends party at M. Hutchinson's; meets novelist George Moore for the first time, enjoys his vitality and disagrees with everything he says (*D*, 9 May).

16 Explains to VSW that 'style' is all 'rhythm', which goes deeper than words: 'A sight, an emotion, creates this wave . . . and then, as it breaks and tumbles in the mind, it makes words to fit it' (to VSW).

17 Works on *TL*, ch. 17 (Mr Carmichael at dinner).

19 Dines at CB's to meet Lord Ivor Churchill, an art collector who impresses VW as a mere dandy, but who comes to the Press the next morning to buy her complete works.

20 Reviews of *Reminiscences of Mrs Comys Carr*, ed. Eve Adam, Arthur Hayward's *The Days of Dickens*, and Violet Hunt's *The Flurried Years*, in *N&A*.

24 Reads Tolstoy's *Anna Karenina* (1877). Dines disastrously with R. Macaulay and friends: VW takes up a remark on the Holy Ghost, finds the discussion is of 'The Whole Coast'; LW picks up a napkin, finds he is lifting a petticoat (*QB* II; in VW's account to VSW, 29 Mar, LW retrieves a sanitary towel).

26 Attends gathering at VB's, with L. Ashton, painters W. Sickert and his wife Thérese Lessore, and others.

27 Review of William Larkins' *Steeple-jacks and Steeplejacking* in *N&A*.

29 Finishes the dinner scene in *TL*; works on an index for *Castles in the Air*, memoirs of Viola Tree, daughter of actor–manager Sir H. Beerbohm Tree (Hogarth, Apr).

'The Life of John Mytton', review of *Memoirs of the Life of John Mytton Esq.*, by Nimrod (pseud. of C. J. Apperley), in *Vogue*.

HOGARTH PRESS: Douglas Ainslie, *Chosen Poems*, preface by G. K. Chesterton; W. Arnold-Forster, *The Victory of Reason*; K. Innes, *How the League of Nations Works Told for Young People*; M. Jaeger, *The Question Mark*; Marius Lyle, *The Education of a Young Man in Twelve Lessons*; R. C. Trevelyan, *The Deluge and Other Poems*; Hubert Waley, *The Revival of Aesthetics*; W. Plomer, *Turbott Wolfe*.

April

7 (Wed) Buys two gross of pen nibs for her Penkala pen.

9 Reads B. Webb's autobiography *My Apprenticeship* (1926) – 'enthralling' – and *The Letters of Sir Walter Raleigh, 1879–1922* (1926) – 'disgusting'. Takes tea with Walter Leaf and family; misses the 'natural happiness' of family life. (*D*; to VSW, to VB.)

12 Works on 'Cinema'.

13–18 On holiday in Dorset.

29 Finishes pt I of *TL*.

30 Begins pt II, 'Time Passes': 'the most difficult abstract piece of writing', but still it goes easily (*D*).

HOGARTH PRESS: P. J. Noel-Baker, *Disarmament*; V. Tree, *Castles in the Air*.

May

1 (Sat) Mineworkers go on strike.

2 The Trades Union Congress proclaims a General Strike in support of the mineworkers; VW records the unnatural atmosphere of the city, 'great activity but no normal life', cold and windy streets full of people trekking to work, no tubes, or regular cabs or busses, no newspapers, and a constant round of unresolved discussions and arguments (see *D*, 5–20 May).

6 Excited by the prospect of dress-buying with Dorothy Todd, the editor of *Vogue*.

7 Reads in the Reading Room of the British Museum for the first

time in many years; likes the 'chill serenity, dignity, & severity' (*D*).

9 In *TL* sketches Mrs MacNab (pt. II, ch. 5). Quarrels with LW over the strike: 'I dislike the tub thumper in him; he the irrational Xtian in me' (*D*).

10 Settles quarrel, but plagued by incessant arguments and interruptions; takes LW's article to the House of Commons, notes there is no violence in the West End; LW gets up a petition calling upon the Government to restart negotiations.

11 Visited by art historian Margaret Bulley, RF and H. Anrep, R. Patridge, CB and others, including G. Brenan, who composes a letter to J. Galsworthy (author of *The Forsyte Saga*), who has refused to sign the petition.

12 Sees armoured cars going down Oxford Street; Harold Laski, professor of political science at the London School of Economics, assures them that the General Strike will be settled that afternoon – it is, but individual negotiations continue and many unions remain out in the days following. VW attends a strike party with CB, RF and others.

14 Works on *TL*, pt II, ch. 6 (spring).

18 V. Tree, 'half sordid half splendid', to dinner to discuss the sales of her book, which have been stifled by the strike.

19 H. Waley visits to discuss his pamphlet *The Revival of Aesthetics* (Hogarth, Mar).

22 Asks VSW to publish *Passenger to Tehran* with Hogarth rather than Heinemann's (pub. Nov).

25 Has 'sketchily' finished *TL*, pt II, 'Time Passes'.

27 Begins pt III, 'The Lighthouse'.

31 Works on ch. 1 (Lily preparing to paint).

Late this month, attends VB's show, amazed by the smaller works, but 'still I think the problems of design on a large scale slightly baffle you' (to VB, 2 June).

Review of *The Letters of Walter Raleigh*, ed. Lady Raleigh, in *Vogue*.

June

1 (Tues) Attends party at E. Sitwell's in honour of G. Stein – 'rather formidable' – who had been invited to address literary societies at Oxford and Cambridge (the lecture, *Composition as Explanation*, pub. Hogarth, Nov).

5 Stricken with 'nerve exhaustion headache' (to M. MacCarthy).

9 Still bedridden, revising 'How Should One Read a Book?' for

the *Yale Review*. LW lunches with H. G. Wells, who tells him VW is '"too intelligent – a bad thing"' (*D*).

19 Dines with M. Hutchinson to meet A. Huxley, just back from a world tour.

21 Works on *TL*, pt III, ch. 3 (Lily in the 'perpetual combat' of imposing form).

26–7 To Garsington. With O. Morrell and A. Huxley visits R. Bridges, Poet Laureate, at Boar's Hill, Oxford; discusses handwriting, Keats and criticism, inspects manuscripts of G. M. Hopkins.

'Cinema' in *Arts*, New York; 'Jones and Wilkinson', drawn from Tate Wilkinson, *Memoirs of his own Life*, in *Bermondsey Book*.

July

1 (Thurs) Meets H. G. Wells at a lunch party at the Keyneses'.

2 Lunches with D. MacCarthy and H. G. Wells, who talks of his new book, *The World of William Clissold*, and reminisces about T. Hardy and H. James, discusses S. Richardson, T. S. Eliot, A. Bennett and Proust, whose book he compares to the British Museum – 'One knows there are delightful interesting things in it, but one does not go there' (*D*).

3 'Romance and the 'Nineties', review of Richard Le Gallienne's *The Romantic Nineties*, in *N&A*.

15 Asks VSW to send H. Nicolson's *Tennyson* and *Venetian Glass Nephew* (1925) by Elinor Wylie, an American writer VW has just met.

22 Has put *TL* aside until Rodmell; works on de Quincey's 'Suspiria de Profundis', struggling to define the difference between poetry and prose. Dines with O. Sitwell.

23 To Dorchester to visit T. Hardy, a genial host who resists all attempts to get him to talk about his books.

26 To Long Barn to visit VSW, who gives VW a spaniel puppy (Pinker), who becomes the model for 'Flush'.

27 To Rodmell for the summer.

28–31 Experiences a 'nervous breakdown in miniature'; notes her return to health is marked by the power to make images again (*D*).

Late this month, reads Maurice Baring's *C* (1924); finds it 'entirely second rate' but possessing merit none the less (*D*). Writes an introduction to *Victorian Photographs of Famous Men and Fair Women*, by her great aunt, Julia Margaret Cameron (Hogarth, Oct).

Hogarth Press: R. Graves, *Another Future of Poetry*; JMK, *The End of Laissez-faire*; Vernon Lee, *The Poet's Eye*; R. Manning-Sanders, *Martha Wish-You-Ill*; E. Muir, *Chorus of the Newly Dead*; C. P. Sanger, *The Structure of Wuthering Heights by C. P. S.*

August

4 (Wed) In *TL* begins pt iii, ch. 4 (the boat becalmed).

8 Finds D. Wellesley's long poem *Genesis* 'cobbled, jerked, patched', though with merits (to VSW).

12 Reading S. Richardson's *Clarissa* (1748); reports, 'Clarissa brightening up – seduced last night – I should say raped – most impressive' (to S. Sydney-Turner).

(Mid-month) Reads H. G. Wells's *The World of William Clissold*: 'rather thin spread – bread comes through' (to E. Sackville West).

17 Works on *TL*, pt iii, ch. 8 (James remembering his symbol of 'striking his father to the heart').

20 Dines at the Keyneses'. Attends Q. Bell's eighth birthday party at Charleston.

26 Works on *TL*, pt iii, ch. 11 (Lily gazing at the bay).

September

1 (Wed) Continues *TL*, pt iii, ch. 11. (Lily remembering Tansley and Mrs Ramsay on the beach).

3 Writes scene of Lily on the lawn, but not sure whether it is the 'last lap' or not; still writing easily.

5 Predicts *TL* will be finished in three weeks; concerned about how to bring Lily and Mr Ramsay together at the end; considers using parentheses so that one has the sense of reading two things at the same time. Finds stories are 'sprouting' from sources such as Clara Pater's remark ' "Don't you find that Barker's pins have no points to them?" ' (*D*), which leads to ' "Slater's Pins have no Points" ' (Jan 1928); plans to return to her book on literature ('Phases of Fiction').

6 Begins *TL*, pt iii, ch. 12 (approaching the lighthouse).

6–10 Works on de Quincey.

12 Continues *TL*, pt iii, ch. 12 (James's reaction to the lighthouse).

13 Confident of *TL*, but still haunted by J. Case's criticism that *MD* was 'all dressing . . . technique' (*D*).

15 Reads proofs of VSW's *Passenger to Tehran*, impressed with the method, though finds 'one or two dangling dim places' (to

VSW). In diary records 'A State of Mind': waves of irrational horror passing over.

16 Finishes *TL*, 'provisionally'. '"Impassioned Prose"', on Thomas de Quincey, in *TLS*.

28 Records bouts of intense depression, due in part to having finished *TL* and not working on anything else; finds these moods frightening, but useful, for 'nothing protects one from the assault of truth' (*D*).

30 Notes there is a mystical side to her dark moods: 'It is not oneself but something in the universe that one's left with. . . . One sees a fin passing far out. . . . it may be the impulse behind another book' – it is: *W* (*D*).

October

3 (Sun) Invites G. Brenan to the 'Bloomsbury Bar', a new society, to meet on alternate Fridays, in which each of the eight hosts, CB, DG, VB, EMF, RF, LS, LW and VW, would be allowed to bring three guests.

9 'The Cosmos', review of *The Journals of Thomas James Cobden-Sanderson, 1879–1922*, in *N&A*.

14 Returns to London for the winter.

15 Writes to S. Sydney-Turner with her distinction between 'vapid' ('heavy, vacant, blank') and 'insipid' (trivial, frivolous, chattering') used in the review of Cobden-Sanderson (9 Oct).

16 'Laughter and Tears', review of Jerome K. Jerome's *My Life and Times*, in *N&A*.

23–4 To Cambridge. Dines with JMK; LW reads a paper to the Heretics' Club.

25 Attends performance of Chekhov's *The Three Sisters*.

27 Attends VSW's lecture to the Royal Society of Literature; annoyed by the smug respectability of the gathering, and especially of Sir E. Gosse – 'the ornament on the tea pot' (*D*).

30 Revising *TL*, beginning to think of a book of a solitary woman musing, a dramatisation of her dark mood at Rodmell, 'an endeavour at something mystic, spiritual; the thing that exists when we aren't there' (*D*). Has received books from M. Baring (*Punch and Judy and other Essays*, 1924; *Daphne Adeane*, 1926; *Cat's Cradle*, 1926; and *The Glass Mender and other Stories*, 1926), from O. Sitwell (*Before the Bombardment*, 1926), and from S. Sitwell (*All Summer in a Day*, 1926). 'George Eliot', review of *The Letters of George Eliot*, intro. R. Brimley Johnson, in *N&A*.

Hogarth Press: J. M. Cameron, *Victorian Photographs of Famous Men and Fair Women*, intro. VW and RF; Mary Edwards, *Time and Chance Poems*; Laura Riding Gottschalk, *The Close Chaplet*; F. L. Lucas, *The River Flows*; E. Muir, *Transition: Essays on Contemporary Literature*; Stanley Snaith, *April Morning*.

November

4 (Thurs) EMF visits to meet French critic Abel Chevalley, whose lecture for the PEN Club on the French contemporary novel EMF is presiding over. VW dines at H. G. Wells's to meet A. Bennett and G. B. Shaw.

6–8 Visits VSW at Long Barn.

7 'Life and the Novelist', review of G. B. Stern's *A Deputy was King*, in the *New York Herald Tribune*.

23 Revising *TL* on the typewriter at the rate of six pages a day, still haunted by the idea of a life of a woman contained in a single incident in which time will be obliterated, 'My theory being that the actual event practically does not exist – nor time either'. Discusses A. Davidson with LW, who concludes, 'he don't do', will never make a manager for the Press (*D*).

Hogarth Press: Joseph Burtt, *The People of Ararat*; B. Dobrée, *Rochester: A Conversation between Sir George Etherage and Mr Fitzjames*; R. Macaulay, *Catchwords and Claptrap*; K. Martin, *The British Public and the General Strike*; VSW, *Passenger to Tehran*; G. Stein, *Composition as Explanation*.

December

3 (Fri) Invited by Lady Colefax to meet A. Bennett, who had attacked her in the *Evening Standard* the previous evening (in 'Am I a Snob?', 1936, VW suggests the book may have been *O*, but it had not yet been written: Bennett criticised her work for poor 'character-drawing', lack of 'logical construction', and 'absence of vital inspiration' on the basis of the 'two and a half' books he had read by her – *CR*, *JR* and *MD*, which 'beat' him; however, VW referred to this review in the manuscript draft of *O*, and Bennett did write a review expressing his disappointment in *O* – see *MOB*, *M&M* and Moore).

4 To Long Barn for the weekend with VSW.

11 Works on *TL*. Reads Laurence Sterne's *Tristram Shandy* (1767) and W. B. Yeats's *Autobiographies* (repr. 1926); finds 'reading

Yeats turns my sentences one way: reading Sterne turns them another' (*D*).

18 'Genius', review of *The Autobiography and Memoirs of Benjamin Robert Haydon*, intro. by A. Huxley, in *N&A*.

22 To Cornwall to spend a very Gold Christmas with K. and W. Arnold-Forster. Reads Margaret Kennedy's *The Constant Nymph* (1924), doggedly, and A. Gide's memoirs *Si le grain ne meurt* (1926), 'voraciously' (to VSW); revises *TL*.

HOGARTH PRESS (month of publication unknown): RF, *Art and Commerce*.

1927

EVENTS AND LETTERS. Charles Lindbergh flies the Atlantic solo; H. Bergson awarded Nobel Prize; EMF publishes *Aspects of the Novel*; E. Hemingway, *Men without Women*; H. Hesse, *Steppenwolf*; M. Proust, *A la recherche du temps perdu* (posth.); VW, *To the Lighthouse*.

January

14 (Fri) Finishes *TL*; feels it is 'a hard muscular book' (*D*).

17–19 Visits Knole with VSW: 'All the centuries seemed lit up, the past expressive . . . & so we reach the days of Elizabeth quite easily' – the genesis of *O* (*D*).

23 LW pronounces *TL* a 'masterpiece'.

24 Dines at Lady Colefax's with V. Tree, D. Wellesley, M. Hutchinson and others; bored by Sir Arthur Colefax on the Trades Union movement (see 'Am I a Snob?', *MOB*).

25 VW's forty-fifth birthday.

26 VSW and W. J. Turner to dinner. CB arrives distraught, announces he is breaking off with M. Hutchinson, leaving immediately for the south of France to write a book; over the next few days VW attempts to mediate, but finds herself blamed by M. Hutchinson as the cause of the rupture.

27 Writes to O. Morrell, winding up the Eliot fund; in early February helps organise a fund for the MacCarthys.

28 Spends the morning with VSW, who leaves for Persia.

29 Stays overnight with S. and B. Webb in Surrey, finds their mechanically efficient minds uncongenial; meets Lord Russell, husband of the best-selling author 'Elizabeth'.

31 VW and LW negotiate with F. Birrell to purchase the

Bloomsbury bookshop founded by him and D. Garnett (finally they do not do so).

Hogarth Press: S. Freud, *The Ego and the Id*, tr. Joan Riviere; Sandor Ferenczi, *Further Contributions to the Theory and Technique of Psycho-analysis*, compiled by John Rickman, tr. Jane Suttie and others.

February

Early this month, attends RF's exhibition at the Lefevre Gallery; says she thinks he has improved 'vastly' only to discover that the pictures she has praised had been painted 10 years before (to VB, 5 Mar).

5 (Sat) Absorbed in 'Phases of Fiction', which is to be about 'how to read all fiction as if it were one book one had written oneself' (to VSW).

9 CB and B. Mayor to dinner; Mayor shingles VW's hair: 'Behind I'm like the rump of a partridge' (*D*).

11 H. G. Wells asks to have *Democracy under Revision* published by Hogarth; relations with A. Davidson continue to be strained; VW feels the Press needs a 'fanatic', 'not this quiet easygoing gentlemanliness' (*D*).

12 Discouraged by the early reception of *TL*: RF disappointed in 'Time Passes', *Harper's* and the *Forum* refuse serial rights, and Donald Brace (of Harcourt Brace) seems less enthusiastic than with *MD* (*D*). Review of Sir James Crichton-Browne's *Victorian Jottings* in *N&A*.

15 Lady Colefax visits to discuss the MacCarthy fund; W. J. Turner visits to ask VW to persuade Cynthia Noble to become his mistress; LS visits to dine and discuss 'Queen Elizabeth, sodomy, love, the Antigone, Othello' (to VSW).

16–18 Agrees with LS and R. Mortimer that D. Garnett's latest book, *Go She Must!*, is 'unspeakably bad' (to VB).

21 Considers a new work: 'away from facts: free; yet concentrated; prose yet poetry; a novel & a play' (*D*). Reads William Cowper's *The Task*; admires the way a single line will emerge from the mass (to VSW). Works on proofs of *TL*; dines at E. Sands's to meet Violet Bonham (daughter of former prime minister Asquith), former president of the Women's Liberal Federation.

26 'George Gissing', review of *The Letters of George Gissing to Members of his Family*, collected and arranged by Algernon and Ellen Gissing, in *N&A*.

27 Lady Dilke asks VW to present the Femina Vie Heureuse Prize (an annual literary award given to one English book and one French); VW declines, though Lady Dilke mentions giving her the prize (VW does win in 1928 for *TL*).

28 Finishing EMF's *A Passage to India*.

HOGARTH PRESS: Horace Alexander, *Justice among Nations*; R. B. Braithwaite, *The State of Religious Belief: An Inquiry Based on 'The Nation and Athenaeum' Questionnaire*; Stephen King-Hall, *The China of To-day*.

March

2 (Wed) Busy at the Press; has decided to combine A. Davidson with Mervyn Arnold-Forster (Will's brother; he dies in May from the delayed effects of his war wounds).

5 Still winding up the Eliot fund (which drags on until Jan 1928). Writes to VB, finalising plans for trip to France and Italy; comments on the exhibition of Flemish and Belgian art at the Royal Academy (likes the Breughels' and on VB's show – feels they are now both mistresses of their respective media (to VB). Review of Seton Gordon's *The Immortal Isles* in *N&A*.

14 Between midnight and 1 a.m. conceives of 'The Jessamy Brides', a work about two women living alone at the top of a house, which will satirise her own 'lyric vein' – a rest before the mystical book which will come next (*D*; to VSW, 8 Mar).

(Mid-month) E. Sitwell to tea; gives VW a copy of her just-published *Rustic Elegies*.

19 Takes tea with Q. Bell at Leighton Park School; plans their next lampoon.

20 Talks with LS about love; practises Italian with gramophone records.

23–8 Suffers high fever from typhoid inoculation.

24 Sends the MacCarthys a cheque for £300.

27 'What is a Novel?' in *Weekly Dispatch*.

30 Departs for a month in France and Italy; first to Cassis to visit CB, VB and DG. Arrives in Palermo 9 April; from train sees N. Douglas and D. H. Lawrence (the closest they come to meeting); meets Cecil Taylor, master at Clifton College. In Syracuse, meets O. Sitwell (13th); two days later meets Adrian Stokes, writer and art critic. Visits Pompeii on the 19th; next day takes a crowded train to Rome; strolls through gardens instead of reading Proust, considers moving to Rome. Leaves

early in the morning on the 27th; travels straight through to London, arriving the next day.

HOGARTH PRESS: R. Graves, *Impenetrability or the Proper Habit of English*; Charles Mauron, *The Nature of Beauty in Art and Literature*, tr. with preface by RF; Lord Olivier, *The Anatomy of African Misery*; E. Sackville-West, *The Apology of Arthur Rimbaud: A Dialogue*; R. C. Trevelyan, *Meleager, Cheiron*; H. G. Wells, *Democracy under Revision*; LW, *Hunting the Highbrow*.

April

2 (Sat) 'A Giant with Very Small Thumbs', review of Avrahm Yarmolinsky's *Turgenev: The Man, his Art and his Age*, in *N&A*.

23 'Two Women', review of Lady Stephen's *Emily Davies and Girton College*, and *Letters of Lady Augusta Stanley*, ed. the Dean of Windsor and Hector Bolitho, in *N&A*.

HOGARTH PRESS: V. A. Demant, Philippe Mairet, Albert Newsome, Alan Porter, Maurice Reckitt, Egerton Swann and W. T. Symons, *Coal: A Challenge to the National Conscience*; K. Innes, *The League of Nations and the World's Workers*.

May

Early this month, contends with M. Hutchinson, who is annoyed that her *Fugitive Pieces* have not yet been published.

5 (Thurs) *TL* published; VW depressed by 'timid' review in *TLS* but pleased that she and LW can now afford a motor car (*D*; see *M&M*).

8 Fascinated by VB's account of the giant moths at Cassis – part of the germination of *W* (to VB; see *QB* II).

18 Travels with VSW to Oxford to deliver a lecture, 'Poetry, Fiction and the Future'; the undergraduates 'sit on the floor and ask innocent questions about Joyce' (to VB).

22 Pleased by VB's praise of the portrait of their mother in *TL*; philosophical about Lord Olivier's quibbles over botanical and biological inaccuracies in the book (to VB).

24 Attends luncheon party at CB's; gives tea party; attends dinner party at LS's, where she discusses Oscar Browning, a Cambridge character mentioned in *Room*.

27 Relieved that RF admires *TL*, assures him, 'I meant *nothing* by The Lighthouse. One has to have a central line down the middle of the book to hold the design together' (to RF).

'The New Dress' in *Forum*, New York.

HOGARTH PRESS: E. Muir, *The Marionette*; Fridtjof Nansen, *Adventure and Other Papers*; Lord Olivier, *The Empire Builder*; LW, *Essays on Literature, History, Politics, etc.*; VW, *To the Lighthouse*.

June

Spends the first week of June in bed with a headache, but with EMF's letter of praise feels *TL* is behind her, and that she is an established figure as a writer; enjoys printing L. Gottschalk's poem *Voltaire* (Hogarth, Nov).

7 (Tues) To Rodmell. Reads 'trash' until, on the 14th, suddenly finds herself 'rhapsodising' the story of the Moths (*W*: 'the play-poem idea: the idea of some continuous stream'; works on it while listening to late Beethoven sonatas (*D*).

15 Reads H. Nicolson's *Some People* (reviewed 30 Oct).

16 Attends presentation of the Hawthornden Prize to VSW for *The Land*.

21 DG and H. Nicolson dine; VW warms to the latter's childlike spontaneity.

23 Notes that A. Bennett in the *Evening Standard* concedes that with Mrs Ramsay her character drawing has improved (see *M&M*).

28 EMF takes exception to her article 'The Novels of E. M. Forster' (Nov); maintains his method is not wrong.

29 With the Nicolsons and E. Sackville-West travels to north Yorkshire to observe the total eclipse of the sun (*D*, 30 June).

HOGARTH PRESS: M Hutchinson, *Fugitive Pieces*.

July

2 (Sat) Visits VSW at Long Barn for the weekend.

8 Finishes rewriting '"Slater's Pins Have No Points"': 'a nice little story about Sapphism, for the Americans' (to VSW).

10 EMF writes asking her to give more praise to *A Passage to India* in her article on his novels (Nov); VW is surprised at his sensitivity (see *QB* II).

(Mid-month) Argues with G. Rylands that F. L. Lucas's *Tragedy in Relation to Aristotle's 'Poetics'* is too academic for the Press, but they publish it (Feb 1928).

15 LW and VW broadcast for the BBC for the first time, and purchase their first car; VW is enthusiastic about the new freedom it brings, and for the rest of the summer attempts to learn how to drive (eventually she gives up).

22 Attends wedding of S. Tomlin and Julia Strachey.
27 P. Morrell declares his love; VW is flattered but does not reciprocate (see *L*, 19 Feb 1928).
27–30 Visits E. Sands and Anna Hudson at Auppegard, Normandy; begins reading A. Maurois's biography of Disraeli; meets Jacques Emile-Blanche, portrait painter, who then writes 'An Interview with Virginia Woolf' for *Les Nouvelles littéraires* (13 Aug 1927).
30 Returns to Rodmell for the summer.

August

5 (Fri) Corrects proofs of 'Street Haunting'; reads K. Mansfield's *Journal* (1827; reviewed 18 Sep).
14 'Poetry, Fiction and the Future' in the *New York Herald Tribune*.
17 'Life Itself', review of James Woodforde's *The Diary of a Country Parson*, vol. III, ed. John Beresford, in the *New Republic*, New York.
21 Writing about romance for 'Phases of Fiction', disappointed in Scott, impressed with Trollope.
22 Asks VSW, who has recently finished a book on Aphra Behn, for Behn's most romantic novel.
24 Reads, and likes, TSE's poem 'Fragment of an Agon' (1927).
29 Reads Ann Radcliffe's *The Mysteries of Udolpho* (1794) – 'remarkably good' (to S. Sydney-Turner).

September

2 (Fri) Grumbling because she should be working on a review of Hemingway (part of a series of articles on American writers for the *New York Herald Tribune*), and she wants to begin *W*. D. Wellesley agrees to sponsor and edit the Hogarth Living Poets series.
3 Reads the manuscript of D. E. Enfield's *L. E. L.: A Mystery of the Thirties* (Hogarth, Mar 1928).
4 An attempt to make the first westbound transatlantic flight fails; VW sketches an imagined scene of the final moments in *D*, also records a Rodmell graveyard scene which becomes the basis of the third picture in 'Three Pictures' (*DM*).
9 With VSW visits Laughton Place, a sixteenth-century moated house which VW considers buying, but which on a second visit seems dreary.
13 Notes death of P. Ritchie, age 28; thoughts of death contend

with thoughts of buying Laughton Place (*D*, 20 Sep). Has finished the Hemingway review and plunged into Walter Peck's study of Shelley (reviewed 23 Oct).

18 'A Terribly Sensitive Mind', review of *The Journal of Katherine Mansfield, 1914–1922*, ed. J. M. Murry, in the *New York Herald Tribune*.

19 Visits VSW at Long Barn.

20 Works on 'The New Biography' (30 Oct). Wants to sketch the outlines of her friends in a work truthful but fantastical: VSW should be Orlando (*D*).

HOGARTH PRESS: Karl Abraham, *Selected Papers of Karl Abraham*, intro. by Ernest Jones, tr. Douglas Bryan and A. Strachey; M. Jaeger, *The Man with Six Senses*; F. O. Mann, *The Sisters and Other Tales in Verse*; The Nation, *Books and the Public*, by the Editor of *The Nation*, JMK, Stanley Unwin, Michael Sadlier, Basil Blackwell, LW, Peter Ibbetson, Henry Saxton, Charles Young and Jeffrey E. Jeffrey; William Stephen Sanders, *Early Socialist Days*; W. Plomer, *I Speak of Africa*.

October

Early this month, VB initiates Sunday-evening gatherings of Old Bloomsbury; relations between LW and A. Davidson at the Press worsen.

5 (Wed) The notion of a fantastical memoir suddenly takes shape as a biography focusing on VSW, beginning in 1500 and continuing to the present – *O*. Visited by the elderly Mrs Grey (cf. the sketch 'Old Mrs Grey', *DM*).

6 Returns to London for the winter.

8 Puts aside 'Phases of Fiction', that 'bloody book' that LW and D. Rylands 'extort' from her, and writes rapidly all morning at *O* (to VSW).

9 'An Essay in Criticism', review of E. Hemingway's *Men without Women*, in the *New York Herald Tribune*.

14 Can think of nothing else but *O*; plans to begin the chapter of VSW and Violet Trefusis (Orlando and Sasha) meeting on the ice.

16 Reads J. Bell's poetry; advises him to avoid cataloguing details, to try to see the whole (to J. Bell). 'Is Fiction an Art?', review of EMF's *Aspects of the Novel*, in the *New York Herald Tribune*.

20 Attends dinner party at CB's; listens to TSE's literary and H. Nicolson's political anecdotes.

22 Enraptured with *O*, has abandoned her schedule for criticism.
23 Asks VSW what she and Lord Lascelles, the model for the Archduchess Harriet in *O*, used to talk about (to VSW). 'Not One of Us', review of W. E. Peck's *Shelley: His Life and Work*, in the *New York Herald Tribune*.
28 Visits Knole with VSW to choose portraits of the Sackville family for *O*.
29 Begins ch. 2 of *O*.
30 'The New Biography', review of H. Nicolson's *Some People*, in the *New York Herald Tribune*.

'Street Haunting: A London Adventure' in the *Yale Review*.

HOGARTH PRESS: Charles Davies, *Welshman's Way*; Robert Hull, *Contemporary Music*; Peter Ibbetson, *Mr Baldwin Explains and Other Dream Interviews*; S. King-Hall, *Posterity*; C. H. B. Kitchin, *Mr Balcony*; L. P. Smith, *The Prospects of Literature*.

November

6 (Sun) VSW sends her latest book, *Aphra Behn*.
10 Begins ch. 3 of *O* (manuscript date, see Moore; cf. *D*, 20 Nov). VSW to dinner; to an unsympathetic VW describes her affair with Mary Campbell, whom her husband, poet Roy Campbell, has threatened to kill.
16 Exchanges letters with EMF on the question of 'art' in the novel, raised by her review of *Aspects of the Novel* (see 16 Oct; revised as 'The Art of Fiction' for *N&A*, 12 Nov).
19 Reads CB's *Civilisation*, thinks it brilliant (to CB; see 31 May 1928).
22 Asks VSW to bring *Gorboduc*, a tragedy by Thomas Norton and her ancestor Thomas Sackville (1561). Criticises J. Bell's play, but advises him to keep writing all sorts of things: 'Anything is better than a novel' (to J. Bell).
30 Attends solo performance by American actress Ruth Draper.

'The Novels of E. M. Forster' in *Atlantic Monthly*.

HOGARTH PRESS: RF, *Cézanne*; P. J. Noel-Baker, *Disarmament and the Coolidge Conference*; H. Edward Palmer, *The Judgement of François Villon*; Laura Riding (Gottschalk), *Voltaire: A Biographical Fantasy*.

December

1 (Thurs) Attends luncheon party at Lady Colefax's with art collector Henry Harris, M. Baring and others.
3 'Ruskin Looks back on Life, *Praeterita*: Serene Thoughts with

the Echoes of Thunder', review of John Ruskin's *Praeterita*, in *T. P.'s Weekly*.

5 Making up the 'last' chapter in *O* (but it goes on).

20 Reads Lord Chesterfield's letters (quoted in *O*; see review, 8 Mar 1928); works on the scene in which Orlando meets Nell in the park (near the end of ch. 3). Considers publishing a *Hogarth Miscellany*, (an idea which recurs but is never implemented).

21 F. Birrel and G. Rylands to dinner before a party at the Keyneses'; Rylands tells VW she lives and writes in an 'opium dream' that is too often about herself (*D*).

24 To Charleston, then on the 28th to Rodmell.

28 Works on de Quincey and Lord Chesterfield.

1928

EVENTS AND LETTERS. The minimum voting age of women in Britain reduced from 30 to 21; T. Hardy dies. TSE publishes *For Lancelot Andrewes*; A. Huxley, *Point Counter Point*; J. Joyce, *Anna Livia Plurabelle*; Radclyffe Hall, *The Well of Loneliness*; D. H. Lawrence, *Lady Chatterley's Lover*, *The Woman Who Rode Away*, *Collected Poems*; W. Lewis, *The Childermass*; S. O'Casey, *The Silver Tassie*; LS, *Elizabeth and Essex*; Evelyn Waugh, *Decline and Fall*; VW, *Orlando*; W. B. Yeats, *The Tower*.

January

2 (Mon) Returns to London.

11 T. Hardy dies.

14–15 Visits VSW at Long Barn.

16 Attends Hardy's funeral; dines at CB's with LS, who declares Hardy's novels are 'poor stuff'.

17 Works on article on G. Meredith (9 Feb), and furbishes up her tribute to Hardy, which B. Richmond had asked her to prepare in August 1921. Bids goodbye to VB and DG, who are leaving to spend the winter in their villa near Cassis (between Toulon and Marseille), which henceforth becomes their winter residence; feels Bloomsbury is more flashy, less substantial, without them.

19 'Thomas Hardy's Novels' in *TLS*.

23–7 Bedridden with headache.

25 VW's forty-sixth birthday.
31 Reading Michelet's *L'Histoire de France* (1833–43), and has been following LS's articles on the historians Macaulay, Hume, Gibbon and Carlyle in the *Nation* (7–28 Jan): 'I can't get into the skip of them. But they enchant the fashionables . . .' (to CB).
Late this month, meets Jean Aubry, professor, biographer of Conrad.
'"Slater's Pins Have No Points"' in *Forum*, New York.

February

Early this month, in bed with a headache from the effort of completing the Meredith and the Hardy articles.
1 (Wed) Begins ch. 5 of *O*.
3 'The Sun and the Fish' in *Time and Tide*.
7 Talks with TSE, recently converted to Anglo-Catholicism, for two hours about God (*D*; to VB, 11 Feb).
9 'The Novels of George Meredith' in *TLS*.
11 'Hacking rather listlessly' at the final chapter of *O*, feels the book is too long. Review of Anthony Hope's *Memories and Notes* in *N&A*.
(Mid-month) Dines with CB and Dorothy Todd, who having lost the editorship of British *Vogue* considers launching her own quarterly. Attends performance of John van Druten's *Young Woodley* with CB, who, in the grip of a mid-life crisis, is 'incessant' in February and March.
23 Visits VSW at Long Barn before she leaves for Berlin.
25 Review of A. K. Hamilton Jenkin's *The Cornish Miner* in *N&A*.
Hogarth Press: F. L. Lucas, *Tragedy in Relation to Aristotle's 'Poetics'*; Allardyce Nicoll, *Studies in Shakespeare*; H. Nicolson, *The Development of English Biography*; Sir Arthur Quiller-Couch, *A Lecture on Lectures*.

March

Early this month, Newnham graduate and writer Elizabeth Jenkins (*Virginia Water*, 1929) to dinner with John Hayward, R. Mortimer and CB, who is captivated by and attempts to captivate her. VW takes French lessons, employs words out of use for centuries (to VB, 5 Mar). At O. Morrell's meets Irish writer James Stephen, who reminisces about Yeats (to VSW, 6 Mar).
6 (Tues) Trying to finish *O*, working on the passage in which

Orlando drives down to the country house. Urges VSW to translate Rilke.

6/8 Lunches with Lady Colefax and meets playwrights Edward Knoblock, who in 1934 dramatises VSW's *The Edwardians*, and Noël Coward, 'a miracle, a prodigy' (to VB, 25 Mar).

8 Review of *The Characters of Lord Chesterfield*, ed. Charles Whibley, in *TLS*.

9–12 At Monk's House, so cold she does no work on *O*; wants to end it, yet finds appendices blossoming in her head (to VSW).

17 Finishes *O* at 1 p.m., though it will need three months of revising; feels sure she will never write a 'novel' again (*D*).

18 Discusses Queen Victoria's letters at Sunday Bloomsbury meeting at CB's.

21 Wonders if her feelings for VSW will change now that she has finished *O*; reads Hazlitt (to VSW).

22 Adds final pages to *O*, judges it 'too long for a joke, & too frivolous for a serious book'. EMF and D. MacCarthy to tea; the latter asks VW to contribute to his new periodical, *Life and Letters*.

24 The Woolfs go to Rodmell, then on the 26th to France, arriving 1 April in Cassis; they stay until the 9th before starting the return journey, arriving home, after enduring snow and several flat tyres, on the 16th (*D*, 17 Apr).

HOGARTH PRESS: B. Bowker, *Lancashire under the Hammer*; Edgar Brookes, *What is Wrong with the League of Nations?*; D. E. Enfield, *L. E. L. A Mystery of the Thirties*; R. M. Fox, *The Triumphant Machine (A Study of Machine Civilisation)*; H. Wilson Harris, *Arms or Arbitration?*; Robert Hull, *Delius*; W. Plomer, *Notes for Poems*; Viscountess Rhondda, *Leisured Women*; Edward Thompson, *Cock Robin's Decease: An Irregular Inquest*; LW, *Imperialism and Civilisation*.

April

7 (Sat) Review of L. C. Dunsterville's *Stalky's Reminiscences* in *N&A*.

11 'Waxworks at the Abbey' in the *New Republic*, New York.

15 'Preference of Four Critics: Virginia Woolf' in the *New York Herald Tribune*.

17 Encounters H. Mirrlees, who tells her J. Harrison has died (15 Apr).

19 Attends funeral of J. Harrison, dines at the Keyneses'.

21 Finding the revision of *O* 'damned rough', hopes to publish in September. 'Mr Yeats', review of W. B. Yeats's *The Tower*, in *N&A*.

23 Reads *Othello*, impressed by the 'volley & volume & tumble' of the words but feels the language is heightened when the dramatic tension is slack (*D*). Has an idea for an article on what we know of French ('On Not Knowing French', 13 Feb 1929).

24 Types *O*, trying to keep to a schedule of ten pages per day.

26 Herbert Croly, editor with *New Republic*, New York, and wife to tea.

27 Thanks VSW for the translations of Rilke (to VSW).

28 Review of *Behind the Scenes with Cyril Maude*, by himself, in *N&A*.

30 Richard Kennedy comes to work at the Press (see Kennedy).

May

2 (Wed) H. Walpole presents VW with the Femina Vie Heureuse Prize for *TL*; neither enjoys the occasion. Talks with Elizabeth Robins (author of *Ibsen and the Actress*, Hogarth, Oct 1928) and others.

5 Gives tea to Crosby Gaige, who is producing a privately printed edition of *O* for his Fountain Press, New York. Review of A. T. Schofield's *Behind the Brass Plate* in *N&A*.

11 Takes tea with Lady Horner, who gossips about E. Burne-Jones; visits VB's show; has H. Walpole, who complains that his books sell but not to the intelligent, to dinner.

16 E. Gosse dies (see *D*, 31 May).

20–3 Meets A. Maurois and A. Bennett at Lady Colefax's, and R. West, whose vitality, intelligence and bad taste she admires, at D. Todd's (to VB, 25 May).

25–9 To Monk's House; advises VB that 22 Hyde Park Gate has now been sold (to VB).

26 Review of *The Book of Catherine Wells*, intro. H. G. Wells, in *N&A*.

31 LW reads *O*, thinks it in some ways better than *TL*. VW now wants to work on 'Dr Burney's Evening Party' (21 and 28 July 1929). Notes CB's *Civilisation: An Essay* is out; concludes, 'In the end it turns out that Civilisation is a lunch party at no. 50 Gordan Square' (*QB*, II).

HOGARTH PRESS: Frances Cornford, *Different Days*; R. Fitzurse, *It was not Jones*; Alice Ritchie, *The Peacemakers*; G. Rylands, *Words and Poetry*, intro. by LS; D. Wellesley, *Matrix*.

June

6 (Wed) O. Morrell to tea, recovering from a jaw operation but cheerful because she has renewed her friendship with D. H. Lawrence.

7/8 Henry Leach, editor of the *Forum*, and Helen McAfee, managing editor of the *Yale Review*, to tea.

13–24 Working five to seven hours a day on proof of *O* and must sign the 800 copies of the limited edition published by C. Gaige; too tired to read Proust.

20 Relieved that VB is back, recognises that she is a necessity to her. J. Bell and novelist Sylva Norman (*Nature Has No Tune*, Hogarth, Nov 1929) to dinner.

30 To Monk's House for the last weekend in June; reads P. Lubbock's *Mary Chomondeley, A Sketch from Memory* (1928) and has been given M. Baring's *Comfortless Memory* (1928). Review of George Arliss's *On the Stage: An Autobiography* in *N&A*.

HOGARTH PRESS: Francis Pollard, *War and Human Values*; S. Snaith, *A Flying Scroll*; Florence Wilson, *The Origins of the League Covenant*, intro. by P. Noel-Baker.

July

5 (Thurs) To Long Barn to visit VSW, 'interested by the gnawing down of strata in friendship' (*D*).

6 Dreams of K. Mansfield; works on an article on Sterne (pub. 23 Sep).

14 Review of Winifred Ponder's *Clara Butt: Her Life Story* in *N&A*.

24 To Monk's House for the summer; guests include EMF, R. Kennedy, D. MacCarthy, VSW, E. Sackville-West and Mrs Woolf.

HOGARTH PRESS: S. Freud, *The Future of an Illusion*, W. D. Robson-Scott.

August

11 (Sat) Review Mrs Aubrey Le Blond's *Day In, Day Out* in *N&A*.

12 Again working on 'Phases of Fiction – Dickens and Austen – with *W* hovering in the background. J. Bell and painter Jane Bussy (daughter of Dorothy and Simon Bussy) to lunch.

14 Visits Long Barn and D. Wellesley's new house, Penns-in-the-Rocks, an eighteenth-century house surrounded by boulders.
20 Buys Scott's Waverley Novels.
25–6 EMF visits, discusses Radclyffe Hall's lesbian novel *The Well of Loneliness* (1928), which has been banned; Hall wants her work defended not merely as serious but as great literature, which poses difficulties for her supporters (to VSW, 30 Aug).
Late this month, reads James, Proust, Dostoevsky and Peacock for 'Phases of Fiction'; plans a trip to France with VSW.
HOGARTH PRESS: F. Wilson, *Near East Educational Survey*.

September
1 (Sat) LW's 76-year-old mother visits; exhausts them by her constant talk, which includes her thoughts on Radclyffe Hall (to VB).
8 Likes VSW's article on Tolstoy in *N&A*; feels she should have pursued the question of how Tolstoy's realism avoids being merely photographic (to VSW). 'The New Censorship', letter to the editor in protest against the banning of Radclyffe Hall's *The Well of Loneliness*, signed by EMF and VW, in *N&A*.
10 Reads H. Melville's *Moby Dick* (1851). J. Bell and D. MacCarthy to lunch; they discuss MacCarthy's condescending remarks on women novelists in his latest *Life and Letters*.
17 Reads Dorothy Osborne's letters (reviewed 24 Oct).
29 Dines at the Keyneses' to meet Lord Gage, JMK's and VB's landlord, and Sidney Cooke, stockbroker, and his wife.
22 Finishes the first draft of 'Phases of Fiction' and writing the review of D. Osborne; not yet feeling pressed to work on *W*, considers reading for a book to be called 'Lives of the Obscure'. Notes *O* is selling poorly because booksellers insist that, because of the subtitle, it must be shelved with biography.
23 'A Sentimental Journey' in the *New York Herald Tribune*.
24 To Burgundy for a week with VSW; initially apprehensive that she and VSW might 'find each other out', she enjoys the trip though she misses LW (see daily letters to LW, 24–8 Sep).
27 Meets John Balderston, American playwright and London correspondent for the *New York World*, with his wife and CB's actress friend Valerie Taylor, in Avallon. Reads J. Hawthorne's *Shapes that Pass* (reviewed 17 Nov).
29 Review of *The Diaries of Mary, Countess of Meath*, ed. by her husband, in *N&A*.

30 Dines at Auppegard with E. Sands.

October

1 (Mon) Returns to Monk's House.
2 With LW returns to Tavistock Square for the winter.
7 Asks M. L. Davies for a copy of the life of her aunt, Sarah Emily Davies, founder of Girton College.
11 *O* published, and, though J. C. Squire dismisses it as a 'pleasant trifle' (*Observer*, 21 Oct) and A. Bennett finds it disappointing after *TL* (*Evening Standard*), most reviewers are closer to R. West, who pronounces it a 'poetic masterpiece' (*New York Herald Tribune*, 21 Oct); it sells better than any of her previous books and brings increased fame – including tea at Lady Cunard's (early Nov); VW has no illusions about the work, feeling that, while she learned continuity, narrative and how to write a direct sentence, she did not explore as she did in *TL* (*M&M*; *D*, 7 Nov).
15 Reads K. Mansfield's letters – 'I didn't realise how gifted she was' (to O. Morrell).
17 Visits TSE, who reads *Ash Wednesday*.
20 Travels with VSW, VB and A. Bell to Cambridge. Stays with P. Strachey, and delivers one of her two papers 'Women and Fiction' (revised to become *Room*); meets Elsi Phare, student, later an authority on Hopkins and Marvell.
21 Lunches with G. Rylands at King's College (see *Room*).
22 Agrees with E. Sackville-West that *TL* is better than *O*, though it is the current fashion to tell her that *O* is superior (to E. Sackville-West; see also *D*, 7 Nov).
24 'Dorothy Osborne's Letters', review of *The Letters of Dorothy Osborne to William Temple*, ed. G. C. Moore Smith, in the *New Republic*, New York.
26 To Cambridge, to deliver a second 'Women and Fiction' paper at Girton College. Lunches with J. Bell to discuss his latest poems; dines with Margaret Thomas, Girton student and one of the organisers of the talk.
27 Reads Fanny Burney's diaries for 'Dr Burney's Evening Party' (21, 28 July 1929).

'The Niece of an Earl' in *Life and Letters*.

HOGARTH PRESS: Robinson Jeffers, *Roan Stallion, Tamar and Other Poems*; E. Robins, *Ibsen and the Actress*; VSW, *Twelve Days: An Account of a Journey across the Bakhtiari Mountains in South-western*

Persia; Basil De Selincourt, *The Enjoyment of Music*; Eric White, *Parnassus to Let: An Essay about Rhythm in the Films*; VW, *Orlando: A Biography*.

November

VB and VW start a series of Tuesday evening at-homes, along the lines of the old Bloomsbury parties, which continue until Christmas.

1 (Thurs) Attends meeting at the studio of architect Clough Ellis to discuss giving evidence in the *Well of Loneliness* case, with VSW, G. B. Shaw, R. Macaulay and others.

7 Plans 'books that relieve other books': wants to write a history of Newnham or the women's movement in the same vein as *O*, and to work on the mystical 'playpoem' *W* (*D*).

8 Corrects review of *The Early Life of Thomas Hardy* (24 Nov) and revises review of Gissing's *Letters* for the introduction to *Selections Autobiographical and Imaginative* (pub. Jonathan Cape).

9 Attends *Well of Loneliness* trial, is impressed with the reason and astuteness of the law; talks with Radclyffe Hall and her lover Lady Troubridge, whom VW had last met when they were children; the magistrate rules that evidence as to literary merit is inadmissible, and on the 16th the novel is declared obscene.

10 Reads novels of Geraldine Jewsbury in preparation for 'Geraldine and Jane' (28 Feb 1929); still correcting Hardy and Gissing. Travels to Cambridge to see L. Lopokova in G. Rylands' production of Milton's *Comus*, with scenery designed by VB and DG.

13 Tuesday-night party at VB's with CB, R. Macaulay, C. P. Sanger, Christabel McLaren, R. Mortimer, VSW, Mr and Mrs A. Clutton Brock and A. Davidson.

17 'Memories', review of Julian Hawthorne's *Shapes that Pass*, and first paragraph under heading 'Plays and Pictures', review of I. Stravinsky's *The Tale of a Soldier*, Shakespeare's *A Lover's Complaint*, and some dancing, by Hedley Briggs (three pieces at the ADC Theatre, Cambridge), in *N&A*.

20 Tuesday-evening party with H. Walpole, who is 'much liked. That is the correct phrase for Hugh', and others (to VSW).

23 Stands surety for £40 for Jonathan Cape, publisher of *The Well of Loneliness*.

24 To Rodmell, where they buy a cottage. LS's *Elizabeth and Essex* is published; VW begins reading it, finding it poor. 'Half of

Thomas Hardy', review of Florence Hardy's *The Early Life of Thomas Hardy*, in *N&A*.

27 Tuesday-night party with A. Stephen, H. Mirrlees, C. McLaren, CB, R. Mortimer, D. Garnett, LS, VSW, V. Taylor and the Hon. Elizabeth Ponsonby (one of the 'bright young people').

28 Experiences superficial pleasure, genuine disappointment, in discovering *Elizabeth and Essex* a bad book. Notes that it is her father's birthday, that had he lived his life would have entirely ended hers – 'No writing, no books; inconceivable' – yet that after writing *TL* she thinks of him more as a contemporary. Slowly starting to work on *W*, holding herself back until she can eliminate conventional narrative and 'saturate every atom'. (*D*.)

Hogarth Press: CB, *Proust*; H. J. C. Grierson, *Lyrical Poetry From Blake to Hardy*; E. Muir, *The Structure of the Novel*; H. Read, *Phases of English Poetry*.

December

2 (Sun) Reads Chaucer's *Troilus and Criseyde* (c. 1380).

9 In exasperation begins a new beginning to 'Phases of Fiction'.

13 Dines with E. Sands; meets M. Beerbohm for the first time, flattered and a little saddened to be treated by him as an equal.

17 Dines with the Hutchinsons and meets G. Moore, who disparages Bennett, Galsworthy, Shaw and Wells, talks of the novel he is dictating, *Aphrodite in Aulis*, and on the whole impresses VW with his serene confidence (*D*).

18 Orders a third edition of *O*, financially secure but finding 'the spending muscle does not work naturally yet'; notes that the determination to make money originated in the night of black despair two years ago (15 Sep 1926). Interrupts work on 'Phases of Fiction' to write eulogy of Lady Strachey (d. 15 Dec). With VB gives party for VSW, who is leaving for Berlin. (*D*.)

22 'Lady Strachey' in *N&A*.

25 Visits S. S. Koteliansky, who talks of K. Mansfield and J. M. Murry, of D. H. Lawrence's *Lady Chatterley's Lover* (pub. Florence during the summer), which he says is disgusting, and of A. Huxley's *Point Counter Point*, which he recommends because of its seriousness. Eats Christmas dinner with RF; during the week exchanges visits with G. Brenan, O. and P. Morrell, M. Strachey and others.

27 To Monk's House until 3 January; plans to add a room, financed by *O*.

HOGARTH PRESS (month of publication unknown): John Rickman, *Index Psychoanalyticus 1893–1926*.

1929

EVENTS AND LETTERS. Wall Street crash; J. Ramsay MacDonald forms Labour government in Britain; T. Mann awarded Nobel Prize. Ivy Compton-Burnett publishes *Brothers and Sisters*; TSE, *Dante*; William Faulkner, *The Sound and the Fury*; R. Graves, *Goodbye to All That*; E. Hemingway, *A Farewell to Arms*; D. H. Lawrence, *Pansies*; Thomas Wolfe, *Look Homeward Angel*; VW, *A Room of One's Own*; W. B. Yeats, *The Winding Stair*.

January

3 (Thurs) Returns to London from Rodmell.

8 A pump on the construction site of the hotel next door shakes her studio (after completion of the hotel a dance band takes over from the pump – see below, Dec). Reading Balzac and Tolstoy, claims it was *Anna Karenina*, not Wells or Galsworthy or any of the 'wishy washy' British realists, that they had to break away from (to VSW).

16 Travels to Berlin to visit VSW and H. Nicolson; joined on the 18th by VB, DG and Q. Bell for a strained, 'rackety' week.

21 Returns to London in a state of collapse, brought on by exhaustion and precipitated by a drug for seasickness recommended by VB; VW spends most of the next month in bed seeing no one, on the orders of Dr Elinor Rendel (daughter of LS's eldest, sister), but composes *W*, and the final version of 'Women and Fiction' seems to make itself up (see *D*, 13 Apr).

25 VW's forty-seventh birthday.

February

4 (Mon) Notes LW and J. Hutchinson plan to protest at the seizing of D. H. Lawrence's poems, *Pansies*, which had been sent from abroad in typescript, opened by Customs, and forwarded to the Home Secretary (to VSW).

10 Reading lives of Beau Brummell, Constable and Trollope, as well as manuscripts for the Press.

13 'On Not Knowing French' in the *New Republic*, New York.
14 Talks with LS; awkward because neither wishes to broach the subject of *Elizabeth and Essex*.
19 Begins writing on the Burneys (21, 28 July). Gives Hilda Matheson (of the BBC) permission to broadcast the frost-and-thaw sequence in *O*.
28 'Geraldine and Jane', review of Geraldine Jewsbury's *Zoe* and *The Half Sisters*, in *TLS*.
HOGARTH PRESS: W. Plomer, *Paper Houses*.

March
20 (Wed) Correcting 'The "Censorship" of Books' (Apr); thinking about *W*, 'an entirely new kind of book' (to Q. Bell).
28 Bids goodbye to VB, who is leaving for four months at Cassis; preparing to attack the 'angular shape' in her mind – *W*.
'Women and Fiction' in *Forum*, New York.
HOGARTH PRESS: *Cambridge Poetry*, ed. Christopher Saltmarshe, John Davenport and Basil Wright; Ida Graves, *The China Cupboard and Other Poems*; F. L. Lucas, *Time and Memory*; Huw Menai, *The Passing of Guto and Other Poems*; VW, *The Voyage Out*, *Night and Day* (Mar or Apr; first Hogarth editions, taking over the sheets from Duckworth).

April
3 (Wed) To Monk's House, now and again later in the month, to arrange the building of her bedroom and workroom.
13 Agrees, because they have raised their price to £50 an article, to do four articles for the *New York Herald Tribune* – work that will assure her the new room: 'Cowper and Lady Austen', 'Beau Brummell', 'Mary Wollstonecraft' and 'Dorothy Wordsworth'; each is published shortly beforehand in *N&A*.
(Mid-month) Invites Richard Braithwaite, later Professor of Moral Philosophy at Cambridge, and writer Lyn Irvine to dinner; meets Hogarth author W. Plomer, recently returned from two and a half years in Japan, for the first time.
21 L. Clifford dies; VW is at Monk's House and does not attend her funeral (to VB, 5 May).
25 Lunches with S. Colefax; talks with M. Beerbohm, H. Nicolson, Sir Philip Sassoon, Under-Secretary of State for Air, and others. Later dashes into a showing of Augustus John's work and is shocked by 'the vulgarity, banality, coarseness and common-

placeness' of the works, 'all costing over £400 and sold in the first hour' (to VB). 'The American Language', letter to the editor in reply to one on 'On Not Knowing French' (which took issue with her remark that H. James wrote English like a foreigner), in the *New Republic*.

28 EMF and C. Mauron, 'obese and almost blind', visit; VW finds him likable but not 'wildly exciting in the intellect or body' (to VB, 5 May).

29 Begins to revise 'Phases of Fiction'.

Late this month, on CB's recommendation reads Maurice de Vlaminck's *Tournant dangereux: souvenirs de ma vie* (1929).

'Phases of Fiction' in the *Bookman*, New York; 'The "Censorship" of Books' in *Nineteenth Century and After*.

HOGARTH PRESS: E. E. Kellett, *The Whirligig of Taste*; Lord Olivier, *White Capital and Coloured Labour*.

May

1 (Wed) Takes her niece, Judith (daughter of A. and K. Stephen) to a variety programme at the Coliseum. Dines at the Keyneses'; discusses the threat by Lord Alfred Douglas (best known as Oscar Wilde's lover) to sue LW over his condemnatory review of *The Autobiography of Lord Alfred Douglas* (*N&A*, 6 Apr), and discusses J. Bell's argument with JMK about Wittgenstein.

2 Resolves to read S. Sitwell's new book, *The Gothick North*.

9 Attends a small literary party with J. Bell, E. Blunden, W. Plomer, RF and H. Anrep, C. Mauron and E. Jenkins.

10 S. Waterlow, back from his post as British minister in Addis Ababa, visits and vociferates on how his life has been changed by Oswald Spengler's *Decline of the West* (tr. 1926, 1928).

11 Notes JMK and H. Henderson have published a pamphlet on unemployment, *Can Lloyd George Do It?*, which will 'turn the scale at the elections' (to Q. Bell).

12 Finishes the final revision of 'Women and Fiction'.

13 Reads Proust for 'that cursed book' – 'Phases of Fiction'; prepares to reread her books for the 'Uniform Edition'. Attends lecture by C. Mauron at Lady Colefax's with a crowd of 'fashion and riff raff'; dines there afterward and talks with G. Moore about her article 'Geraldine and Jane', which he admires, and H. James, whom he does not, about libel suits,

and about his own books; Moore later sends VW a copy of his *The Making of an Immortal* (1929).

(Mid-month) H. Walpole to tea to discuss A. Davidson, who has applied so diffidently for a job as Walpole's secretary that Walpole thinks he is not interested and given it to someone else.

28 Writes a little sketch every morning; wants an unspecified 'She' to think *W*, but is afraid that would be too 'arty' (*D*). Excited about the coming general election and about the forthcoming trip to Cassis.

30 To Rodmell to vote. Visits R. Mortimer and F. Birrell, who are renting Charleston while VB and DG are in France, and who are writing a domestic comedy.

31 VW is shocked to discover that both she and N. Boxall (the Woolfs' cook) want the Labour Party to win. Baldwin's Conservative government is defeated; R. MacDonald, Labour, returns for a second time as Prime Minister.

HOGARTH PRESS: G. S. Dutt, *A Woman of India: Being the Life of Saroj Nalini (Founder of the Women's Institute Movement in India)*, intro. by C. F. Andrews, foreword by Rabindranath Tagore; H. G. Wells, *The Common Sense of World Peace: An Address Delivered in the Reichstag at Berlin, on Monday, April 15th, 1929*.

June

3 (Mon) LS visits and they talk for the first time about why VW dislikes *Elizabeth and Essex*.

4 To Cassis by train; they consider buying a villa, but eventually decide that three houses would be unmanageable. VW, 'lifting the words with difficulty in the heat', writes an article on Cowper (*D*, 21 Sep).

6 Reads R. Murry's *Hard Liberty* (1929); cannot see the point of 'facts about life' in novels (to M. Davies).

14 Arrives back in Tavistock Square.

15 Corrects *Room*. D. MacCarthy visits; talks about J. Bell's abortive speech to the Apostles and about LS's books. P. Sassoon sends a copy of his book *The Third Route: A Description of a Voyage to India by Air* (1929).

19–23 At Monk's House rereads *CR*, horrified by her looseness. Begins to see *W* more clearly: thinks it will start with dawn and childhood; wonders if she could get the waves to be heard all through it. (*D*.)

Late this month, attends a Labour Party party; meets, among

others, William Jowitt, re-elected as a Liberal but persuaded to join the Labour Party as Attorney-General, and Mary Bell, President of the Board of Education.

30 Correcting *Room*, condensing the last pages. Reads D. MacCarthy's review of J. Boswell's *The Hypochondriak* (1777–83), in the *Sunday Times*, excited by the planned publication of the 18 volumes of Boswell's diaries (1928–34).

HOGARTH PRESS: Ernst Benkard, *Undying Faces*, tr. Margaret Green; Wilfred Benson, *The Foreigner in the Family*; Edmund Blunden, *Nature in English Literature*; John Stephens, *Danger Zones of Europe*.

July

2 (Tues) Begins first draft of *W*, entitled 'the Moths?' or 'Moments of Being' or 'The Waves'.

5 Meets Augustine Birrell at Charleston; he later sends his *Collected Essays*, and VW, delighted with them, resolves to write an article on his essays (June 1930).

21 'Dr Burney's Evening Party' in the *New York Herald Tribune*.

27 To Rodmell for the summer.

August

4 (Sun) K. and A. Arnold-Forster spend the night; VW reflects on the futility of talking to impress.

5 Works on the article on M. Wollstonecraft. Distressed by the continuing rows with N. Boxall, the cook, and by VSW's intimacy with H. Matheson.

14 Geoffrey Scott, author of *The Architecture of Humanism* and *The Portrait of Zélide* and editor of the first six volumes of the Boswell papers, dies (*D*, 21 Aug).

17–18 W. Plomer visits for the weekend; VW embarrasses him at Charleston by announcing that he claims to be descended from Shakespeare and Blake; they talk of W. Lewis and Joyce, of G. Moore and Yeats.

19 Finishes correcting proofs of *Room*.

22 Reads La Fontaine and Wordsworth; copies out an excerpt from the *Prelude* (VII.458–66).

September

2 (Mon) Reads from *The Notebooks of Samuel Butler* (1912) as relief from *Alice Meynell: A Memoir* (1929) by her daughter Viola

Meynell. L. Irvine visits at Monk's House; impresses VW with her austere self-reliance.

3–4 Visits VSW at Long Barn; when LW picks her up they discuss H. Nicolson's letter advising her against publishing *King's Daughter*, which includes some lesbian poems (Hogarth, Oct).

4 Considers putting 'The Lonely Mind' in *W* as if it were a person (*D*; see Graham).

(Mid-month) reads H. Walpole's *Hans Frost* (1929), in which she appears as Jane Rose, and R. West's *Harriet Hume* (1929), which she finds affected but more enduring than Walpole's novel (to VSW).

16 Tired from correcting proofs, feels 'The Moths' (*W*) forming, which she now knows will not have that title; wants not to write it but to think it for two or three weeks (*D*).

18–19 F. L. Lucas visits; talks too exclusively of copulation and King's College, Cambridge. VW wants to write a story – 'The Lady in the Looking Glass: A Reflection' (Dec).

21 'Cowper and Lady Austen' in *N&A*.

22 Makes a new beginning on *W*, but immediately faces the problem, 'Who thinks it?' (*D*, 25 Sep).

23 Agrees with E. Sackville-West that Hogarth should not have rejected I. Compton-Burnett's *Brothers and Sisters*.

26 Uniform Editions of *VO*, *JR*, *CR* and *MD* issued.

28 'Beau Brummell' in *N&A*.

30 Attends Labour Party conference in Brighton; listens to debate on Family Allowances.

Hogarth Press: E. E. Kellett, *The Northern Saga*; C. H. B. Kitchin, *Death of my Aunt*; Sylva Norman, *Nature Has No Tune*.

October

2 (Wed) Again attends Labour conference; listens to survey of Government foreign policy.

2–10 Meets Charles Buxton (with LW on the Labour Party Advisory Committees on International and Imperial Affairs). Exchanges visits with VB, RF, D. Cecil, VSW.

4 Writes to G. Brenan (still living in the mountains of southern Spain), offering encouragement, analysing her own impulse to write.

5 'Mary Wollstonecraft' in *N&A*.

7 Robinson Jeffers, American poet, and wife Una to tea (Hogarth, Oct).
11 Surprised, having thought she had learned to write quickly, that *W* goes so slowly.
12 Attends performance of G. B. Stern's *The Matriarch* (with Mrs Patrick Campbell). 'Dorothy Wordsworth' in *N&A*.
(Mid-month) Reads E. Jenkins' *Virginia Water*, J. M. Murry's *God: An Introduction to the Science of Metabiology*; continues reading in La Fontaine and Racine.
19 'Charles Lamb', letter to the editor, in *N&A*.
22 Dines with S. and B. Webb; talks with Hugh Macmillan, lawyer, about writer John Buchan (*The Thirty-Nine Steps*, 1915); LW discusses Labour promises to finance education and roads in Kenya with the Webbs.
23 Thinks 'The Moths' will be called 'The Waves' (*D*).
24 *Room* published by Hogarth and Harcourt Brace.
28 Reaches end of manuscript book I of *W* (episode 2, Rhoda in the looking glass).
29 Begins manuscript book II (*W*); continues with episode 2.
HOGARTH PRESS: G. D. H. Cole, *Politics and Literature*; C. Day Lewis, *Transitional Poem*; Thomas J. Hewitt and Ralph Hill, *An Outline of Musical History*; R. Jeffers, *Cawdor*; VSW, *King's Daughter*; Mark Starr, *Lies and Hate in Education*; Italo Svevo, *The Hoax*, tr. with intro. by Beryl de Zoete; Humbert Wolfe, *Notes on English Verse Satire*.

November
3 (Sun) Asks CB, who is in Paris, to subscribe to *Les Nouvelles littéraires* for her.
5 Feels there is 'something' in *W* but can't get at it with the speed and certainty that she did in *TL*, though she has written 66 pages in the last month. Painter Stephen Tennant and orientalist A. Waley to tea.
12 Attends party at Elizabeth Courtauld's; flirts with O. Sitwell, O. Morrell, C. McLaren, M. Hutchinson and others (to VSW).
15 'Women and Leisure', letter to the editor of *N&A* in reply to the review of *A Room of One's Own*.
20 'Beau Brummell', talk broadcast in the BBC *Miniature Biographies* series; VW angry over cuts insisted upon by H. Matheson.
22 Excerpt from *A Room of One's Own* in *Time and Tide*.
25 Corrects *TL* for the Uniform Edition.

27 'Beau Brummell', text of BBC talk, in the *Listener*.
29 Begins episode 3 of *W*, Bernard at college (entitled 'Chapter Two' and referred to as 'the second part' in *D*, 30 Nov). Dines out at the Red Lion with J. Bell, L. Irvine, H. Mirrlees, W. Plomer, aesthete and poet Brian Howard, and others; Plomer describes the murder of his landlady five days previously, the basis of his novel *The Case is Altered* (Hogarth, July 1932).
HOGARTH PRESS: K. Innes, *The Reign of Law*.

December
Disturbed by the dance band in the Royal Hotel (whose pump had offended while it was under construction), LW takes legal action, eventually winning the case. Sales of *Room* are unprecedented, exceeding even those of *O*.
8 (Sun) Preparing to read little-known Elizabethan writers for what becomes 'The Strange Elizabethans' in *CR* II: George Puttenham's *The Arte of English Poesie* (1589) William Webbe's *A Discourse of English Poetrie* (1586), Gabriel Harvey's *Works*, *Commonplace Book*, *Letter Book* (1573–80).
10 Straining at *W* – after a morning's work has only 200 words, 'and those as crazy as broken china'; dislikes Hemingway and R. Graves (to D. Garnett).
(Mid-month) Dines with LS; reflects that if she had married him she never would have written.
15 Attends performance of Edgar Wallace's *The Calendar*.
19 Attends party at the Keyneses'; listens to G. B. Shaw on G. Moore, women, rhythm in *Heartbreak House*, and other topics.
21 To Rodmell for two weeks; continues to read the Elizabethans and struggles with *W*, writing and rewriting until her writing book is like a 'lunatic dream' (*D*, 26 Dec).
29 Works on *W*, interlude 4 (birds singing at dawn).
30 Considers VB's proposal to publish T. Stephen's letters (they do not do so).
'The Lady in the Looking Glass: A Reflection' in *Harper's Magazine*.
HOGARTH PRESS (month of publication unknown): *The Diary of Montaigne's Journey to Italy in 1580 and 1581*, tr. with intro. and notes by E. J. Trechmann.

1930

EVENTS AND LETTERS. Sinclair Lewis awarded Nobel Prize; W. H. Auden publishes *Poems*; W. Faulkner, *As I Lay Dying*; TSE, *Ash Wednesday*; William Empson, *Seven Types of Ambiguity*; D. H. Lawrence, *The Virgin and the Gypsy*; W. Lewis, *The Apes of God*; G. B. Shaw, *The Apple Cart*.

January

3 (Sun) Continues with *W*, episode 4 (Bernard).
4 Reads Joan Easdale's poems (Hogarth, Feb 1931).
5 Returns to Tavistock Square, to a round of visiting.
9 Attends performance of Mozart's opera *La Finta Giardiniera*.
7 Continues *W*, episode 4 (Louis and Jinny).
12 Can now hardly stop making up *W*; began to write the 'Phantom party' a week ago (*D*).
15 Dines at Henry ('Bogey') Harris's; meets Prime Minister R. MacDonald, Lady Londonderry, Sir Robert Vansittart and others.
18 Begins *W*, interlude 5. Attends VB's costume party for A. Bell's twelfth birthday: the theme is *Alice in Wonderland* and VW goes as the March Hare.
19 Finishes *W*, interlude 5; begins episode 5, the death of Percival; uses the image of the fin in the waste of waters for the first time (see 30 Sep 1926).
20 Takes A. Bell to performance of *Puss in Boots*.
21 Dines with E. Sands; meets Lord Buckmaster, member of the Judicial Committee of the Privy Council.
25 VW's forty-eighth birthday. Reads *Henry Chaplin: A Memoir* (1926) by his daughter Edith Chaplin, now Lady Londonderry (see 15 Jan).
26 Thinks of ending *W* with a 'gigantic conversation' (*D*).

February

3 (Mon) Reads Lady Frances Balfour's *Ne Obliviscaris: Dinna Forget* (1930) – feels she 'should have asked her kitchenmaid's advice before she took to the pen' (to E. Smyth).
8 C. P. Sanger dies: 'I shall miss some peculiar thing – loyal, worn, romantic; flowing with affection' (*D*, 10 Feb).
10 Suffers from influenza.
16 Making up the Hampton Court scene in *W*, has been in bed

for a week and feels that if she could stay in bed for another fortnight she could see the whole of *W*. Reads A. Maurois's *Byron* (1930), and *Childe Harold's Pilgrimage* (1812); analyses the elements in Byron's poetry. (*D*.)

17 W. Empson visits, 'A raucous youth [age 24], but I think rather impressive'; he publishes *Seven Types of Ambiguity* this year (to J. Bell).

18 Artist Margaret Snowden to tea (*D*, 20 Feb).

20 Meets E. Smyth for the first time, 'a bluff, military old woman', who talks of her life and music for four hours (*D*).

21 Visited by G. Duckworth – since 1927 Sir George – who tells complacent stories about himself, and LS, who tells fantastic stories about Christopher Columbus (*D*, 22 Feb).

22 Conceives idea of publishing a broadsheet of 2000–4000 words on art, politics, literature, music, to be printed at irregular intervals (a project that never materialises).

28 Offered £2000 by Doubleday Doran publishers to write a life of Boswell, she declines.

HOGARTH PRESS: Wilfred Benson, *Dawn on Mount Blanc*; F. O. Mann, *St James's Park and Other Poems*; Sherard Vines, *The Course of English Classicism from the Tudor to the Victorian Age*; H. G. Wells, *The Open Conspiracy*.

March

1 (Sat) Ill with headache for the last week, unable to write but feels it is perhaps the best thing for *W*; begins Henry Brewster's *The Prison: A Dialogue*, with a memoir by E. Smyth (1930).

2 Reads E. F. Benson's *Dodo* (1893), in which the character of Edith Staines is based on E. Smyth. D. H. Lawrence, three years younger than VW, dies at Vence, France.

3 Reads Mary Hamilton's *Special Providence* – 'I don't know how she conveys such a sense of the secondrate without gift' (*D*).

6 Works on *W*, episode 6 (Susan on her domestic, rural life).

9 Begins episode 8 (the reunion dinner at Hampton Court).

11 Works 'fairly well' at *W* in the morning; sketches impression of the dreariness of the aging M. L. Davies and L. Harris (*D*).

17 Notes the test of a book for a writer is whether it makes a space in which she can say, without compression or alteration, what she wants to say, and *W* now does so as she works on Rhoda (*D*).

25 Works on *W*, interlude 8.

28 Finding *W* the most complex and difficult of her books, has not yet mastered the speaking voice, and wonders how to end, 'save by a tremendous discussion' (*D*).

HOGARTH PRESS: A. Ritchie, *Occupied Territory*; Horace Samuel, *Unholy: Memories of the Holy Land*.

April

4 (Fri) Tries unsuccessfully to sketch the last chapter of *W*.

7 Begins episode 9 (Bernard's summing-up).

9 Entering what she feels may be the last lap of *W*; notes that the 'abandonment' she experienced with *O* and *TL* is checked by the extreme difficulty of form, as in *JR*, 'But I think it possible that I have got my statues against the sky' (*D*).

10 Lunches with LW's brother, Philip, manager of James de Rothschild's estate, and visits the Waddesdon greenhouses.

13 Continues *W*, episode 9 (Bernard at the hairdresser's). Reads Shakespeare immediately after writing, amazed at his speed and word-coining power, even in the lesser plays.

16 To Rodmell for Easter.

23 Has reached the 'final stride' of *W*: Bernard 'will go straight on now, & then stand at the door; & then there will be a last picture of the waves' (*D*).

29 Finishes first draft of *W* with an interlude of the sea just before dawn, aware the book will need much remodelling; works on W. Hazlitt (7 Sep).

HOGARTH PRESS: Edward Arlington Robinson, *Cavender's House*.

May

1 (Thurs) Accepts *The Private Letter-books of Sir Walter Scott*, ed. Wilfred Partington, for review in *TLS*; dislikes it and returns it. Considers writing on Fanny Burney's half-sister (28 Aug). Finds that, unlike with her other books, she is eager to begin rewriting *W*.

4–11 Tours south-western England, travelling books for the Press.

13 Offers to send TSE's *Ash Wednesday* and Roy Campbell's *Adamastor* (both 1930) to J. Bell.

18 '"Luriana Lurilee"', letter on the refrain in *TL*, in the *Sunday Times*.

22 Works on Hazlitt; attends presentation of Hawthorndon Prize to D. Cecil for *The Striken Deer* (1929), his biography of Cowper.

23 With VSW visits the Nicolsons' future home, Sissinghurst Castle; spends the night at Long Barn.

29 A new printing press installed at the Press; the old one goes to Sissinghurst Castle.

Late this month, writes an introductory letter to M. L. Davies' edition of letters by Co-operative working women, *Life as We Have Known It* (Mar 1931); gives tea to Sir Ronald Storrs, Governor of Cyprus.

HOGARTH PRESS: *Cambridge Poetry 1930*, ed. J. Davenport, Hugh Sykes and Michael Redgrave; John W. Graham, *Britain and America*; R. Money-Kyrle, *The Meaning of Sacrifice*; VSW, *The Edwardians*.

June

11 (Wed) Attends performance of *Othello* (with Paul Robeson, Sibyl Thorndike and Peggy Ashcroft).

13 Sketches plan for second draft of *W*.

15 Sets type for 'On Being Ill'. E. Smyth visits, as she does frequently at this time, driving LW frantic with her non-stop monologues.

16 Notes that, although VSW's *Edwardians* is not a very good book, its gigantic sale guarantees them a good income next year.

'Augustine Birrell', review of *The Collected Essays and Addresses of Augustine Birrell*, in the *Yale Review*.

HOGARTH PRESS: H. B. Samuel, *Beneath the Whitewash: A Critical Analysis of the Report of the Commission on the Palestine Disturbances of August, 1929*.

July

3 (Thurs) To Woking, Surrey, for a party at E. Smyth's; meets M. Baring, the Duchess of Sermoneta, lady-in-waiting to the Queen of Italy and contributor to the *Daily Mail*, and Joyce Wethered, British Ladies Open Golf champion.

21 Converting the two parts of '"Evelina's" Step Sister' (*New York Herald Tribune*, 14, 21 Sep) into a single article for *TLS*.

22 Attends tea party at E. Sitwell's with Thomas Balston of Duckworth's, Lady Lavery, 'the uncrowned king of Barcelona', and others (*D*).

25 Spends the night at Long Barn with VSW.

28 Attends performance of *The Importance of Being Earnest* (with J. Gielgud), at the Lyric Theatre.

29 To Rodmell for the summer.
30 Rewrites *W*, episode 2 (Rhoda on summer holiday).
HOGARTH PRESS: S. Freud, *Civilization and its Discontents*.

August
4 (Mon) Completes *W*, interlude 3.
5 Begins episode 3 (college).
6 Enjoys being at Rodmell: 'The rain pelts – look at it (as the people in The Waves are always saying) now' (*D*).
19 To Charleston for Q. Bell's twelfth birthday and the traditional fireworks.
20 Notes *W* is 'resolving itself (I am at page 100) into a series of dramatic soliloquies'; reads Dante at the end of her own writing (*D*).
25 Rewriting Hazlitt, having stopped *W* 'at the break'; sketches E. Smyth, 'the indomitable old crag', who has declared her love (*D*).
28 Reads Rosamond Lehmann's new novel, *A Note in Music*, with admiration, but is 'as usual appalled by the machinery of fiction: its much work for little result' (*D*). 'Fanny Burney's Half-Sister' in *TLS*.
29 Faints and is ill for 10 days.

September
2 (Tues) begins *W*, episode 4 (farewell dinner); notes she is writing to a rhythm, not to a plot. Sums up her friendships: sees little of LS, never sees S. Sydney-Turner, keeps constant with JMK and keeps up spasmodically with EMF, enjoys her close relations with VB, DG and the children. (*D*.)
7 'Wm Hazlitt the Man', review of *The Complete Works of William Hazlitt*, ed. P. P. Howe, in the *New York Herald Tribune*.
8 Her illness has meant two weeks' break from *W*, but she feels the season of silence and brooding has been fertile. S. Spender sends his poems.
10 Resumes work on *W*, episode 4 (Bernard on the train).
15 Makes notes for episode 4. Assures E. Smyth she has read her diary and her autobiographical volume *A Final Burning of Boats* (1928) to E. Smyth).
20–2 EMF spends the weekend: VW confides to E. Smyth that, though his books once influenced hers, she thinks them 'impeded, shrivelled and immature' (to E. Smyth).

23 To London to interview applicants to replace N. Boxall.
24 Reading Dante at the rate of one canto a week.
26 LW's mother visits for the second time this month, ruins the day.
27 Finishes her morning's work of 'fearful labour' on *W*, episode 4, with the words '"listen," she said, "Look"' (to E. Smyth).

'Memories of a Working Women's Guild' in the *Yale Review*.

October

Reads M. MacCarthy's *Fighting Fitzgerald and other Papers* (1930).

3 (Fri) Returns to London for the winter.
6 Works on *W*, interlude 5 (the sun in the middle of the sky).
8 Asks VSW to lend her *The Hamwood Papers of the Ladies of Llangollen*, ed. John Travers (1930).
11 Watches the coffins of the 48 passengers killed on the experimental flight of the R101 aircraft from Britain to India pass by; dislikes all the ceremony (*D*).
14 Dines with R. Mortimer; discusses W. Lewis's novel *The Apes of God* and his pamphlet *Satire and Fiction* (both 1930).
15 Works on an article on C. Rossetti (6 Dec). Finds it difficult to settle to *W*, so returns to Rodmell for the weekend.
18 TSE sends a copy of the limited-edition reprint of *'London: A Poem' and 'The Vanity of Human Wishes' by Samuel Johnson LL.D.*, with an introductory essay by TSE (1930).
22 Takes the day off writing and goes to Hampton Court. E. Smyth visits; proposes to leave VW some of her letters in her will, interests VW in becoming her literary executor.
23 Works in *W*, episode 5 (Neville's account of Percival's death).
27 'Grinding out' *W*. Has decided with LW to stop the Press.
28 Drafts notes for 'The death chapter' (*W*, episode 5).

HOGARTH PRESS: W. Benson, *As You Were*; Maurice Dobb, *Russia To-day and To-morrow*; R. M. Fox, *Drifting Men*; John Hoyland, *History as Direction*; Norman Macleod, *German Lyric Poetry*; Herbert Palmer, *The Armed Muse: Poems*; Louis Racine, *Life of Milton together with Observations on 'Paradise Lost'*, tr. with intro. by Katherine John; *Letters to Frederick Tennyson*, ed. Hugh Schonfield.

November

3 (Mon) Drafts scheme for the remainder of *W*. CB, H. Matheson and VSW to dinner; VSW agrees J. Bell's poems, *Winter Movement* (1930), are not good; H. Walpole comes in later,

agonising over the scathing portrait of him as Alroy Kear in S. Maugham's novel *Cakes and Ale* (1930).

7 At O. Morrell's meets W. B. Yeats for the first time in over 20 years; with W. de la Mare they discuss dreams and poetry; VW impressed by the directness, terseness and the vitality of Yeats, which is so much greater than that of TSE. Reads W. de da Mare's collection of stories *On the Edge* (1930); finds them 'wobbly' (*D*).

11 Begins *W*, episode 7 (middle age); attends party at H. Mirrlees'.

12 Finds herself 'too numb brained' to go on with Bernard's soliloquy; gives N. Boxall notice, then relents for three months (*D*).

16 Reads VSW's poem *Sissinghurst*; likes its 'air of rings widening widening until they imperceptibly touch the bank' (to VSW).

20 Lunches with Viscountess Rhondda.

21 Lunches at the Garrick Club to celebrate H. Nicolson's forty-fourth birthday; spends the night at Long Barn.

24 Begins *W*, episode 8 (reunion dinner).

29 '"The Book of Beauty": A Protest', letters to the editor, 29 Nov and 20 Dec, in *N&A*.

HOGARTH PRESS: *The Art of Dying: An Anthology*, ed. F. Birrell and F. L. Lucas; J. C. Flugel, *The Psychology of Clothes*; R. Jeffers, *Dear Judas and Other Poems;* I. Svevo, *The Nice Old Man and the Pretty Girl and Other Stories*, tr. L. Collison-Morely; D. Wellesley, *Deserted House: A Poem-Sequence; A Broadcast Anthology of Modern Poetry*, ed. D. Wellesley; VW, *On Being Ill*.

December

1 (Mon) Dines at E. Sands's; meets A. Bennett, tries to detect signs of genius but cannot, yet finds the next morning she cannot write a difficult pasage in *W* ('how their lives hang lit up against the Palace') all because of Bennett (*D*).

4 A 'slight snub' in a review of *On Being Ill* in *TLS* determines her to alter the whole of *W* (*D*).

5 Completes *W*, episode 8.

6 '"I am Christina Rossetti"', review of Mary Sandars' *The Life of Christina Rossetti*, and Edith Birkhead's *Christina Rossetti and her Poetry*, in *N&A*.

8 Types 'Inaccurate Memories' (cf. 'The Searchlight', 1939). Takes a week off from writing *W*.

(Mid-month) E. Blunden sends a book on C. Rossetti (probably D. M. Stuart's *Christina Rossetti*, 1930).

14 Begins *W*, interlude 9 (the sun at dusk). Dines at M. Hutchinson's to meet Rupert Hart-Davis, who may come to the Press (he does not; at present working for Heinemann, he later founds his own publishing company).

15 Dines at the Colefaxes', bored by A Colefax on *The Letters of Queen Victoria* and the Dyestuffs Act (see 'Am I a Snob?', *MOB*); resolves to burn her evening dress.

17 D. Cecil, LS and CB visit; discuss James Jeans's *The Mysterious Universe*, G. M. Trevelyan's *Blenheim*, Grace Stone's *Bitter Tea*, *The Letters of Queen Victoria*, ed. G. E. Buckle (all 1930), Lady G. Cecil's ongoing *Life* of her father, and possible titles for LS's forthcoming book of essays (*Portraits in Miniature and Other Essays*, pub. May 1931).

20 K. Martin to lunch; announces the *Nation* and the *New Statesman* are to amalgamate; asks LS to become literary editor, but he declines.

21 While listening to a Beethoven quartet, decides to 'merge all the interjected passages into Bernard's final speech, & end with the words O solitude' (*D*).

22 Copies out passage from Dante's *Inferno*, XXVI.94–102 (*D*).

23 To Monk's House. Bedridden with influenza, unable to work on *W*, reads D. Defoe's *Tour Through the Whole Island of Great Britain*, 3 vols (1724–7), *The Autobiography of Archibald Hamilton Rowan* (1840), E. F. Benson's *A Victorian Peep-Show* (1930), J. Jeans's *The Mysterious Universe* or *The Universe around Us*, and *The Journal of a Somerset Rector*, ed. Howard Coombs and the Revd Arthur Bax (1930) (see sketch *D*, 29 Dec; 'The Rev. John Skinner', *CR* II).

30 Wants to run the scenes of *W* together more, 'by rhythm, chiefly . . . changes of scene, of mood, of person, done without spilling a drop' (*D*). Continues reading Defoe.

31 Works on *W*, episode 9 (Bernard sitting by the willow tree).

1931

EVENTS AND LETTERS. Britain abandons gold standard; A. Bennett dies. Pearl Buck publishes *The Good Earth*; W. Faulkner, *Sanctuary*;

Robert Frost, *Collected Poems* (Pulitzer Prize); E. O'Neill, *Mourning Becomes Electra*; VSW, *All Passion Spent*; LS. *Portraits in Miniature*.

January

1 (Thurs) Reads S. Benson (probably *The Man who Missed the Bus*, 1928), thinks her 'extremely good' (to VSW; but see letter to E. Smyth, 18 May: 'the repulsion of the early book . . . poisons my mind').

3 Makes brief notes for *W*, episode 9 (Bernard's summing-up).

7 Returns to London, writing *W* at such high pressure that she can only work at it for about one hour each morning; wants to make Bernard's soliloquy move 'as prose has never moved before: from the chuckle & the babble to the rhapsody' (*D*). Has ideas for articles on Gosse (1 June), 'the armchair critic' (cf. 'All about Books', 28 Feb) and other topics; reads e e cummings' *The Enormous Room* (1922), and *Lettres de la Marquise de Deffand à Horace Walpole*, published by Mrs Paget Toynbee (1912).

10 Reads her 'Poetry in Fiction' and Dante, which she continues to read after her own writing.

20 Out of her speech for the National Society for Women's Service (21 Jan) conceives a sequel to *Room* 'about the sexual life of women: to be called "Professions for Women" (*D*) – the conception of what eventually becomes, after great complications and nearly a dozen changes of title for each volume, *The Years* (1937) and *Three Guineas* (1938) (shortened version of speech pub. in *DM*; original version repr. in *'The Pargiters': The Novel–Essay Portion of 'The Years'*, ed. Leaska, 1978; for an account of the novel's development see Leaska's intro. and Radin).

21 J. Lehmann starts work at the Press.

23 Too excited by her new book on women to work on *W*: 'the didactive demonstrative style conflicts with the dramatic' (*D*).

25 VW's forty-ninth birthday.

26 Suffering from influenza, but has shaken off the obsession of her new book and returned to *W*, which she plans to have finished in three weeks; reads manuscript of W. Plomer's *The Fivefold Screen* (Hogarth, May 1932).

30 Sketches notes for the final pages of *W*, episode 9.

Late this month, W. Plomer visits, talks about his new novel, *Sado* (pub. Sep).

February

2 (Mon) Works on *W*, episode 9 (Bernard without a self), incapable of other reading and writing. Attends rehearsal at Lady Lewis's of E. Smyth's setting for voice and orchestra of her friend H. Brewster's poem *The Prison*; finds the music too literary and didactic (*D*).

4 Dr Elinor Rendel visits to determine the cause of VW's temperature, delaying *W*, in which Bernard is 'within 2 days' of saying 'O Death' (*D*).

7 Finishes second draft of *W*: 'I wrote the words O Death fifteen minutes ago, having reeled across the last ten pages with some moments of such intensity & intoxication that I seemed only to stumble after my own voice . . . (as when I was mad). . . . I have netted that fin in the waste of waters . . .' (*D*; see 30 Sep 1926).

13 J. Case, who taught VW Greek 30 years ago, visits.

14–15 Drives with VB to Cambridge. Attends performance of Purcell's opera *The Faery Queen*; visits EMF, G. Rylands and others.

16 Finds the opening chapters of E. Sackville-West's *Simpson* (1931) too much like A. Bennett (to CB). A. Huxley and his wife Maria visit, talk of their travels in India, their plans to go to Russia and America, and their current research on industrial Britain.

17 Has undertaken to write six articles for *Good Housekeeping*, 'about what?' (*D*; these become the series 'The London Scene', Dec 1931–Dec 1932).

21 Reads William Rothstein's *Men and Memories*, 2 vols (1931–2).

24 Attends performance of E. Smyth's *The Prison*, which is a critical failure, and then a party for Smyth at the Countess of Rosebery's; talks with Lady Oxford, who wants her to review her next book.

27 Spends the night at Sissinghurst with VSW.

28 'All about Books' in the *New Statesman and Nation* (amalgamated this day under the editorship of K. Martin, who remains editor until 1960).

Late this month, suffers the usual depression after completing a book.

HOGARTH PRESS: *Cambridge Women's Verse*, compiled by Margaret Thomas; Lord Derwent, *Fifty Poems*; J. Easdale, *A Collection of Poems (Written between the ages of 14 and 17)*; John Hampson, *Saturday*

Night at the Greyhound; C. H. B. Kitchin, *The Sensitive One*; R. M. Rilke, *The Notebook of Malte Laurids Brigge*, tr. John Linton.

March

13 (Fri) Barbara Hutchinson (daughter of Mary and Jack Hutchinson), and J. Bell to dinner – 'Julian in a stew about his poems'; E. Jenkins comes in afterward (*D*).

16 Begins sketching 'Houses of the Great'; visits Carlyle's house and Keats's house. Notes Winifred Holtby is writing a book on her (*Virginia Woolf*, 1932).

18 E. Smyth visits; discusses her counter-attacks on reviewers. VW dines with CB and Benita Jaeger (CB's companion in the 1930s), C. McLaren, D. Cecil, J. Bell, VB and VSW.

20 Visits the docks with H. Nicolson, VSW and the Persian ambassador (for 'The Docks of London', Dec).

22 Reads *Alice Meynell: A Memoir* (1929) by her daughter Viola Meynell.

27 Takes niece Ann Stephen and a friend to see the light opera *Tantivy Towers*, by A. P. Herbert and T. Dunhill.

28 Saddened by the death of A. Bennett (27 Mar, age 63): 'A lovable genuine man' with 'a shopkeepers view of literature' but yet 'some real understanding power. . . . he abused me; & I yet rather wished him to go on abusing me; & me abusing him' (*D*).

28–9 Visits S. and B. Webb. Later in the week Beatrice sends a chapter of autobiography, which VW encourages her to develop into a book (probably *Our Partnership*, 1948).

30 Visits House of Commons (for '"This is the House of Commons"', Oct 1932).

31 Attends memorial service for A. Bennett.

HOGARTH PRESS: *Life as We Have Known It, by Co-operative Working Women*, ed. M. L. Davies, introductory letter by VW; C. E. M. Joad, *The Horrors of the Countryside*; Rupert Trouton, *Unemployment: Its Causes and their Remedies*, Foreword by JMK.

April

2 (Thurs) To Monk's House for Easter.

9 Agrees wtih E. Smyth's dislike of O. Sitwell's *Collected Satires and Poems*: 'All Foliage and no filberts' (to E. Smyth).

10 P. Strachey and F. L. Lucas visit; VW talks about Violet Hunt's

The Wife of Rossetti, her Life and Death, which had been rejected by Hogarth (pub. 1932 by John Lane).

11–15 Attends performance of S. Maugham's play *The Circle*; notes that J. M. Murry has written a book on D. H. Lawrence (*Son of Woman*, 1931), 'making out that he is Judas and Lawrence, Christ' (to E. Smyth).

16 VW and LW depart for tour of western France, travelling via La Rochelle south of Périgueux; they visit, among other monuments, the château at St Michel-de-Montaigne, where Montaigne lived and wrote, and the Château du Milieu at Chinon, in which Joan of Arc stood before Charles VII. VW reads TSE's *Thoughts after Lambeth* (1913) and, between flat tyres, D. H. Lawrence's *Sons and Lovers* (1913), realising with regret 'that a man of genius wrote in my time and I never read him', noting that 'the fact about contemporaries . . . is that they're doing the same thing on another railway line: one resents their distracting one'. They return to England 30 April. (To E. Smyth, 20 Apr; *D*, 16–17 Apr.)

23 'Lockhart's Criticism', review of *Lockhart's Literary Criticism*, intro. M. C. Hildyard, in *TLS*.

May

3 (Sun) Plans to regulate 'seeing people' in the months ahead, and to finish off *W* in 'a dashing masterly manner'; notes 'D. H. Lawrence has given me much to think about – about writing for writings sake' (*D*).

13 Typing *W* at the rate of seven or eight pages a day, 'It is like sweeping over an entire canvas with a wet brush' (*D*).

(Mid-month) Attends performance of A. Huxley's play *The World of Light*, and screening of *Le Million*, dir. René Clair. D. MacCarthy comes to dinner, leaves his collection of essays *Portraits*, which he later decides to publish with Putnam (Nov 1931), because it is a more 'durable' publisher than Hogarth (*D*, 30 May).

19 Admires LS's new book, *Portraits in Miniature and Other Essays*, noting 'the compressed yet glowing account' suits him far better than the larger scale; loathes the 'vulgarity' and 'frivolity' of L. P. Smith's *Afterthoughts*. LS and R. Mortimer to dinner (*D*).

20 E. Smyth visits; rants for three hours about her iniquitous treatment by Adrian Boult, Director of Music at the BBC, who

has refused to conduct *The Prison* for broadcast, and leaves VW with a headache for two days.

21 To Rodmell for Whitsun holiday. Reads Princess Daisy of Pless's *From My Private Diary* (1931) and D. H. Lawrence's *The Man who Died* (1931) – 'something sham' in spite of 'the lovely silver-bright writing here & there' (*D*, 28 May); finds herself making up *3G*.

HOGARTH PRESS: Charles Buxton, MP, *The Race Problem in Africa*; R. Macaulay, *Some Religious Elements in English Literature*; VSW, *All Passion Spent*; Jean Stewart, *Poetry in France and England*; R. C. Trevelyan, *Three Plays: Sulla, Fand, The Pearl-Tree*.

June

Early this month, dreams of meeting K. Mansfield beyond death (*D*, 8 June).

1 (Mon) Likes VSW's *All Passion Spent* (1931) better than *The Edwardians* (1930) (to M. L. Davies). 'Edmund Gosse', review of Evan Charteris's *The Life and Letters of Sir Edmund Gosse*, in the *Fortnightly Review*.

10 Attends party at VB's for DG's show at the Cooling Galleries, opened by O. Morrell.

14 LW finishes *After the Deluge* (Hogarth, Oct).

22 Finishes retyping *W*, 'Not that it is finished – oh dear no. For then I must correct the re-re-typing' (*D*, 23 June).

23 Attends gala performance of Sir Thomas Beecham's 'Season of Russian Opera and Ballet', with C. McLaren and Lady Abingdon; meets M. Baring, who defends Gosse.

27 Thinks Rudolph Besier's *The Barretts of Wimpole Street* (1930) 'rather feeble' (to E. Smyth).

'Aurora Leigh' in the *Yale Review*.

July

During this month, VW sits restively to sculptor Stephen Tomlin, who produces the well-known portrait head: original plaster model at Charleston, lead casts at Monk's House and the National Portrait Gallery (see *D*, 7 Aug).

1 (Wed) Works on opening interlude of *W*. Attends concert at Bumpus's bookshop: J. Easdale performs her poems set to her brother's music. M. Hutchinson, S. Tomlin and O. Morrell to dinner.

7 Corrects interludes in *W*; reads Byron's *Don Juan*; notes 'Fr.

G.' (possibly Fräulein Ruth Gruber, who was to publish a pamphlet on VW in 1935) is studying her works in the British Museum (*D*).

14 Finishes correcting the Hampton Court scene in *W*. Visited by R. C. Trevelyan, who asks her to help obtain a pension for poet H. Palmer (see Hogarth, Oct 1925, Nov 1927, Oct 1930); receives request for a copy of her new book from Conte Umberto Morra (author of several articles on VW in Italian literary journals, 1927–46).

17 Finishes correcting the typescript of *W*; nervously preparing to submit it to LW.

19 LW, though anticipating difficulties for the common reader, pronounces *W* a masterpiece, and the best of her books (*D*).

21 Begins *F*.

25 Visits S. Waterlow, now British Minister in Athens, at his house in Wiltshire.

30 To Rodmell for the summer.

Hogarth Press: VSW, *Sissinghurst*.

August

Visitors to Monk's House include S. Colefax, George and Margaret Duckworth, E. Smyth and VSW.

7 (Fri) Has been writing *F* to ease the strain of correcting *W*. Learns that H. Nicolson is leaving the *Evening Standard* to become editor of *Action*, the journal of Sir Oswald Mosley's New Party.

10 Begins correcting proofs of *W*; writes a little at *F*; cannot settle to read Donne, Sidney and Greville.

14 S. Colefax visits for two hours of 'barren gossip' (*D*).

15 Continues proof-reading *W*; as when first writing it, finds it so concentrated she can only work on a few pages at a time. Sets up some of G. Rylands' *Poems* (Dec); notes JMK visits Downing Street and spreads sensational rumours (the international financial crisis leads to R. MacDonald's resignation on the 24th to form a coalition government, and to Britain's abandonment of the gold standard, 21 Sep.

16 Works on proofs of the last chapter of *W*; thinks it good to write biographies so as to use her powers of accurate representation, and to reserve novels for expressing the general and poetic (*D*).

18 Sends off proofs of *W*.

20 Asks VSW to send H. Nicolson's *Swinburne and Baudelaire* (1930); later in the month asks her to send his *People and Things* (1931).
30 Plagued by headaches, spends the next week in bed.

September

1 (Tues) Reads H. Walpole's *Judith Paris* (1931), and W. Scott's *Ivanhoe* (1819); enthusiastic about neither, but judges Scott better than Walpole because at least his book has 'roots': 'My anger that S[cott] won't be more intense partly the result of England's crisis this summer' (*D*).
2 Listens to a Bach concert on the radio; 'bathes' herself in the Elizabethan prose of Thomas Dekker: a 'nobler instrument than Scott or the 18th Century' (*D*).
3 Reads a passage in Montaigne on the passion of women; begins making up *3G* when she was hoping to begin thinking about an article on the Elizabethans for *CR* II; annoyed by D. MacCarthy's comment in *Life and Letters* that in contemporary novels such as *MD* 'events have become merely interruptions in a long wool-gathering process' (*D*).
15 Depressed because H. Walpole dislikes *W*. To Tunbridge Wells, travelling books for the Press; buys a volume of John Skelton's poetry, visits D. Wellesley and the Easdales.
16 Elated because J. Lehmann likes *W*; is inspired to write 'A Letter to a Young Poet' (July 1932). Plans to read S. Spender and W. H. Auden.
19 Works on 'Donne after Three Centuries' for *CR* II.
21 Britain goes off the gold standard and VW writes about Donne: '& if everybody had spent their time writing about Donne we should not have gone off the Gold Standard' (*D*). Talks with economist Richard Kahn, and JMK, who in *The Economic Consequences of Mr Churchill* (Hogarth, 1925) had warned against the return to the gold standard.
27 Plans to publish *W* 8 October, in spite of the forthcoming general election (27 Oct).
30 Reads S. Spender's novel, which she advises him to scrap.

HOGARTH PRESS: C. Day Lewis, *From Feathers to Iron*; L. M. Fraser, *Protection and Free Trade*; Allen Havens, *The Trap*; Denis Ireland, *Ulster To-day and To-morrow . . . A Study in Political Re-evolution*; J. Lehmann, *A Garden Revisited and Other Poems*; W. Plomer, *Sado*;

Marjorie Wise, *English Village Schools*; LW, *The Village in the Jungle* (1913; first Hogarth edition).

October

Early this month, returns to Tavistock Square for the winter; works intermittently at 'Letter to a Young Poet'. Pleased by the positive response to *W* by her friends and by reviewers – though puzzled that *TLS* praises her characters when she meant to have none (see *M&M*, *D* and *L* for Oct); by mid-October *W* has sold 5000 copies, beating any of her previous books, and a second impression is printed.

14 (Wed) Dashes off a sketch entitled 'The Cook', a portrait of Sophia Farrell, the family cook of VW's youth (MHP). Attends performance of E. Smyth's *The Wreckers*; with VSW takes Smyth to dinner at the Eiffel Tower restaurant, where the proprietor tells them anecdotes about Austrian writer Arthur Schnitzler.

15 W. Plomer and B. Dobrée, professor and critic, 'a nimble secondrate man' (*D*), to dinner.

(Mid-month) F. L. Lucas visits; has not read *W* but talks about his own forthcoming poem, *Ariadne*, and play, *The Bear Dances* (pub. 1932).

17 Attends Motor Show.

19 Lays in 'a stock of Elizabethans', for 'The Strange Elizabethans'.

23 Diffident about mentioning the positive review of *W* in the *Manchester Guardian* because LW's *After the Deluge*, though praised in *NS&N*, receives a short, unenthusiastic review in *TLS* and he resolves to abandon the work (*D*).

27 Attends party at J. Strachey's to hear the election results.

29 Attends family party for LW's mother's eighty-first birthday.

Hogarth Press: EMF, *A Letter to Madam Blanchard*; E. Jones, *On the Nightmare*; R. M. Rilke, *Duineser Elegien: Elegies from the Castle of Duino*, tr. VSW and E. Sackville-West; LW, *After the Deluge*; VW, *The Waves*.

November

5 (Thurs) R. Lehmann visits to discuss her novel *Invitation to the Waltz* (pub. 1932).

8 Reads G. Eliot's *Middlemarch* (1932) and F. Madox Ford's memoir *Thus to Revisit* (1931).

15 Reads B. Disraeli's *Coningsby* (1944); plans to read Trollope.

16 EMF's letter of praise for *W* confirms her decision 'to go on along this very lonely path'; avoids meeting RF and LS, whom she suspects do not like the book (LS, already ill with what proves to be cancer, never reads it). Reads CB's *An Account of French Painting* (1931), and Philip Sidney and Gabriel Harvey for *'The Countess of Pembroke's Arcadia'* and 'The Strange Elizabethans' in *CR* II, for which she wants to devise a new, less formal method (*D*).
24 Attends performance of Ibsen's *The Master Builder*; contracts a headache that disables her for most of December.

December
6 (Sun) Plans to read Gerald Heard's *The Emergence of Man* (1931), and *The Science of Life* (1931) by H. G. and G. P. Wells and J. Huxley.
(Mid-month) Learns that LS is seriously ill.
22 To Monk's House for Christmas, phoning each day for news of LS.
25 Lunches at the Keyneses', where the talk is of LS and death in general.
29 Thinks D. MacCarthy's *Portraits* (1931) 'too much in the style of Gosse' (to VSW). Notes *After the Deluge* has sold 450 copies; *W*, 9400.
30 Remarks on the 'impeccably well bred' portrait of P. Strachey in E. Jenkins' novel *The Winters* (1931) (to P. Strachey).
31 Works on 'Letter to a Young Poet'. The Keyneses and the Bells to tea; they talk of LS, of the possibility of Carrington committing suicide, of the death of Elizabeth Courtauld, and of the demise of *Action*.
'The Docks of London' in *Good Housekeeping*.
HOGARTH PRESS: N. Leys, *A Last Chance in Kenya*; G. Rylands, *Poems*.
Month of publication unknown: Aneurin Bevan, MP, E. J. Strachey, MP, George Strauss, MP, *What We Saw in Russia*; Viscount Cecil, *A Letter to an MP on Disarmament*; E. W. White, *Walking Shadows: An Essay on Lotte Reiniger's Silhouette Films*.

1932

Events and Letters. Lady Gregory, G. L. Dickinson and LS die; J. Galsworthy awarded Nobel Prize; W. Faulkner publishes *Light in August*; E. Hemingway, *Death in the Afternoon*; A. Huxley, *Brave New World*; R. Lehmann, *Invitation to the Waltz*; R. Macaulay, *They were Defeated*.

January

10 (Sun) Returns to Tavistock Square from Monk's House.
13 Katherine Thring, wife of G. H. Thring, secretary to the Society of Authors, calls to ask for donations.
14 Visits LS at Ham Spray, where she had not been since October 1924.
17 W. Plomer and A. Ritchie to dinner; they discuss Mrs Kapp (pseud. of Yvonne Cloud) and her sapphic novel *Nobody Asked You* (1932): 'so dull, so improper' (to D. Carrington, 18 Jan).
20 LS dies, age 52; VW attends a gloomy fancy dress party for A. Bell at VB's.
25 VW's fiftieth birthday.
29 O. Strachey to dinner; discusses LS, J. Jeans.
31 Finishes 'Letter to a Young Poet' (pub. June). Visits RF and H. Anrep; meets G. Heard, writer and broadcaster on science, who strikes VW as all fact and no feeling (*D*).

'Oxford Street Tide', second essay in 'The London Scene', in *Good Housekeeping*.

Hogarth Press: F. Birrell, *A Letter From a Black Sheep*; R. Mortimer, *The French Pictures: A Letter to Harriet*; L. A. G. Strong, *A Letter to W. B. Yeats*.

February

2 (Tues) Reads H. G. Wells's *The Science of Life* (1930), on sex reversal in a chicken.
2 Dines at CB's with RF, VB and DG; they discuss G. Heard, LS and his circle, the war between China and Japan over Manchuria, P. Buck's *The Good Earth* (1931), and other topics.
3 Corrects 'Donne after Three Centuries' for *CR* ii. Visits O. and P. Morrell; talks about Dryden, LS, *W* and about O. Morrell's portrait in B. Russell's autobiography – as well as those in D. H. Lawrence's *Women in Love* (1920), A. Huxley's *Crome*

Yellow (1921), O. Sitwell's *Triple Fugue* (1921) and G. Cannan's *Pugs and Peacocks* (1921).

6 'The Rev. William Cole: A Letter', review of *The Blecheley Diary of Rev. William Cole*, ed. Francis Griffen Stokes, in *NS&N*.

11 Inspired to work on *3G* by H. G. Wells's remarks in *The Works, Wealth and Happiness of Mankind* (1932) on how women must be 'decorative and ancillary'.

12 Attends lecture on French art by RF; talks with M. Hutchinson about the case of 'Count' Geoffrey Potocki, who has been sentenced to six months in prison for trying to commission a printer to print his indecent poems: LW helps organise an appeal and M. Hutchinson's husband, St John Hutchinson, KC, is to appear for the defence (see 7 Mar).

13 Reads Donne's 'An Anatomie of the World'.

16 Finishes Donne's after Three Centuries'; 'itching' to write *3G*, 'for which I have collected enough powder to blow up St Pauls' (*D*).

18 W. Plomer, G. Potocki and Derrick Leon, author of *Livingstones: A Novel of Contemporary Life* (Hogarth, Feb), to dinner.

26 Finishes Sidney's *The Countess of Pembroke's Arcadia*; corrects 'Letter to a Young Poet'. Visited by S. Colefax, H. Walpole and Elizabeth Williamson, great-niece of E. Smyth.

28 Explains her violent reaction to Charles Morgan's *The Fountain* (1932): 'I suspected him of wrapping up tame little reputable platitudes in words of twenty-five syllables, and thus posing, and thus undermining the health of English letters, as Mrs Ward did and others' (to H. Walpole). Attends Camargo Society ballet, which includes Walton's *Façade* (with L. Lopokova and Frederick Ashton).

29 Invited to deliver the Clark lectures at Cambridge next year; pleased because her father gave the first Clark lectures in 1883, but declines because it would take too much time from her other writing. Lunches with Mary Dodge (a wealthy American friend of E. Smyth's) who gives her Donne's copy, with his signature and notes, of Alberico Gentilis's *Regales Disputationes Tres* (1605). Reads Julia Strachey's 'remarkable acidulated story' *Cheerful Weather for the Wedding* (Hogarth, Sep), and Gamel Woolsey's 'indecent novel' *One Way of Love*, which Hogarth rejects (to CB).

HOGARTH PRESS: G. T. Garrett, *The Mugwumps and the Labour Party*; J. Hampson (pseud. of John Hampson Simpson), *O Providence*;

C. Isherwood, *The Memorial*; René Lafourgue, *The Defeat of Baudelaire*; H. J. Laski, *The Crisis and the Constitution: 1931 and After*; C. M. Lloyd, *Russian Notes*; L. B. Pekin, *Public Schools*; *New Signatures: Poems by Several Hands*, ed. Michael Roberts.

March

3 (Thurs) Wishes she had accepted the Clark lectureship and polished up 'Phases of Fiction'; LW advises against it.

7 Attends court appeal of G. Potocki, which is denied; next day finds herself unable to continue revising 'Dorothy Osborne's "Letters"' for *CR* II because of attending court.

9 Lunches with R. Mortimer to meet Alice Keppel, mother of Violet Trefusis and former mistress of King Edward VII.

10 Travels to Ham Spray to talk to D. Carrington.

11 D. Carrington, unable to face life without LS, commits suicide (*D*, 12 Mar; to O. Morrell, 15 Mar).

12–14 Travels to Cambridge to see G. Rylands' production of *Hamlet*; returns through East Anglia, visiting RF at his house in Suffolk.

17 Visits W. Plomer and painter Anthony Butts; meets journalist Louise Morgan, Eslanda Goode (wife of singer P. Robeson) and others.

18 Visits VB, J. Bell and his friend Lettice Ramsey; discusses his dissertation on Pope, which has just been rejected by King's College, Cambridge.

19 Advises an American student that she has not studied Freud or any psychologist, and that 'Bloomsbury Group' is a 'journalist phrase which has no meaning' (to Harmon Goldstone, 19 Mar, 16 Aug).

20 Reads Floris Delattre's *Le Roman psychologique de Virginia Woolf* (1932); observes, 'Its difficult to see one self as a mummy in a museum' (to W. Plomer).

21 Attends performance of *The Enchanted Grove*, by the Vic-Wells Ballet, with scenery and costumes by DG. Reads M. Baring's autobiography, *The Puppet Show of Memory* (1922).

23 To Rodmell for Easter.

24 Notes two books on her have appeared – Delattre's, and Ingeborg Badenhausen's *Die Sprache Virginia Woolfs*; resolves, 'I must not settle into a figure' (*D*).

26 To Sissinghurst to visit VSW.

28 To Rottingdean to tea at M. Baring's with E. Williamson, E.

Smyth and Alistair Grant, a partner in Peter Davies Ltd, who are to publish E. Smyth's *Female Pipings in Eden* (1933).

Late this month, works on 'De Quincey's Autobiography', 'Dr Burney's Evening Party' and other articles for *CR* II.

'Great Men's Houses', third essay in 'The London Scene', in *Good Housekeeping*.

HOGARTH PRESS: J. Easdale, *Clemence and Clair*.

April

Early this month, sees VSW and H. Nicolson (who is looking for a job), E. Smyth, K. Martin, and J. and A. Strachey, who are sorting through LS's papers. Reads and rejects Mary Sargant-Florence's book, which proves 'that colour is the same as sound' – *Colour Coordination* (pub. 1940) (to VB, 11 Apr).

1 (Fri) Has 'invented the skeleton of another novel: but it must wait, buried, at least a year' (to E. Smyth; probably *The Pargiters* – see 11 Oct).

3 Returns to London from Rodmell.

12 Reads and admires, but does not publish, poems by Lilian Bowes-Lyon, niece of the Duchess of York, the future Queen Elizabeth (to W. Plomer).

15 With LW, RF and his sister Margery, departs by train for Venice, where they sail for Athens. VW reads Max Eastman, J. M. Murry, H. G. Wells and Jean-Jacques Rousseau; records visits to Sunium, Aegina, Corinth, Delphi and other places before their return via Belgrade, on the Orient Express, to England (12 May). VW wants to come to Greece every year. (See *D* and *L*, 19 Apr–15 May.)

HOGARTH PRESS: M. Dobb, *On Marxism To-day*.

May

15 (Sun) Returns to Tavistock Square from Monk's House.

17 Wonders how to react to the attack by Muriel Bradbrook in 'Notes on the Style of Mrs Woolf', *Scrutiny*, May (see *M&M*).

19 Discusses J. Lehmann's complaints about his position at the Press (see Lehmann).

23 Refurbishes *'David Copperfield'* (which, however, she does not ultimately include in *CR* II).

26 Attends party at A. Stephen's; meets Solly Zuckerman, who has just published *The Social Life of Monkeys and Apes*, R.

Hughes (author of *A High Wind in Jamaica*, 1929), painter Doris Chapman and others.

31 Attends dinner party at CB's with artist Rex Whistler, writer Beatrice Howe, D. Cecil and Mrs Peter Quennell.

'Abbeys and Cathedrals', fourth essay in 'The London Scene', in *Good Housekeeping*.

HOGARTH PRESS: W. Plomer, *The Fivefold Screen*; R. C. Trevelyan, *Rimeless Numbers*; D. Wellesley, *Jupiter and the Nun*.

June

1 (Wed) Attends Derby Day party at D. Cecil's with E. Bowen, A. Asquith, John Sparrow, barrister and editor of Donne's *Devotions*, and others; discusses Naomi Mitchison's review of W. H. Auden's *The Orators* (1932).

2 Lunches at the Keyneses' with G. B. Shaw, who talks about *Ellen Terry and Bernard Shaw: A Correspondence*, ed. C. St John (1931), and Frank Harris's *Bernard Shaw* (1931).

5 Declines K. Martin's invitation to write the 'World of Books' page in *NS&N*. Dines at CB's; discusses Hector Bolitho's *Albert the Good: Life of the Prince Consort* (1932).

6 Attends Camargo Society ballet (with L. Lopokova).

14 Attends private view of recent paintings by DG, VB and Keith Baynes; meets Robert Tatlock, editor of the *Burlington Magazine*, and others.

18 Attends party at the Hutchinsons'; meets David Lindsay (Lord Balniel), Trustee of the Tate Gallery, George Johnstone (Baron Derwent), diplomat and author of *Fifty Poems* (Hogarth, Feb 1931), and others.

27 Prince Mirsky, lecturer in Russian literature at the University of London, visits and tells VW and LW he is going back to Russia; they predict he will be killed (and in fact he later disappears). VSW delivers the manuscript of *Family History* (Hogarth, Oct) and A. Strachey delivers the translation of Melanie Klein's *The Psycho-analysis of Children* (Hogarth, Nov).

28 Finishes the De Quincey article, trying to complete *CR* II before the end of June. Dines with Dame Katharine Furse (whom she had known in her youth, now director of the World Association of Girl Guides and Girl Scouts) and her friend American philosopher Mary Follett; meets Richard Cabot, Professor of Medicine and of Social Ethics at Harvard, who is writing *The*

Meaning of Right and Wrong (1933), and his wife Ella Cabot, writer and teacher of ethics and psychology.

'A Letter to a Young Poet' in *Yale Review*.

July

2 (Sat) Watches the German dirigible, *Graf Zeppelin*, pass over London.

3 Finishes 'The Novels of Thomas Hardy'; prepares to revise '"I Am Christina Rossetti"' for *CR* II.

7 Thanks VSW for her latest book, *The Death of Noble Godavary* (1932).

11 Finishes *CR* II, with 'no sense of glory; only of drudgery done' (*D*).

12 Reads E. F. Benson's *Charlotte Brontë* (1932), thinks it fifth-rate, not first-rate, as E. Smyth does (to E. Smyth); later in the month receives a book by a 'lunatic' proving that Branwell Brontë wrote *Wuthering Heights* – Alice Law's *Emily Jane Brontë and the Authorship of 'Wuthering Heights'* (1925) (to Lady Cecil, 25 July).

13 Reads *The Life of Joseph Wright* (compiler of the six-volume *English Dialect Dictionary*) by his wife, Elizabeth Wright (1932).

14 Reads the newly published *S. T. Coleridge's Unpublished Letters*, ed. E. L. Griggs.

15 Stella Benson visits; talks about the slave trade in Hong Kong, where she has been living, and about the prizes awarded her novel *Tobit Transplanted* (1931).

22 Has been 'experimenting with little stories' (*D*); thanks E. Bowen for sending her latest novel, *To the North* (1932).

26 To Monk's House for the summer.

31 Corrects proofs of *CR* II; 'nibbles' at *F*, feeling 'the point is rather gone, as I meant it for a joke with Lytton, and a skit on him'; responds to J. Lehmann's remarks on 'A Letter to a Young Poet' (to J. Lehmann).

HOGARTH PRESS: Henry Brailsford, *If We Want Peace*; W. Plomer, *The Case is Altered*; H. Walpole, *A Letter to a Modern Novelist*; VW, *A Letter to a Young Poet*.

August

4 (Thurs) Saddened to learn G. L. Dickinson, 'that fine charming spirit', has died; resolves not to let friendships lapse (*D*, 5 Aug; to E. Smyth, 7 Aug).

9 Reads *Reminiscences of Lord Kilbracken* (1931).
11 Faints and is unwell for several days.
17 Works on proofs of *CR* II.
Late this month, records reading 'Souvenirs de Tocqueville, any number of biographies, Coleridge – one or two poems, Lord Kilbracken memoirs, Shaw Pen portraits, Ainslie memoirs, Vita's novel, MSS. (Livingstones), Nothing much good – except de T. Coleridges letters; but failed to finish the 2nd vol.'; and records visitors: VB, CB, J. Bell, Frances Marshall, the Stephens, the Keyneses, RF, J. T. Sheppard, A. Ritchie, TSE and wife, VSW and H. Nicolson (*D*).

September
2 (Fri) Enjoying work on *F*. TSE and Vivienne Eliot visit, 'she wild as Ophelia'; J. Lehmann resigns from the Press (*D*).
7 Thinks Viscount Cecil's *A Letter to an MP on Disarmament* (1931) and L. A. G. Strong's *A Letter to W. B. Yeats* (1932) 'd——d dull' (to E. Sands).
10 Reads 'The Waterfall' from E. Smyth's *Female Piping in Eden* (pub. 1933).
12 Thanks H. Walpole for his anthology of Scott, *The Waverley Pageant*, which he has dedicated to her; notes *The Bride of Lammermoor* (1819) and *The Antiquary* (1816) are her favourites; would like to write on the 'Shakespearian' dialogue in Scott (to H. Walpole; see also 27 Sep 1934).
15 Takes plums to old Mrs Grey (cf. 'Old Mrs Grey', DM).
16 Distraught, botches the penultimate chapter of *F*, because LW's snapshot instead of the Lenare photograph is to be used as the frontispiece of W. Holtby's study of VW: 'My legs show; & I am revealed to the world (1,000 at most) as a plain dowdy old woman' (*D*).
Late this month, entertains A. Davidson, E. Smyth, the Keyneses; exchanges visits with VB, DG and others at Charleston; W. Plomer and Charles Siepmann, who has replaced H. Matheson as Director of Talks at the BBC, visit, and they drive to Sissinghurst to see a performance of *The Land*.
HOGARTH PRESS: R. D. Charques, *Soviet Education*; B. Dobrée, *St Martin's Summer*; Lyn Irvine, *Ten Letter-Writers*; Julia Strachey, *Cheerful Weather for the Wedding*.

October

1 (Sat) Returns to Tavistock Square for the winter; reads *The Letters of D. H. Lawrence*, ed. A. Huxley (1932), with 'the usual frustration . . . its the preaching that rasps me' (*D*); acknowledges the 'genius' of *Sons and Lovers*, thinks it the 'pinnacle' though admits she has read nothing else (to VSW, 8 Nov; see 18 Aug 1912 and 20 June 1921 for other works by Lawrence).

3–5 Attends annual conference of the Labour Party, at Leicester.

6 Glances through W. Holtby's *Virginia Woolf*, which makes her 'roar with laughter' (to E. Smyth).

11 Begins 'The Pargiters: An Essay based upon a paper read to the London/National Society for Women's Service'.

13 *CR* II published. Stephen Spender visits: 'a rattle headed bolt eyed young man, raw boned, loose jointed who thinks himself the greatest poet of all time' (*D*, 2 Nov).

23 Begins second essay in *P*.

Late this month, in response to J. B. Priestley's 'To a Highbrow' (BBC, 10 Oct) and H. Nicolson's 'To a Lowbrow' (BBC, 24 Oct) writes 'Middlebrow', which LW advises her not to send to the *NS&N* (pub. posthumously, *DM*).

'"This is the House of Commons"', fifth essay in 'The London Scene', in *Good Housekeeping*.

HOGARTH PRESS: Leonard Barnes, *The New Boer War*; Louis Golding, *A Letter to Adolf Hitler*; J. C. Hardwick, *A Letter to an Archbishop*; J. A. Hobson, *From Capitalism to Socialism*; D. Graham Pole, *India in Transition*, intro. by the Rt. Hon. Wedgwood Benn; P. Quennell, *A Letter to Mrs Virginia Woolf*; VSW, *Family History*; Sir Michael Sadler, *Modern Art and Revolution*; VW, *The Common Reader: Second Series*.

November

Early this month, V. Trefusis visits to talk about her forthcoming novel, *Tandem* (pub. 1933).

1 (Tues) VW's heart begins 'galloping'; Dr Rendel advises her to restrict her activity.

2 Finishes the essay on L. Stephen (28 Nov). Enthusiastic about working with facts again for the first time since *N&D* in 'The Pargiters', which is to be an 'Essay–Novel,' taking in 'everything, sex, education, life &c; & come, with the most powerful & agile leaps, like a chamois across precipices from

1880 to here & now' (*D*; here designated as *P* until 2 Feb 1933, when she abandons the essay chapters).

4 O. Morrell comes to tea to discuss her memoirs, which VW has encouraged her to write (pub. 1963, 1974).

5 Continues second essay in *P*.

10 Finishes the scene of the man exposing himself (*P*, ch. 2).

11 Begins third essay in *P*.

13 Mocks E. Smyth for thinking the review of *Jane Austen's Letters* in the *TLS* (10 Nov) was hers (it was by EMF); declares Austen is not one of her favourites: 'I'd give all she ever wrote for half what the Brontës wrote – if my reason did not compel me to see that she is a magnificent artist' (to E. Smyth, 13, 20 Nov).

17 Begins third chapter in *P*.

23 Works on fourth essay in *P*.

24 Begins fourth chapter in *P*.

28 'Leslie Stephen, the Philosopher at Home: A Daughter's Memories' in *The Times*.

30 Begins fifth essay in *P*; gives a private-view party, 'notable for its peeresses its chatter, its cocktails', at the exhibition of furnishings, fabrics and decorations by VB and DG at the Lefevre Gallery (*D*).

Hogarth Press: M. Klein, *The Psycho-analysis of Children*; Arthur Ponsonby, *Disarmament*.

December

4 (Sun) Plans to finish the '1880' section of *P* in a day or two.

9 Begins fifth chapter in *P*.

11 Reads *Little Innocents*, ed. Alan Pryce-Jones (1932), a volume of childhood reminiscences by E. Smyth, VSW, H. Nicolson, E. Sackville-West, and others.

13 R. West, 'a very clever woman . . . with a great supply of worldly talk', to dinner (*D*).

15 L. P. Smith, 'a dogmatic cultivated American bore', to tea (*D*).

16 Begins sixth essay in *P*; dines with H. Mirrlees.

17 Has written out her 'first fury' – 234 typewritten pages since 10 October and 'the fun of the book is to come, with Magdalena & Elvira [later Sara]' (*D*).

19 Having written *P* 'to the verge of total extinction' (the complete first draft of what is to become the '1880' section of *Y*), takes up *F* as relief, but is finding *P* much easier than *W* (*D*).

20 To Rodmell for Christmas.
22 Reading J. Austen's letters, finds they steadily improve.
23 Reads *F* and finds it a waste and a bore; works at finishing it at the rate of ten pages a day. Talks with A. Bell about Mrs Gaskell and Thackeray.
24 Reads Catherine Carswell's *The Savage Pilgrimage: A Narrative of D. H. Lawrence* (1932), which the author had asked her to 'puff' (to O. Morrell, 25 Nov); finds her 'servile and supine adoration' distasteful (to O. Morrell, 26 Dec; see also *D*, 2 Oct).
28 Reads Axel Munthe's *The Story of San Michele* (1929) and S. Benson's *Christmas Formula* (1932); asks E. Smyth about Mrs Pankhurst and the suffrage movement, and Lady Radnor's memoirs, *From a Great-grandmother's Armchair* (1927), for *P* (to E. Smyth); thanks H. Walpole for his book of reminiscences, *The Apple Tree* (1932).

Late this month, mosaicist Boris Anrep represents VW as Clio in 'The Awakening of the Muses' on one of the vestibule landings of the National Gallery.
'Portrait of a Londoner', sixth essay in 'The London Scene', in *Good Housekeeping*.
Hogarth Press (month of publication unknown): Dr Helene Deutsch, *Psycho-analysis of the Neuroses*, tr. W. D. Robson-Scott.

1933

Events and Letters. Hitler appointed German Chancellor; J. Galsworthy, G. A. Moore and S. Benson die. TSE publishes *The Use of Poetry and the Use of Criticism*; George Orwell, *Down and Out in Paris and London*; G. Stein, *The Autobiography of Alice B. Toklas*; VW, *Flush*.

January

2 (Mon) Attends A. Bell's fourteenth birthday party; talks with N. Hudson, E. Sands and others, including Wogan Philipps (husband of R. Lehmann), who suggests *W* should be filmed. Receives a letter from Virginia Isham, who suggests *W* should be broadcast.
5 Has rewritten the Whitechapel scene in *F* for the third time; notes, without jealousy, the positive review in *TLS* of D. Garnett's *Pocahontas or The Nonpareil of Virginia*; plans to spend

another week on *F* and then 'come to grips with my 20 years in one chapter problem' in *P* (*D*).

6 Advises against publishing J. Hampson's latest novel (which seems to have been resubmitted and again rejected; see *D*, 29 Oct).

14 Finishes typing *F*, all the while speaking aloud phrases of *P*. Reads R. Barry O'Brien's *The Life of Charles Stewart Parnell* (1898).

18 While LW visits a skin specialist in Wimpole Street, VW verifies details of the houses for *F*. W. Plomer and M. Strachey dine before attending *Pomona*, a ballet at Sadler's Wells (choreography by F. Ashton, set and costumes by VB), and a party afterward at VB's studio, where RF questions VW about his forthcoming book, *Characteristics of French Art* (Chatto and Windus, 1933).

19 Has 50 pages left to correct of *F*; scenes from *P* keep springing up.

21 *F* 'lingers on'; VW attends performance of Mozart's *Don Giovanni*, G. A. Moore dies – 'I liked his incorruptible conscience in art, combined with the corruption of all the rest' (to E. Smyth, 27 Jan).

25 VW's fifty-first birthday.

26 Despatches *F*. Has arranged with Bianca Weiss for Italian lessons (early Feb–mid Apr), in preparation for a trip to Italy in May; W. Holtby to tea.

31 Returns to *P* with additions to first chapter ('1880'). J. Galsworthy – 'That stark man' – dies (*D*, 2 Feb).

Late this month, the Woolfs take delivery of a new Lanchester car, 'shaped like a fish, green on bottom, silver on top' (to G. Rylands).

February

Early this month, Margaret West succeeds Scott Johnson as manager of the Hogarth Press.

2 (Thurs) Finishes revising ch. 1 of *P*; plans to leave out the 'interchapters' (i.e. essays), 'compacting them in the text': thus VW abandons the idea of the 'Essay–Novel', to develop the novel (which will become *Y*) and the essays (which will become *3G*) separately (*D*).

(Mid-month) Gives manuscript of *Room* to the Women's Service Club. Reads J. M. Murry's *Reminiscences of D. H. Lawrence* (1933):

'Murry's last spurt of oil and venom and other filth seemed to me his foulest' (to O. Morrell, 14 Feb).

16 E. Smyth visits; exhausts VW. EMF, who is writing the life of G. L. Dickinson, to dinner.

17 Launched on *Y* in this 'blank season of the year' – VB at Charleston, CB in Jamaica, RF in Tangier, VSW in America.

25 Lady G. Cecil dies (to E. Smyth, 1 Mar).

27 Attends concert by Hungarian violinist Jelly d'Aranyi in Westminster Abbey. S. Tomlin visits.

28 Visits art collectors Bertha and Frank Stoop.

HOGARTH PRESS: T. Bosanquet, *Paul Valéry; The Hogarth Letters;* D. Leon, *Livingstones: A Novel of Contemporary Life;* A. Prophett, *The Twilight Age;* Hebe Spaull, *How the World is Governed*.

March

Early this month, meets Lady Patricia Ramsay and quizzes her for an hour about being royal (to E. Smyth, 12 Mar; to VSW, 18 Mar).

3 (Fri) Writes to Jonathan Cape, publisher, who has advised VW that A. C. Gissing objects to some of VW's remarks in her articles on his father, G. Gissing (reprinted as an introduction to Cape's edition of *By the Ionian Sea*); the dispute, conducted in *TLS*, culminates in VW's letter of 4 May.

25 Dines with Susan Lawrence (Labour politician), Mary Stocks (lecturer at Manchester University), Evelyn Sharp (writer and suffragist) and her husband, journalist Henry Nevinson; discusses her intention to refuse an honorary Doctor of Letters from Manchester University.

26 Dines with Lady Rhondda, discussing her weekly journal, *Time and Tide*; visits CB, just back from Jamaica.

27 Writes letter of refusal to Manchester, noting that her situation parallels that of Elvira [Sara] Pargiter in *Y* ('1910').

Late this month, meets painter Ethel Walker, age 73, who has a 'rough raddled charm' (to VSW, 1 Apr).

HOGARTH PRESS: Ivan Bunin, *The Well of Days*, tr. Gleb Struve and Hamish Miles; C. Day Lewis, *The Magnetic Mountain;* H. R. G. Greaves, *The Spanish Constitution; New Country: Prose and Poetry by the Authors of 'New Signatures'*, ed. M. Roberts; R. West, *A Letter to a Grandfather*.

April

3 (Mon) Begins '1907' chapter in *Y*. Takes her nieces, Ann and

Judith Stephen, to see Paul Robeson and Flora Robson in E. O'Neill's *All God's Chillun Got Wings*.

4 Drive to Bedford, travelling books.

5 Lord Sydney Olivier, one of the founders of the Fabian Society, author of *The Myth of Governor Eyre* (Hogarth, Oct), to dinner.

6 Too exhausted by *Y* to write the scene of Elvira [Sara] in bed ('1907'); begins reading the four volume *Miscellaneous Works of Oliver Goldsmith* (1837), making notes for an article (Mar 1934).

13 To Monk's House for 10 days. Exchanges visits with the Keyneses and the Bells; works almost daily on Goldsmith; plans to write on Turgenev (14 Dec).

20 'Gissing's "By the Ionian Sea"', letters to the editor, 20 Apr and 4 May (see letter from A. C. Gissing in 8 Apr issue), in *TLS*.

25 Correcting proofs of *F*, doubting its worth; in *Y* wants to give 'the whole of the present society – nothing less: facts, as well as the vision. . . . The Waves going on simultaneously with Night & Day' (*D*).

27 Meets G. B. Shaw, age 76, just back from a world tour.

28 Meets Bruno Walter, director of the Städtische Oper in Berlin, embittered because he has been forced by the rise of Hitler to leave Germany.

HOGARTH PRESS: C. L. R. James, *The Case for West-Indian Self Government*.

May

5 (Fri) LW and VW depart in their new car for Italy, stopping to visit the Bussys at their villa overlooking Monte Carlo (19 May). VW decides that Shelley, who lived between San Terenzo and Lerici, chose better than M. Beerbohm, who lives in Rapallo. In Siena (14 May) reads H. James's *The Sacred Fount* (1901), finding it rarefied, but lean and muscular none the less, particularly in comparison with *The Creevey Papers* (1928), the letters and diaries of Whig politican Thomas Creevey (1768–1838). Visits D. H. Lawrence's grave at Vence (21 May) but is anxious to get home and resume work on *Y*. Learns that *F* is to be the Book Society's choice for October and of the death of Lady Cynthia Mosley (16 May). Returns to Monk's House 27 May. (See *L* and *D*, 9–23 May.)

29 Forces herself to resume work on the Goldsmith article.

31 Feels she can now work straight ahead at *Y* for four months;

is concerned with how to give intellectual argument the form of art (*D*).

June

6 (Tues) Suggests revisions for E. Smyth's *Female Pipings in Eden* (1933); advises in particular against autobiography (to E. Smyth).

9 Attends Simon Bussy's exhibition 'Pastels of Morocco and Zoo Studies' at the Leicester Galleries.

12 In 'full flood', with *Y*. Dines with A. and K. Stephen and painter E. X. Kapp (see review, 9 Jan 1920); H. Mirrlees comes in afterward.

15 Lunches at G. B. Shaw's with Laurence Binyon, Keeper of Prints and Drawings in the British Museum, about to succeed TSE as Charles Eliot Norton Professor of Poetry at Harvard, and his wife.

16 Finishes the 'Elvira scene' (*Y*, '1910').

20 Attends the Jubilee Congress of the Women's Co-operative Guild, 'all wind blown, gaseous, with elementary emotions' (*D*). Begins reading manuscript of Edgar Meredith's *The Wainwrights: A Novel, not a Saga* (pub. 1935, Grayson and Grayson).

24 'London Squares', letter to the editor suggesting that London squares, reserved for local residents, might be opened for part of the summer to those unable to leave town, in *NS&N* (see *D*, 16 June).

26 Reading *Henry the Fourth, Part I*, and a poem by Leopardi; about to begin novelist Archibald Marshall's recently published *Out and About: Random Reminiscences*.

27 Attends gala ballet performance at Covent Garden, put on by the Camargo Society in honour of delegates to the World Economic Conference.

July

5 (Wed) Works on 'Oliver Goldsmith' – 'two days of misery . . . forced respite from Pargiters'; attends exhibition of pictures by RF (*D*).

6 Attends annual general meeting of the London Library.

7 R. West and husband Henry Andrews to dinner; J. Hutchinson and W. Plomer come in afterward; VW and R. West discuss suffragette leader Emmeline Pankhurst, whom West is writing

on for *The Post-Victorians* (1933); Hutchinson tells them that TSE has returned to England but not to his wife.

8 Thanks D. Brett for sending *Lawrence and Brett: A Friendship* (1933), but does not read it; plans to read through his works when there is less 'coloured dust about his horizon' (to D. Brett).

13 Attends *Les Présages*, a new ballet choreographed by Massine, set to Tchaikovsky's Fifth Symphony.

20 Working well on *Y* after a sparse week; thinks it tends more to drama, and that the next lap should be more objective and realistic, 'in the manner of Jane Austen' (*D*). Dines with M. and J. Hutchinson; tells M. she will put her in *Y*; meets André Masson, who designed the set for *Les Présages*.

25 Attends Burne-Jones centenary exhibition at the Tate Gallery.

26 Trying to finish 'Oliver Goldsmith'; E. Bowen to tea.

27 To Rodmell for the summer.

Flush, pt 1, in *Atlantic Monthly*.

August

Early this month, visits Charleston, the Keyneses, LW's mother at Worthing; gives tea to social worker Elizabeth Read.

5 (Sat) Reads E. Smyth's biography of E. Pankhurst for *Female Pipings in Eden*.

8 John and Elizabeth Nef, she 'a positive dangerous woman lunatic from Chicago', visit to discuss her memoirs ('writes rather well . . . but all at sea'); afterward VW is exhausted and bedridden for two days. Reads Geoffrey Faber's *Oxford Apostles: A Character Study of the Oxford Movement* on John Henry Newman's nervous breakdowns. (To VSW, 9 Aug; *D*, 8 and 12 Aug.)

12 Takes J. and A. Bell to see Sir Alan Cobham's air show; afterward again bedridden with headache.

14 E. Smyth visits; outraged at not being allowed to see VW.

15 Reads VSW's *The Edwardians* (1930), E. Arnot-Robinson's *Ordinary Familes* (1933) and Antonia White's *Frost in May* (1933).

16 Reads Turgenev, which prompts reflections on form (*D*); thanks J. Nef for sending his book *The Rise of the British Coal Industry* (1932).

18 Begins rearranging the first part of *Y*.

23 J. Bell, F. Marshall and CB visit; CB leaves Arsène Houssaye's *Confessions* (1885, 1891).

24 Finishes death of Mrs Pargiter in *Y*; cannot switch moods and 'shoot ahead' to Oxford ('1880'). Continues reading Turgenev.

30 Leopold Campbell-Douglas (clergyman), William Robson (joint editor with LW of the *Political Quarterly*), Neil Lyons (journalist, novelist, and dramatist) and VSW visit at different times throughout the day.

Flush, pt 2, 'Mr Browning in Wimpole Street', in *Atlantic Monthly*.

September

2 (Sat) Plans to compress 'Eleanor's day' ('1891'); thinks of 'Here & Now' as title for *Y*, a title that will not compete with H. Walpole's *Herries Chronicle* (the fourth volume of which, *Vanessa*, he has just sent VW) or J. Galsworthy's *Forsyte Saga* (1922). Reading 'with extreme greed' Vera Brittain's *Testament of Youth* (1933), neglecting Turgenev and I. Compton Burnett.

9 TSE, looking much younger ('a glorified boy scout in shorts & yellow shirt'), spends the night; talks about his poetry, his marriage, Keats's letters, the 'infamy' of teaching English literature, and other topics (*D*).

10 Reads *Twelfth Night* in preparation for L. Lopokova's performance.

19 F. L. Lucas and wife, sculptor Prudence Wilkinson, visit.

20 To London to see L. Lopokova as Olivia in Tyrone Guthrie's production of *Twelfth Night* at the Old Vic.

23 Reads M. Oxford's *More Memories* (1933), M. Hamilton's *Sidney and Beatrice Webb* (1933) and Turgenev's *Smoke* (1867); roughs out review of *Twelfth Night*; attends meetings of the Memoir Club at Tilton, where she and EMF read papers. Having led a very social life, for the last two weeks has done no work on *Y* (*D*).

26 Conceives of a biographical fantasy on the theme of George Crabbe (cf. 'Crabbe', *CDB*); writes on Turgenev (14 Dec).

30 '*Twelfth Night* at the Old Vic', dramatic review, in *NS&N*.

Flush: An Autobiography, pt 3, 'Wimpole Street and Whitechapel', in *Atlantic Monthly*.

October

3 (Thurs) Attends annual conference of the Labour Party at Hastings, 'a buzzing bursting humming perfectly self dependent other world' (*D*); meets William Gillies, secretary of the International Department of the Labour Party, Philip Noel-

Baker, assistant to the president of the Disarmament Conference at Geneva, Charles Buxton, chairman of the Advisory Committees on International and Imperial Affairs of (which LW is secretary), Frederick Pethick-Lawrence, campaigner for women's suffrage and disarmament, and others.

4 In bed with headache, reads Marguerite Steen's *Hugh Walpole: A Study* (1933).

5 *F* published in Britain by Hogarth and in America by Harcourt Brace; VW pleased *TLS* detects no signs of whimsicality. Visits VSW at Sissinghurst; meets Gwendolen St Aubyn, H. Nicolson's sister and VSW's intimate friend.

6 Somewhat cast down by R. West's criticism in the *Daily Telegraph* of *F* as a 'family joke' that had better not have left the house; works on Turgenev.

7 Cheered by D. Garnett's praise in *NS&N* of the humour and perfect proportions of *F*, and by EMF's letter praising her memoir; hopes to bring off *Y* in that style.

9 Notes D. MacCarthy praises *F* in the *Sunday Times*, while the acerbic Geoffrey Grigson condemns it as 'tiresome' in the *Morning Post*; continues 'writhing with Turgenev' (*D*).

13 Attends performance of Chekhov's *The Cherry Orchard*; doubts whether it can be acted in English: 'Even the dog is English' (to Q. Bell).

16 Notes she stopped inventing *Y* about 20 August and then rewrote; delivers Turgenev article to the typist.

17–18 LW ill with influenza; VW unable to work.

19 Resolves to stop the Hogarth Press.

20 Reads G. Brenan's new novel, *Jack Robinson* – 'unmitigated trash' (*D*).

28 'The Protection of Privacy', letter to the editor, in *NS&N*.

29 Too tired to go on with Bobby and Elvira's meeting at St Paul's in *Y* (early '1914'), checked by a review in the *Granta* (25 Oct) that says the progress to popular success represented by *W*, *O* and *F* represents the death of a potentially great writer. Reads in the New Testament; attends family dinner for LW's mother's eighty-third birthday.

31 Reads traveller and writer G. Borrow (1803–81).

Flush, pt 4, 'A Cocker Recaptures his Youth', in *Atlantic Monthly*.

Hogarth Press: *The Worker's Point of View: A Symposium*, preface by C. T. Cramp; Imre Madách, *The Tragedy of Man*; Margaret Miller and Douglas Campbell, *Financial Democracy*; Benito Mussolini, *The*

Political and Social Doctrine of Fascism, tr. Jane Soames; Lord Olivier, *The Myth of Governor Eyre*; K. M. Panikkar, *Caste and Democracy*; VW, *Flush*.

November

3 (Fri) Takes VB and QB to Croydon aerodrome for a flight to Geneva, where Q. Bell will be treated for tuberculosis, then travels to Brighton to see F. Birrell (recuperating from an operation for a brain tumour) and his father A. Birrell (who dies 20 Nov).

9 J. Bell, now writing on 'The Good' and running a 'No More War Exhibition' at Cambridge, comes to tea with poet Kathleen Raine.

11 Spends the night with W. and R. Phillipps, in Ipsden, Oxfordshire; meets economist Roy Harrod.

13 VSW and D. Leon to dinner; VW too 'dissipated' to write next morning (VW comes to recognise this as a persistent pattern: see 19 Dec 1935).

14 D. Garnett visits to discuss 'the hoax': he has printed a paragraph in *NS&N* entitled 'A Dinner', ostensibly by a fourteen-year-old schoolgirl, which is in fact a passage from *Room*. VW reads TSE's *The Use of Poetry and the Use of Criticism* (1933), and T. and D. C. Sturge Moore's *Works and Days: Extracts from the Journal of Michael Field* (1933), instead of going to hear E. Smyth's *March of the Women* at a meeting on the right of married women to earn.

15 Thanks D. Cecil for his essay on Scott in *The Raven Miscellany* (1933).

23 Dines with M. and J. Hutchinson to meet Michael Arlen, author of the best-selling *The Green Hat* (1924); talks with Princess Bibesco, V. and B. Rothschild and others; too tired to work next morning.

24 Dips into VSW's *Collected Poems* (1933).

25 Wants a pause before going on to the scene of Kitty's party (*Y* '1914'). Visits the retrospective of pictures by Walter Sickert with an eye to writing about them (*Walter Sickert: A Conversation*, Oct 1934, and, with some variations, 'A Conversation about Art', Sep 1934).

28 TSE to tea; talks of his pageant *The Rock*. RF and H. Anrep to dinner; they discuss the use of criticism, and RF's inaugural lecture as Slade Professor at Cambridge, 'Art History as an

Academic Subject'. VW finds it difficult to work next morning on Sickert.

30 Travels to Oxford to spend the night with her cousin, historian H. A. L. Fisher, and his wife Lettice; meets student Marie Lynd (daughter of R. and S. Lynd) and philosopher Isaiah Berlin.

HOGARTH PRESS: S. Freud, *New Introductory Lectures on Psychoanalysis*, ed. E. Jones, tr. W. J. H. Sprott; VSW, *Collected Poems: Volume One* (a second volume is never published).

December

6 (Wed) S. Benson dies; VW feels as she did after K. Mansfield's death that the response to her own writing is thereby diminished, 'as if the thinking stuff were a web that were fertilised only by other peoples (her that is) thinking it too' (*D*, 7 Dec).

14 'The Novels of Turgenev' in *TLS*.

15 Dines with CB to meet W. Sickert and his wife, artist Thérèse Lessore; they talk about Goldoni and Flaubert. At home VW talks with D. Leon, whose second novel, *Wilderness*, which she read in manuscript, did not impress her (pub. Heinemann, 1935).

17 Finishes 'part 4' of *Y* ('1914'); rereads some of her old diaries to freshen her memory of the war for the next section.

19 S. Spender, who has the makings of a 'long winded bore', and M. Lynd to dinner; W. Plomer and K. Raine come in afterward.

21 To Rodmell for Christmas; worried about transitions in Goldstein article.

25 The Keyneses to lunch; VSW and her two sons to tea.

1934

EVENTS AND LETTERS. O. Mosley addresses Fascist meetings in Britain; Hitler and Mussolini meet in Venice; first Soviet Writers' Congress held in Moscow under M. Gorky; L. Pirandello awarded Nobel Prize. F. Scott Fitzgerald publishes *Tender is the Night*; Jean Cocteau, *La Machine infernale*; E. Pound, *ABC of Reading*.

January

Early this month, at Monk's House, 'divinely happy & pressed with ideas' for *Y* (*D*); exchanges visits with writer Enid Bagnold (Lady Jones).

15 (Mon) VSW to dinner; they discuss John Sparrow's *Sense and Poetry: Essays on the Place of Meaning in Contemporary Verse* (1934).

16 'Floating rather rapturously in the Raid scene' in *Y* (mid '1917').

17 L. Irvine asks VW to write for her new magazine, the *Fortnightly*; VW is relucant, and in the event Irvine writes the ten issues herself.

22 R. Macaulay and Ivy Davison, who later comes 'to write letters' for VW, to tea (*D*, 14 Feb).

23 Dines with M. and J. Hutchinson; meets gossip columnist Viscount Castlerosse.

24 Writing about 'sodomy' in *Y* ('1917'; to Q. Bell). Dines at Lady Colefax's with connoisseur Lord Ivor Spencer Churchill, and others, including N. Coward, who sings 'like a tipsy crow' from his new romantic comedy, *Conversation Piece* (to Q. Bell, 15 Feb).

25 VW fifty-second birthday.

29 Reads Arthur Young's *Travels in France during the Years 1787, 1788, and 1789.*

30 Continues work on 'the Raid Scene', which 'draws out'; the strain brings on a headache which forces her to spend the next ten days lying down; S. Tomlin and TSE to dinner.

Late this month, VB begins work on an oil portrait of VW (see American edition of *QB*, and Spater and Parsons).

February

Early this month, while recuperating, dips into Thackeray, A. Young's *Travels*, Lord Berners' *First Childhood* (1934), E. de Selincourt's *Dorothy Wordsworth* (1933) and J. E. Neale's *Queen Elizabeth* (1934).

8 (Thurs) Has finished 130,000 words of *Y* in ten months.

14 Revises article on Sickert, refuses offer by the National Portrait Gallery to draw her.

(Mid-month) Politics dominates conversation in the wake of the coup d'état by Austrian Nazis: 'Everybody here says this is the beginning of the end. We are to have Mosley within five years' (to Q. Bell, 15 Feb).

15 Finishes Sickert article in spite of a 'great row' with N. Boxall, the Woolfs' cook.

18 Begins *Y* again, revising the talk during the raid, notes that the civil war in Vienna 'somehow comes closer than usual to our safe London life' (*D*). J. Lehmann, just back from Vienna, has submitted his book *The Noise of History* (Hogarth, Sep).

HOGARTH PRESS: Parmena Githendu Mockerie, *An African Speaks for his People*, foreword by Julian Huxley; L. B. Pekin (pseud. of Reginald Snell), *Progressive Schools*; R. M. Rilke, *Poems*, tr. J. B. Leishman; James Sutherland, *The Medium of Poetry*; Laurens van der Post, *In a Province*; Y. Z. (pseud. of Freda Utley), *From Moscow to Samarkand*.

March

1 (Thurs) 'Oliver Goldsmith', review of Goldsmith's *The Citizen of the World and The Bee*, intro. Richard Church, in *TLS*.

3 Attends performance of E. Smyth's Mass in D and other works at the Albert Hall, in honour of Smyth's seventy-fifth birthday.

4 Plans to begin work on *Y*, Kitty and Edward in Richmond (after '1918', deleted during revision of proofs; see Radin). Withdraws from BBC Advisory Committee on Spoken English; attends performance of Ibsen's *A Doll's House* (with L. Lopokova as Nora).

7 Attends private view of an exhibition of recent paintings by VB and Elwin Hawthorne (for which she has written a foreword to the catalogue).

14 Suffering from influenza, cannot work on 'the Kitty–Eleanor scene'.

18 To Cambridge to see G. Rylands' production of *Antony and Cleopatra*; lunches with Rylands, R. Lehmann and W. Philipps.

19 The situation with N. Boxall weighing on her, cannot settle to work on *Y*.

27 Gives notice to N. Boxall for the last time, who leaves on 28 March, after 18 tempestuous years of service, although squabbles continue into April.

28 To Rodmell until 19 April.

HOGARTH PRESS: *Charles Lamb: His Life Recorded by his Contemporaries*, ed. E. Blunden.

April

7 (Sat) EMF visits to attend Memoir Club meeting at Tilton next day.

16 Attends dinner at the Hutchinsons' and performance of opera

based on *Macbeth* at Sadler's Wells; talks with Lady Macnaghten and Sir Frederick Pollock, acquaintances from VW's youth. Too jaded next morning to work on Sickert or *Y*.

18 JMK and TSE dine to discuss the latter's new book, *After Strange Gods: A Primer of Modern Heresy* (1934); J. Bell and E. Bowen come in afterward and the discussion turns to communism and Ricardo's economic theories.

26 The Woolfs depart for tour of Ireland by car. VW is struck by the poverty and general dreariness, but fascinated by the Irish genius for conversation and moved to wonder, 'Why aren't these people the greatest novelists in the world?' (*D*, 3 May). Visits E. Bowen, where she encounters Cyril Connolly, and his first wife Jean Bakewell, both of whom she dislikes. Reads Proust's *Sodome et Gormorrhe* (1922) *en route*. Returns to Tavistock Square 9 May. (See *D* and *L*, 30 Apr–9 May.)

May

11 (Fri) Falls ill; spends the week in bed.

20 Thanks E. Bowen for sending her novel *The Last September* (1929).

21 Reads E. Wharton's memoirs, *A Backward Glance* (1934), and Proust, his work 'so magnificent that I cant write myself within its arc'. Feels *Y* will be bad: 'At lunch I told L: who said anyhow one could burn it' (to E. Smyth). To Charleston, to an animated discussion of Stanley Spencer's paintings.

22 Begins 'part 7' of *Y*, 'Elvira [Sara] & George, or John, talking in her room' ('Present Day'); notes the 'narrative part' of composition is finished, now wants to 'enrich & stabilise' (*D*).

25 Falls ill again; bedridden until 3 June.

27 Reads A. Huxley's *Beyond the Mexique Bay* (1934).

'Why?' in *Lysistrata*, Oxford.

HOGARTH PRESS: W. G. Ballinger, *Race and Economics in South Africa*; W. F. Watson, *The Worker and Wage Incentives*.

June

8 (Fri) Attends performance of *Figaro* at Glyndebourne Festival in Sussex.

(Mid-month) Begins twice-weekly French lessons with J. Bussy.

15 A. Huxley to tea, 'a most admirable, cool, antiseptic distempered, but humane & gentle man' (*D*), who has just spent the

weekend at Welwyn with the Society for Sexual Information and Progress.

18 'In flood' with *Y*, making up the scene with Renny and Maggie ('1917').

30 Hitler crushes the Brown Shirts, over 1200 people are killed, 'And for the first time I read articles with rage, to find him called a real leader' (*D*, 2 July).

July

11 (Wed) O. Sitwell to tea; tells VW the story of the 'Lady with the Pink Feather' (included in *Penny Foolish: A Book of Tirades and Panegyrics*, 1935).

20 Listens to Monteverdi's *Ballet of the Ungracious Ladies* on the BBC, which gives her 'a little fresh water' in her well for *Y*.

21 Finishes the first chapter of *The Truth Tellers* ('Phases of Fiction'); has been reading *Pericles, Titus Andronicus* and *Coriolanus*.

23 Attends dinner at the Hutchinsons' with D. MacCarthy, TSE and others; talk ranges from TSE's *The Rock*, to Crashaw, to Hitler, and TSE reads poems by George Barker, 'chanting, intoning': 'He thinks there is some melody some rhythm some emotion lacking in the Audens, & Spenders' (*D*; see Barker's *Thirty Preliminary Poems* and the prose *Alanna Autumnal*, Faber and Faber, 1933).

24 Inserts a paragraph on Beerbohm and others into her article on Sickert, 'A Conversation about Art', for the *Yale Review*.

26 To Rodmell for the summer.

28 Having visited LW's mother in Worthing the day before, feels free to begin the last chapter of *Y*; is conscious that she is breaking the mould of *W*.

31 To Charleston, concerned that F. Birrell is dying of cancer.

Late this month, reads the life of eighteenth-century divine Henry Venn (VW's great-great-grandfather) by his son John Venn, reissued with selected letters by J. Venn (1837), and Prosper Mérimée's *Carmen* (1847), which she thinks far better than M. Baring's new novel, *The Lonely Lady of Dulwich* (to E. Smyth, 8 Aug).

Hogarth Press: S. K. Ratcliffe, *The Roots of Violence*.

August

2 (Thurs) Worried that *Y* is 'too shrill & voluble' and too long. E. Bagnold visits to discuss her forthcoming book about 'the

effect of winning the Grand National on a child' (*National Velvet*, 1935). (*D*.)

7 Tea with the Keyneses; JMK talks of his trip to New York ('An impossible climate. . . . Nobody could produce a great work in America') and how Germany refuses to pay its bill for cotton but is buying copper, no doubt for armaments. VW, considering how to end *Y*, wants 'a Chorus, a general statement, a song for 4 voices'. (*D*.)

11–12 S. Sydney-Turner visits for the weekend; they discuss Shakespeare, Artistole and writing in general.

17 Sees the end of *Y*: 'Its to be all in speeches – no play . . . & it ends with a supper party in the downstairs room' (*D*).

21 Reads de Maupassant's *Une Vie* (1883), finds it 'rather marking time & watery' in comparison with *Y* (*D*).

24 Reads Hector Bolitho's *Victoria the Widow and her Son* (1934).

26–7 W. Plomer and L. Irving visit for the weekend, read Susan Miles's *Blind Men Crossing a Bridge* (1934), which has been pronounced a work of genius by the *TLS* and 'totally absurd' by VW; they talk of Plomer's forthcoming novel, *The Invaders* (1934), which was not offered to Hogarth.

30 Trying to finish Eleanor's speech (at Delia's party in 'Present Day', deleted in final version of *Y*); still reading Dante, as well as *Lost London: The Memoirs of an East End Detective* by ex-Detective Sergeant B. Leeson (1934), H. James's Preface to *Portrait of a Lady*, A. Gide's *Pages de Journal, 1929–32*, and Saint Simon.

HOGARTH PRESS: Peter and Irma Petroff, *The Secret of Hitler's Victory*.

September

1 (Sat) Gives tea party for the Keyneses, who bring economist Richard Kahn, K. and O. Martin, CB and Q. Bell; they discuss LW's gloomy predictions for civilisation in his review of G. B. Shaw's *Prefaces* (*NS&N*, 8 Sep).

2 Excited by the scene in *Y* 'where Peggy listens to them talking & bursts out' (*D*; latter half of 'Present Day').

9 RF dies; VW feels 'the poverty of life now . . . a thin blackish veil over everything', resolves to 'live more . . . see people . . . create' (*D*, 12 Sep).

13 Attends RF's funeral.

18 John L. Graham visits to talk about his forthcoming book, *Good Merchant* (Hogarth, Sep).

23 Reads VSW's *The Dark Island*; feels her characters are less successfully drawn than the landscape (to VSW).
27 Writes to G. Rylands, elaborating her notion that the great Victorian novelists had a sense of audience and created their characters through dialogue, whereas novelists since G. Eliot have retreated from the spoken word.
28 To Tunbridge Wells, travelling Hogarth books; buys a first edition of G. Eliot's *The Mill on the Floss* (1860) and visits VSW at Sissinghurst.
30 Finishes *Y*, still nameless, and needing much rewriting, but at least 'the design is there' (*D*).

'A Conversation about Art' in the *Yale Review*.

HOGARTH PRESS: J. Graham, *Good Merchant*; J. Lehmann, *The Noise of History*.

October

4 (Thurs) Notes books read or being read: Shakespeare's *Troilus and Cressida, Pericles, The Taming of the Shrew* and *Cymbeline*; in recent prose, J. Cowper Powys's *Autobiography*, H. G. Wells's *Experiment in Autobiography*, Her Highness the Ranee of Sarawak (Sylvia Leonora)'s *Good Morning and Good Night*, B. Dobrée's *Modern Prose Style*, *Alice James: Her Brothers – her Journal*, ed. Anna Robeson Burr (all 1934); and scraps of de Maupassant, de Vigny, St Simon, and Gide.
5 Wants to condense the last chapters of *Y*, to achieve 'a summing up: a solution' (*D*).
7 Returns to Tavistock Square for the winter.
10 Improvises a new method for 'Phases of Fiction' – it is to be phases of the reader's mind, in different situations, and thus avoid formality.
11 Notes appearance of W. Lewis's *Men without Art*; shrinks from reading it.
13 Turns to J. Thomson's *The Seasons* (1726–30) in a 1773 edition of his works owned by J. Austen (see *D*, 31 Oct), after E. Sackville-West's 'ridiculous rhodomontade' *The Sun in Capricorn* (1934).
14 Reads the chapter on herself in *Men without Art*, which mocks her for 'peeping' timorously at life; determines not to rearrange *Y* to meet Lewis's criticisms, but is unable to write for two days (see *M&M* for Lewis, S. Spender's 19 Oct review defending VW, and Lewis's rebuttal, 2 Nov).

15 Begins reading a life of J. Boswell, making notes for biography.
17 EMF to tea to discuss the meeting of the National Council for Civil Liberties next day to protest at the Sedition Act.
20–1 With LW and K. Martin, travels to Maidstone to attend conference of the New Fabian Research Bureau.
24 Works on 'Royalty' (pub. 1 Dec). H. Read, now editor of *Burlington Magazine*, R. Lehmann and S. Spender come for the evening; Spender sends VW a copy of his poem *Vienna* later in the week.
25 At O. Morrell's meets, among others, W. B. Yeats, who talks of the occult, Stendhal, Balzac, Tolstoy, Proust (his 'slow motion novel'), and of getting the Irish back to the great eighteenth-century men of letters; he advises VW to read Swift's *Drapier's Letters* (1724) and mentions he has been writing about VW's *W* in the introduction to his play *Fighting the Waves* (*D*).
29 Reads Sophocles' *Antigone*; finds the Greek language still has a powerful 'spell . . . an emotion different from any other' (*D*).
30 Dines with H. Anrep, who tentatively asks VW to write a biography of RF.
31 Dines at CB's with A. Huxley, Kenneth Clark, director of the National Gallery, and his wife Jane; talk ranges from the dinner service the Clarks had commissioned from VB and DG, to Coward, Yeats and Auden, whom Huxley dismisses as nothing but a demagogue.

HOGARTH PRESS: Constance Butler, *Illyria, Lady*; M. Gorky, *Reminiscences of Tolstoy, Chekhov and Andreev*, tr. K. Mansfield, S. S. Koteliansky and LW; C. H. B. Kitchen, *Crime at Christmas*; Raymond Postgate, *How to Make a Revolution*; Geza Roheim, *The Riddle of the Sphinx or Human Origins*, tr. R. Money-Kirle, preface by E. Jones; A. L. Rowse, *The Question of the House of Lords*; VSW, *The Dark Island*; VW, *Walter Sickert: A Conversation*.

November

2 (Fri) Stung by W. Lewis's reply to Spender, and by review of *Walter Sickert: A Conversation*, in *Spectator*.
8 H. Anrep visits, confirms her request to have VW write a life of RF.
11 Attends performance of TSE's *Sweeney Agonistes*; likes the

performance better than the reading but doubts 'that Tom has enough of a body & brain to bring off a whole play' (*D*).

15 Begins rewriting *Y*; in the coming days oscillates from euphoria to despair, completing eight or nine pages a day and intermittently reading Dante after writing (*D*, 21 Nov and 2 Dec).

25 Attends private view of photographs by Man Ray, who invites her to be photographed; meets Victoria Ocampo, wealthy Argentinian publisher, and throughout December is increasingly charmed by her.

December

1 (Sat) Reads C. E. M. Joad's article. 'The End of an Epoch' in *NS&N* on the decline of Bloomsbury as a cultural influence. 'Royalty', review of *The Story of my Life* by Marie, Queen of Romania, in *Time and Tide*.

2 Continues to revise *Y*, working on 'the scene at the Lodge'; plans to rewrite *Freshwater* for Christmas (see 18 Jan 1935). Notes D. Cecil's new study *Early Victorian Novelists* is a good book for readers but not for writers. Visited by Louis Gillet, editor of the *Revue des deux mondes*, who later writes an introduction to C. Mauron's 1935 French translation of *F*.

17 Visits F. Birrell, who knows he is dying.

21 To Rodmell for three weeks.

22 Reads V. Ocampo's essay on A. Huxley; VW likes his mind but not his imagination: 'When he says "I Aldous . . ." I'm with him: what I don't like is "I Rampion [of *Point Counter Point*]"' (to V. Ocampo).

30 Rewrites the scene of Maggie and Sarah in the bedroom (*Y*, '1907'); plans to work next on Martin's visit to Eleanor ('1908'), and then on the day that ends with the King's death ('1910'). Visits Charleston to rehearse *Freshwater*.

1935

Events and Letters. Nuremberg Laws against Jews passed in Germany; London publisher Victor Gollancz founds Left Book Club. E. Bagnold publishes *National Velvet*; S. and B. Webb, *Soviet Communism: A New Civilisation?*; W. H. Auden and C. Isherwood, *The Dog beneath the Skin*; TSE, *Murder in the Cathedral*; Clifford Odets,

Waiting for Lefty; T. Wolfe, *Of Time and the River*; John Steinbeck, *Tortilla Flat*.

January

Early this month, busy with rehearsals of *Freshwater*.

1 (Tues) Reads Ernest Renan's *St Paul* (1868) and *The Apostles* (1866); adds letter from Princess Bibesco, about why the woman question was being ignored in a proposed anti-Fascist exhibition, to the volume of material relating to *3G*.

2 F. Birrell dies, age 44 (*D*, 6 Jan; to E. Smyth, 8 Jan). VW lunches with the Keyneses; JMK talks about the new book he is writing, which, he claims, will revolutionise economics: *The General Theory of Employment, Interest and Money* (1936).

11 Plans to condense *Y* and to finish retyping by May; finds it difficult to read Dante after working on fiction.

13 Returns to London from Monk's House.

18 *Freshwater*, first written July 1923, performed in VB's studio, before an audience of 80 friends; VW talks with H. Anrep, D. Garnett, C. McLaren, D. Cecil, Cory Bell, E. Bowen, B. Mayor, ENF, O. and M. Strachey, R. Lehmann (whose play *No More Music* has been postponed because of the success of J. Gielgud's *Hamlet*) and others.

19 Has an idea for a '"play" Summers night. Someone on a seat. And voices speaking from the flowers' (*D*; cf. *BA*).

23 Taking a fortnight off *Y*, reading C. M. Yonge's *The Heir of Redclyffe* (1853), A. Huxley's *Point Counter Point* (1928) – 'all raw, uncooked, protesting . . . makes people into ideas' (*D*) – and Spenser's *Faerie Queen* (1590, 1596); plans to write about the last ('*The Faery Queen*', *M*).

25 VW's fifty-third birthday.

30 Advices S. Buchan to expand *Funeral March of a Marionette* (Hogarth, Oct).

February

2 (Fri) Concerned because she has had no reply to her letter to R. West praising her new book, *The Harsh Voice* (West finally replies 15 Mar).

4 TSE to tea; they discuss his criticism of A. A. Milne's recent anti-war tract, *Peace with Honour*.

5 Finishes 'the difficult song chapter' in *Y*.

6 In her diary copies out a passage on the ephemerality of

earthly fame from Dante's *Purgatorio*, canto XI (from *La Divina Commedia*, ed. Hermann Oelsner, tr. Thomas Okey, 1933; later in the month in her reading notes records the passage from canto XV that occurs at the end of '1911' in *Y*).

7 Ralph Wright comes to lunch to discuss the anti-Fascist exhibition, for which VW has been helping to raise money.

19 Quarrels with CB, who believes the committee for the anti-Fascist exhibition is dominated by communists. Dines with H. Read and his wife Ludo, in the company of sculptor Henry Moore and his wife Irena; cannot write next morning.

20 Struggling with the 'chop house scene' (*Y*, '1914'), wants to avoid propaganda: 'I have a horror of the Aldous [Huxley] novel' (see 23 Jan). E. Bowen and H. Walpole to dinner; Walpole talks of Hollywood, where he had gone the previous June to write a scenario of *David Copperfield* and to act the Vicar of Blunderstone for Metro Goldwyn Mayer.

26 Working over 'the scene by the Round Pond' before moving on to 'the dinner party & Kitty in the country' (*Y*, '1914'). Plagued by a sudden desire to write an anti-Fascist pamphlet.

27 Wants to stop reading *The Faerie Queen* and read Cicero's letters and Chateaubriand's *Mémoires d'outre tombe* (1849–50).

28 Attends party with Ann Stephen, Richard Llewelyn Davies (nephew of Margaret Llewelyn Davies), David Gourlay and his wife Janet Vaughan (daughter of Madge Vaughan), a doctor, whose account of how she lost the Beit Memorial Fellowship – because it was decided that women could not do research work – interests VW for *3G*.

HOGARTH PRESS: S. H. Baily, *Mr Roosevelt's Experiments*; H. J. Laski, *Law and Justice in Soviet Russia*; Thomas Sharp, *A Derelict Area: A Study of the South-west Durham Coalfield*, intro. Hugh Dalton.

March

3 (Sun) With E. Smyth attends a performance conducted by Sir Thomas Beecham at the Queen's Hall which includes a portion of Smyth's opera, *The Wreckers*.

5 Attends party in honour of painter E. Walker with Henry Tonks (former professor at the Slade School, who had taught VB briefly in 1904), Sir C. J. Holmes (former director of the National Gallery), C. Morgan (novelist and drama critic for *The Times*) and others.

10 To Sissinghurst in a snowstorm; realises her friendship with

VSW is over, 'Not with a quarrel, not with a bang, but as ripe fruit falls' (*D*).

11 Works on the episode of Eleanor in Oxford Street (deleted in *Y*); has read herself 'to a standstill' in *The Faerie Queen*; reads Chateaubriand and an Italian novel.

16 Glances at O. Sitwell and Margaret Barton's *Brighton* (1935); depressed by the detractions of Prince Mirsky in *The Intelligentsia of Great Britain*, tr. 1935, and F. Swinnerton in *The Georgian Literary Scene*, 1935 (see *M&M*). TSE and S. Spencer to tea; TSE talks of a play he is working on (*Murder in the Cathedral*) and of how he wrote the last verses of *The Waste Land* in a trance; Spender talks of the negative reviews of *Vienna*.

14 Reads E. Smyth's article on Lady Ponsonby (for *As Time Went On*, 1936).

20 Meets André Malraux at a meeting at the home of Amabel and Clough Williams-Ellis to engage support for an International Congress of Writers in Defence of Culture in Paris which Malraux is organising; VW hides her anchovy sandwich in her bag and flees, vowing 'This is my last dabble in politics' (to Q. Bell, 3 Apr).

24 To VB's; with CB and others discusses M. Eastman's *Artists in Uniform* (1934) and Jacob Epstein's exhibition of sculpture at the Leicester Galleries.

25 Rewrites the 'raid chapter' (*Y*, '1917'), which has been troubling her for the last week, in a 'spasm of desperation' (*D*).

26 Cheered by the review of Swinnerton in *The Times*, which declares he fails to understand VW.

27 Reads Henry Greene's *Life* (1935) of Irish composer Charles Villiers Stanford (1852–1924).

28 Finishes rewriting the 'raid chapter' ('1917'); has been using her diary as a transition between revising *Y* and reading Dante.

29 C. Morgan to dinner; VB, DG and J. Graham come in afterwards; they discuss Morgan's first book, *The Gunroom* (1919), which dealt with the bullying of midshipmen, and the Dreadnought Hoax (see 10 Feb 1910).

30 Takes tea with TSE in his depressing room in the home of Father Eric Cheetham, Vicar of St Stephen's Church (of which TSE is vicar's warden, 1934–59).

HOGARTH PRESS: I. Bunin, *Grammar of Love*, tr. John Cournos; C. Day Lewis, *Collected Poems 1929–1933*, *A Time to Dance and Other*

Poems; C. Isherwood, *Mr Norris Changes Trains*; Anna Whyte, *Change your Sky*.

April

1 (Mon) Wants to compact the scene of Eleanor and Kitty in *Y* (deleted); despairs of finishing the *Purgatorio*. Ann Stephen wins a scholarship at Newnham; the Woolfs take her to dinner and to see Gary Cooper in *Lives of a Bengal Lancer*, 'but the virility & empire building bored her' (*D*).

2 Receives E. Bagnold's 'much applauded' *National Velvet*.

5–8 To Rodmell for a weekend of 'almost incessant conversation', with F. R. Hancock at the Rodmell Labour Party meeting, JMK at Tilton, H. Anrep at Monk's House, and CB and others at Charleston.

8 Meets EMF in the London Library; is outraged by his news that the library committee has decided no women should be allowed on the committee.

14 Meets W. Robson, whose tales of the legal profession excite VW to work on *3G*, but she has decided not to begin until *Y* is finished, because it is impossible to write propaganda and fiction at the same time. Reads eighteenth-century Italian dramatist Vittorio Alfieri, John Summerson's *John Nash, Architect to King George IV* (1935) and Annie Swan's *My Life* (1934); cheered by R. Ellis Roberts' defence of Bloomsbury in the *Sunday Times*.

17 Plans to read Violet Markham's *Paxton and the Bachelor Duke* (1935), L. H. Myers' trilogy, *The Root and the Flower* (1935), G. Barker's *Poems* (1935) and Marianne Moore's *Selected Poems*, intro. by TSE (1935).

18 To Rodmell for Easter.

20 Finds S. Spender's critical study *The Destructive Element* (1935) has 'swing & fluency . . . but peters out in the usual litter of an undergraduates table'. Notes there are 'incessant conversations' on the possibility of war. (*D*.)

21 Ralph Wigram, of the Foreign Office, and his wife Ava to tea to discuss the Woolfs' forthcoming trip through Germany; he describes his encounter with Hitler ('very impressive very frightening') in March, but advises them to go (*D*; *LW* IV).

22 K. Martin visits, agonising (as he had been for several months and will for many more) over whether to accept the Chair of International Relations at Aberystwyth (University of Wales).

25 Suffering from headache, reads Pirandello and resolves not to write any fiction until June.

27 J. and A. Strachey to dinner; they discuss whether one can give people a substitute for war. VW composes some of *3G*.

May

1 (Wed) The Woolfs cross to Holland, where they spend a week. VW is impressed by the spruce houses and the fact that there is no sign of crisis or war; reads Howard Sturgis's *Belchamber* (1904) – 'superficial' but 'finished' – and E. Smyth's new book, *Beecham and Pharaoh*. They enter Germany easily, the customs officials diverted by LW's marmoset, and find themselves amid anti-Jewish banners, driving through a reception organised for Goering (9 May). VW reads D. H. Lawrence's *Aaron's Rod* (1922). They cross the Brenner Pass into Italy, joining VB, QB and A. Bell in Rome 16 May. VW reads N. Mitchison's *We Have Been Warned* (1935); receives a letter from the Prime Minister's Office offering to recommend her for the Companion of Honour, an offer she declines; learns of the death of T. E. Lawrence ('of Arabia', 19 May). In Aix-en-Provence on the way home reads Alberto Moravia's *Gli Indifferenti* (1933), Stendhal's *Rome, Naples et Florence* (1817), and dips into *The Letters of Katherine Mansfield* (1928). Returns to Monk's House 31 May; receives a copy of Ruth Gruber's pamphlet *Virginia Woolf: A Study* (1935). (See *L* and *D*, 6 May–2 June.)

HOGARTH PRESS: *The Brontës: Their Lives Recorded by their Contemporaries*, ed. E. M. Delafield (pseud. of Edmée De La Pasture); C. Mauron, *Aesthetics and Psychology*, tr. RF and Katherine John; R. M. Rilke, *Requiem and Other Poems*, tr. with intro. by J. B. Leishman; LW, *Quack, Quack!*

June

2 (Sun) Returns to Tavistock Square. Resumes work on *Y*; sees that the last 200 pages will force her 'to write a play more or less: all broken up' (*D*).

6–12 To Monk's House for Whitsun. Attends performance of Mozart's *Magic Flute* at Glyndebourne, 11 June.

12 K. Panikkar and EMF visit, the latter to urge the Woolfs to join the British Delagation (which he is to head) to the Writers' Congress in Paris; they decline.

13 Finds that, as with *W*, she can only do a little on *Y* at a time; plans to finish the article on *The Faerie Queen*.

19 TSE visits; talks of *Murder in the Cathedral* and about *The Dog beneath the Skin*, the new play by Auden and Isherwood (pub. Faber and Faber).

20 M. Fry asks VW to open an exhibition of RF's paintings (see 12 July) and confirms that she wants VW to write the life of RF.

24 Geoffrey Tillotson sends a copy of his hand-printed edition of Arthur Drake's seventeenth-century poem *The Larke*.

25 Reads Harriet Martineau's *Retrospect of Western Travel* (1838); writes to S. Spender on *The Destructive Element*, suggesting that he sees writers 'too much from the 1935 angle'. Iris Origo comes to tea to discuss her book *Allegra* (Hogarth, Oct).

26 Dines with R. West and her husband, H. Andrews; J. Graham and LW come in afterward.

27 Dines with D. Cecil; talks with I. Origo, novelist Leo Myers and others.

HOGARTH PRESS: W. R. Lester, *Poverty and Plenty: The True National Dividend*.

July

2 (Tues) Spends the night near Oxford with Susan Buchan (now Lady Tweedsmuir, her husband having been created first Baron Tweedsmuir on being appointed Governor-General of Canada in May); dines with E. Bowen and her husband Alan Cameron, Isaiah Berlin – 'very clever, much too clever, like Maynard in his youth' – and others (to VB).

7 TSE sends a copy of *Murder in the Cathedral*.

8 CB and writer Odette Keun to dinner; G. Brenan and his wife Gamel Woolsey come in afterward.

9/10 Ellis Roberts invites VW to succeed H. G. Wells as president of PEN; she declines and J. B. Priestley assumes the post.

12 Travels to Bristol to deliver the opening address for the Roger Fry Memorial Exhibition at the Bristol Museum and Art Gallery.

16 Feels her speech was a failure; is unable to write; turns to one of Shakespeare's late plays. Has been reading J. M. Murry's autobiography, *Between Two Worlds* (1935); cannot bear to read his *Shakespeare* (1935) (to O. Morrell). J. Bell drops in to announce he has been offered a professorship at the National University of Wuhan in China.

17 Finishes retyping *Y*; finds it still comes to 740 pages; plans to condense and wants to form the last chapter around North's speech (end of 'Present Day').

19 E. Sitwell, E. Playfair, O. Morrell, Q. and J. Bell to dinner; Sitwell talks of sitting to W. Lewis for her portrait, and of her work in progress, *Victoria of England* (pub. 1936).

25 To Monk's House for the summer.

August

Early this month, reads Florence Marryat's *The Life and Letters of Captain Marryat* (1872), which leads to 'The Captain's Death Bed' (26 Sep).

16 (Fri) Pressed with rewriting of *Y*, trying to type 100 pages a week.

21 Notes return of Stanley Baldwin (who succeeded MacDonald as Prime Minister on 7 June) after breakdown of the three-power talks on Abyssinia in Paris.

22 Finishes reading Marryat. Dines with the Keyneses; talks of Abyssinia.

27 To Sissinghurst, where H. Nicolson, just returned from staying with the Lindberghs in America, gives *VW* Ann Lindbergh's *North to the Orient* (1935) and tells her of the American fame of *Room*, which inspires her to write *3G*.

28 Attends farewell dinner for J. Bell at Charleston.

29 Rewrites the scene of 'Eleanor's day' (*Y*, '1891'); now has three boxes of RF's papers but wants to write *3G*. Reads Emily Young's *Miss Mole* (1930), Abbé Dimnet's *My Old World* (1935), J. Dryden's *The Hind and the Panther* (1687).

30 Works on 'the Law Courts passage' (*Y*, '1891').

31 Works on Eleanor and the death of Parnell (*Y* '1891'); reads *D. H. Lawrence: A Personal Record* by E. T. (Jessie Chambers). Concerned about the situation in Abyssinia.

September

4 (Wed) Decides to call her book *The Years*. Notes the newspapers say it is the most critical day in the history of the League of Nations, which is meeting in Geneva to try to find some way of averting the use of force by Mussolini in Abyssinia.

6 Writes a new transition scene, Maggie looking at the Serpentine (*Y* '1907'); reading, in addition to other books in progress, *Dr Salter: His Diary and Reminiscences from the Year 1849 to the Year*

1932, compiled by J. O. Thompson (1933), and S. Benson's unfinished novel *Mundos* (1935). Notes the talks continue back and forth in Geneva.

7 Opens *John Baily, 1864–1931, Letters and Diaries* (1935) and is annoyed to read that it was D. MacCarthy who introduced her to Cowper's poetry.

12–13 Continues work on *Y*, reading Italian or Dryden after writing; reads W. Congreve's *Love for Love* (1695) and Sir Charles Mallett's *Anthony Hope and his Books* (1935).

18 Begins reading RF's papers.

21–3 TSE visits for the weekend; in this and recent visits VW finds she has grown very fond of him, and is not at all 'knocked off her perch' by him as she was when she was writing *JR* (see 26 Sep 1920).

26 Struggling with the scene of Sally and Maggie in the bedroom (*Y*, '1907'). 'The Captain's Death Bed' in *TLS*.

29 Reads John Ford's *The Lover's Melancholy* (1629); dips into Mrs Easdale's 'silly' memoir *Middle Age: 1855–1932* (1935), and is shocked to find their tea together (of 27 Sep 1931) described. W. Holtby, author of the first biography of VW, dies: 'Holtby I only saw 2 or 3 times – nice enthusiastic woman, but feather pated I thought' (to V. Dickinson, 21 Apr 1936; see 6 Oct 1932).

30 Attends Labour Party conference in Brighton.

HOGARTH PRESS: Arthur Calder-Marshall, *Challenge to Schools*; R. Postgate, *What to do with the BBC*; Frederick Verinder, *Land and Freedom*.

October

1 (Tues) Attends Labour meeting at which Ernest Bevin attacks party leader George Lansbury's pacifist stance on enforcing sanctions against Italy in her dispute with Abyssinia (*D*).

2 Her work on *Y* disrupted, VW refuses to attend the third day of the Labour conference; 'Happily, uneducated & voteless, I am not responsible for the state of society' (*D*).

4 Thinks E. Bowen's *The House in Paris* (1935) the best of her work. Mussolini attacks Abyssinia.

5 Returns to London; excited by the Labour conference dashes off a chapter of 'The Next War' (*3G*). During the next ten days works at *Y* in the morning, reads RF letters between tea and dinner, visits or is visited by CB, VB, DG, H. Anrep, EMF, E. Williamson and others.

7 Visited by J. Bussy and François Walter to discuss an anti-Fascist organisation.

14 Reads A. Stephen's essay in *We Did Not Fight*, ed. J. Bell (1935), a collection of autobiographical essays by conscientious objectors in the First World War.

15 R. Gruber visits to discuss a book on women and fascism.

16 Works on Crosby (*Y*, '1913').

21 Visits with R. Macaulay and with E. Bowen, too tired next day to continue with the scene of Sal and Martin in Hyde Park (*Y*, '1914').

24 Reads George Herbert's *The Temple, or Sacred Poems and Private Ejaculations* (1652); prepares to read G. L. Prestige's *Life* of Charles Gore (1853–1932), Bishop of Oxford (1935).

25 Notes W. Empson has written a new critical book, *Some Versions of Pastoral* (1935), 'but I shant read it' (to J. Bell).

26 Visits birthplace of RF, in Highgate.

27 Enjoying work on Kitty's party (*Y*, '1914'), but feels pressure of other books 'kicking their heels in the hall' (*D*).

29 Attends conference of National Peace Council, 'for a joke'; receives the three-volume *Correspondence of Thomas Gray*, ed. P. Toynbee and L. Whibley (1935). A. Whyte, author of *Change your Sky* (Hogarth, Mar), to tea (*D*).

31 Lunches at CB's with C. McLaren and D. MacCarthy, with whom VW talks about George Santayana's book (his latest was *The Last Puritan: A Memoir in the Form of a Novel*, 1935). Dines at M. Hutchinson's with the Rothschild's and the Huxleys; A. Huxley scorns the signing of anti-Fascist documents and talks about biology.

HOGARTH PRESS: Mary Birkinshaw, *The Successful Teacher*; R. Brewster, *The 6,000 Beards of Athos*, preface by E. Smyth; S. Buchan, *Funeral March of a Marionette: Charlotte of Albany*; C. Day Lewis, *Revolution in Writing*; G. P. Gooch, *Politics and Morals*; I. Origo, *Allegra*; R. C. Trevelyan, *Beelzebub and Other Poems*.

November

4 (Mon) Attends *Sunday Times* book exhibition; meets publisher Stanley Unwin. Baroness Helene von Nostitz-Wallwitz, niece of late German president Paul von Hindenburg, visits the Woolfs on behalf of a German organisation of writers.

9 At the book exhibition attends C. Day Lewis's speech, which

deals with the need for poetry to communicate with the common people.

12 Attends performance of TSE's *Murder in the Cathedral* at the Mercury Theatre, which 'acts far less well than reads: cant manage the human body: only a soliloquy' (to E. Smyth, 16 Nov).

14 Travels to Rodmell for the General Election; S. Baldwin and the Conservatives win a majority.

(Mid-month) Visits E. M. Delafield, author of *The Brontës* (Hogarth, May).

18 Dines at R. Mortimer's before party at A. Huxley's; Mortimer insists that men are unfairly treated because they have to maintain a wife – VW realises her next book, *3G*, will need courage; meets N. Mitchison and poet Robert Nicols.

21 Works on the scene of Kitty and Edward in Richmond (*Y*); visits Mrs Bridges (Monica, *née* Waterhouse), widow of poet Robert Bridges.

25 A. Whyte and S. Spender to dinner; Elizabeth Graves, niece of poet Robert Graves, H. Anrep and her son Igor come in afterward.

December

3 (Tues) C. Day Lewis writes to say his agent advises him to leave Hogarth for a larger firm, which revives the question of continuing the Press. VW attends performance of *Romeo and Juliet* (with J. Gielgud, P. Ashcroft, Laurence Olivier and Edith Evans).

10 Has promised to deliver *Y* by 15 February and is feeling pressed; continues to read through RF's letters; notes S. Colefax has cut her (see 'Am I a Snob?', *MOB*). A Davidson and Mary Fisher (daughter of H. A. L. and Lettice Fisher) to dinner; H. Anrep and A. Strachey come in afterward.

11 Spends two hours having her palm analysed by Dr Charlotte Wolff at the Huxleys'; VW is sceptical (to J. Bell, 17 Dec). In her *Studies in Hand-reading* (1936), Dr Wolff notes that VW's palm reveals 'a desire to escape reality' and an 'over-stress of the imagination' which 'forces her to adopt a defensive attitude' (see letter to E. Smyth, 16 Jan 1936).

13 Dines with the Huxleys; meets biologist Julian Huxley and his wife Juliette, learns that A. Huxley is getting on well with his novel *Eyeless in Gaza* (pub. 1936).

16 E. Graves to tea; it is decided she is to write on socialism (*A History of Socialism*, Hogarth, 1939).
18 Dines at E. Sands's with B. and E. Richmond, Sir Eric Maclagan, director of the Victoria and Albert Museum, Leigh Ashton, of the Department of Ceramics at the museum, and others.
19 With VB discusses why they cannot paint or write after a dinner party; VB asserts, '"Its because one changes one's values"' (*D*, 20 Dec).
20 To Monk's House for Christmas.
22 Intrigued by an article by H. Nicolson in *What is a Book?*, ed. D. Warren (1935), which hints at unknown facts surrounding Byron's decision to leave England late in his life.
29 Finishes first revision of *Y*.
30 Developing an 'odd posthumous friendship' with RF as she reads his papers; considers making *3G* a series of articles on diverse subjects (*D*).

HOGARTH PRESS: S. Freud, *An Autobiographical Study*, tr. J. Strachey.

1936

EVENTS AND LETTERS. Hitler occupies the Rhineland; Spanish Civil War begins; London University moves to Bloomsbury; BBC London inaugurates television service; R. Kipling, A. E. Housman, G. K. Chesteron, M. Gorki, L. Pirandello, Federico García Lorca and King George V die; E. O'Neill awarded Nobel Prize. A. Huxley publishes *Eyeless in Gaza*; EMF, *Abinger Harvest*; R. Frost, *A Further Range* (Pulitzer Prize, poetry), R. Lehmann, *The Weather in the Streets*; Margaret Mitchell, *Gone with the Wind* (Pulitzer Prize, novel); Dylan Thomas, *Twenty-five Poems*.

January

Early this month, anxious to begin work on *3G*, still holding off until she has finished *Y*, but the strain of revising the novel has her in and out of bed with headaches. Continues reading RF's papers; notes she can no longer write for newspapers because she immediately adapts the work (VW published only one article in 1935, 26 Sep).

1 (Wed) Thanks S. Spender for his story 'The Burning Cactus'.
4 Reads T. Hardy's *The Trumpet Major*; finds it flat and tedious.

5 Reads RF's criticism of Chinese art in his letters; thinks his off-hand criticism is sometimes better than the printed.
6 Begins final revision of *Y*.
8 Returns to Tavistock Square from Monk's House.
9 I. Origo to tea; talks of the situation in Italy, where women are donating their wedding rings to the war effort.
10 Reads Harry Greenwall's *The Strange Life of Willy Clarkson* (1936) – Clarkson had supplied the disguises for the Dreadnought Hoax (see 10 Feb 1910).
11 Asks E. Smyth to send Alphonse Daudet's *Lettres de mon moulin* (1868); reads novels by G. Borrow, including *Wild Wales* (1862).
15 Reads over the end of *Y* and thinks it 'feeble'; in the morning thinks it 'full' and 'bustling', but she continues to have misgivings.
16 Reads John Mctaggart, Cambridge philosopher and friend of RF's: 'I'm surprised to find how interesting mystic Hegelianism is to me' (to E. Smyth).
18 R. Kipling dies (*D*, 19 Jan).
20 Dines with A. Ritchie, now editor of *International Women's News*. King George V dies (*D*, 21 Jan).
24–6 To Monk's House and to Canterbury where LW lectures to the Worker's Educational Association.
25 VW's fifty-fourth birthday.

Late this month, works slowly on *RF*; enjoys the quarrel in the *Sunday Times* between E. Sitwell and G. Grigson, editor of the *Morning Post*, over the merits of the new poets (she supports TSE and Dylan Thomas, he S. Spender and W. H. Auden); travels to Cambridge to visit Ann Stephen and to see G. Rylands' production of Aristophanes' *The Frogs*.

HOGARTH PRESS: Friends Anti-War Group, *The Roots of War*.

February

8 (Sat) Reading Dickens' *David Copperfield* (1849–50) 'for the 6th time with almost complete satisfaction', and Thomas Wright's *Life of Charles Dickens* (1935), 'which makes me dislike [Dickens] as a human being' (to H. Walpole).
9 Attends meeting at A. Stephen's of the group 'For Intellectual Liberty', founded as a counterpart to the French Comité de Vigilance.

(Mid-month) Continues to correct the typescript of *Y*, to the exclusion of all other work and social engagements.

Late this month, M. Oxford asks VW to write her obituary (see 'Am I a Snob?', *MOB*).
HOGARTH PRESS: C. Day Lewis, *Noah and the Waters*.

March

3 (Tues) Attends performance of Ibsen's *A Doll's House*, with L. Lopokova as Nora, at the recently opened Cambridge Arts Theatre (conceived and financed by JMK – 'an interesting play, wh. throws light on some of my own efforts; but I wish I'd gone to Figaro instead' (*D*).
7 Hitler's troops march into the demilitarised zone of the Rhineland: 'We are all under the shadow of Hitler at the moment' (to J. Bell, 11 Mar).
10 Takes the unusual step of sending the first batch of typescript of *Y* to the printers (R. and R. Clark of Edinburgh) without first letting LW read the novel. Attends performance of *Hedda Gabler* at Criterion Theatre.
11 Pleased to read in A. Bennett's *Letters to his Nephew* that 'Virginia's all right' (*D*).
12 Discusses politics with LW, who supports the League of Nations' sanctions against Italy, whereas A. Huxley opposes them; 'Its odd, how near the guns have got to our private life again . . . though I go on, like a doomed mouse, nibbling at my daily page' (*D*).
14 Attends meeting of Intellectual Liberty group.
16 Continues to retype *Y*; alternates between feeling it is an utter failure and that it is her best book.
17 Visited by S. S. Koteliansky, K. Stephen and E. Williamson; unable to work on *Y* next morning.
18 Considers the scene at Witterings (*Y*, '1911') 'about the best, in that line, I ever wrote' (*D*).
19 Lady Simon, cousin Harry Stephen and R. Mortimer visit.
21–3 To Rodmell; reads D. Cecil's 1935 Leslie Stephen lecture on J. Austen; notes *Persuasion* was her favourite last time she read it (to D. Cecil).
24 So absorbed in 'Two Guineas' (*3G*) feels she must be verging on insanity; has not had time to read EMF's *Abinger Harvest*, which has just been published.
25/27 E. Robins visits; VW rereads her *Ibsen and the Actress* (1928).
28 Attends performance of Ibsen's *The Master Builder*; disap-

pointed in L. Lopokova, who 'cant swing from the real to the poetic' (*D*).

31 Visits Gerald Duckworth; wishes she could have attended Prime Minister Baldwin's speech on behalf of the Newnham College building fund (a speech VW draws on in *3G*, ch. 2).

HOGARTH PRESS: L. Barnes, *The Future of Colonies*; J. Bell, *Work for the Winter and Other Poems*; L. Tolstoy, *On Socialism*, tr. Ludvig Perno; Irene Cooper Willis, *The Authorship of Wuthering Heights*; LW, *The League and Abyssinia*.

April

2 (Thurs) Takes EMF from the nursing home where he had been recovering from a prostate operation to his home at Abinger Hammer, Surrey.

3 To Monk's House for Easter.

8 Sends the last batch of typescript of *Y* to the printers.

9 Dines at Charleston to discuss CB's article 'Inside the *Queen Mary*: A Business Man's Dream' (*Listener*, 8 Apr); next day collapses and spends the rest of the month largely recumbent with severe headaches at Monk's House. Relieved that Harcourt Brace cannot produce *Y* before October, she ignores the proofs.

23 Reading TSE's *Collected Poems, 1909–35*, held off from 'understanding' by the 'enchantment, incantation' (to TSE; to J. Bell, 2 May).

30 A. E. Housman, classical scholar and author of *The Shropshire Lad* (1896), dies ('Do you like his Muse? . . . Always too laden with a peculiar scent for my taste'), leaving TSE 'now the titular head of English–American letters' (to J. Bell, 2 May).

May

Early this month, visited by VB, CB, QB, and others at Charleston; J. Lehmann visits the Press to collect work for his biannual anthology, *New Writing* (pub. Bodley Head until 1938, thereafter by Hogarth). Reads J. M. Murry's *Shakespeare*, Hesketh Pearson's *Labby: The Life of H. Labouchere*, and E. Sackville-West's *A Flame in the Sunlight: The Life and Work of Thomas de Quincey* (all 1936); dreams of war (to J. Bell, 2 May).

1 (Fri) Considers a proposal to publish R. Brooke's letters (no full edition appears until 1959, ed. G. Keynes).

2 Replies to V. Ocampo, pleased that she has published *Room* (in her magazine *Sur*, tr. Jorge Luis Borges).
3 Returns to Tavistock Square.
8 On Dr E. Rendel's advice, VW and LW embark on a motor tour to Cornwall.
11 Reading E. Smyth's *As Time Went On* (1936, dedicated to VW); telegraphs 'enthralled by book' to Smyth; to VB writes, 'Considering she writes like an old turkey cock scattering the gravel with its hind legs, the picture of Ponsonbys and Vernon Lees and HBs [Henry Brewster] is rather amazing'.
22 Returns to Tavistock Square.
26 Begins correcting proofs of *Y*, allowed to work no more than 45 minutes a day.
29 To Rodmell, on Dr Rendel's recommendation. Reads T. B. Macaulay, and Flaubert's *Correspondence (1830–80)* (9 vols, 1926–33).

HOGARTH PRESS: F. C. R. Douglas, *Land-value Rating*; Mary Gordon, *Chase of the Wild Goose: The Story of Lady Eleanor Butler and Miss Sarah Ponsonby, Known as the Ladies of Llangollen*; K. Innes, *The League of Nations: The Complete Story Told for Young People.*

June

10 (Wed) Returns to London from Rodmell.
11 Writing in her diary for the first time since 9 April, notes the last two months of 'almost catastrophic' illness have been the worst since her nervous breakdown and attempted suicide of 1913. Begins reading VSW's just-published *Saint Joan of Arc* – 'Why 20 words where 2 are enough?' (to E. Smyth; to VSW, 29 June).

(Mid-month) Continues to suffer from headaches, slowly correcting *Y*, reading Flaubert's letters, which she finds 'consoling, admonishing'; receives visits from R. Macaulay, E. Bowen and VB. No diary entries from 23 June until 30 October, but she writes regularly to E. Smyth.

23 Reads the typescript of E. Smyth's *Inordinate(?) Affection*; advises her for commercial reasons to publish it with another press.
25 Reads an article about Anna de Noailles by Colette, 'floored by the extreme dexterity insight and beauty' of her writing (to E. Smyth).
29 Finishes *Saint Joan of Arc* – 'massive and wholesome' (to VSW).

HOGARTH PRESS: Securitas (Financial Editor of *Time and Tide*), *Adventures in Investing by 'Securitas'*.

July

9 (Thurs) Feels 'badgered' by all the political activity in London, including LW's meetings in their flat, so they go to Rodmell for the summer earlier than usual (to E. Smyth, 25 July, 3 Aug).

14 Reads Wilfred Blunt's *My Diaries* (1919, 1920) and Macaulay.

19 Reads Maud Diver's *Honoria Lawrence: A Fragment of Indian History* (1936). Q. Bell comes to visit with A. Bell and J. Bussy, who later in the week sends Colette's recent memoir *Mes apprentissages* (1936).

22 Tells VB of a visit 'long long ago from Tom Eliot, whom I love, or could have loved, had we both been in the prime and not in the sere' (to VB, 22 July).

25 Returns Daudet's letters to E. Smyth; thinks about the need for praise, 'this desire for reverberation', in connection with *3G* (to E. Smyth). Now working six hours a day on the proofs of *Y*.

August

Early this month, disagrees with E. Smyth on the merits of novelist M. Baring, whom Smyth adores and VW finds unreadable, and on 'Bloomsbury', which Smyth abuses and VW hotly defends (see *L*, Aug–Sep).

14 (Fri) Enthralled by Elizabeth Lynn Linton (whether by her 1885 fictionalised *Autobiography of Christopher Kirkland* or the 1901 biography by G. S. Layard, *Mrs Lynn Linton*, is not clear; to VB).

17 Sally Graves, niece of writer Robert Graves, visits.

20 Excited by VSW's next subject for a biography, her grandmother, the Spanish dancer, and her mother, Lady Sackville (*Pepita*, Hogarth, Oct 1937), and by B. Russell's edition of his parents' memoirs, (*The Amberley Papers*, Hogarth, Mar 1937).

27 Drives herself to a headache trying to finish the proofs; fails, 'so thank God, cant send them in time to print this autumn. . . . The Mess, the repetition, the diffusion, the carelessness were, and still are, inconceivable' (to VSW).

30 Attends performance at Charleston of Q. Bell's play *A Guided Tour* (of Charleston in 2036).

September

2 (Wed) Asks VB for A. C. Gissing's *Holman Hunt: A Biography* (1936).

15 B. Russell to lunch to discuss publication of *The Amberley Papers*.

18 Rereads Wordsworth's *The Prelude* with delight; wonders why the present age has no great poet, only 'a few pipers on hedges like Yeats and Tom Eliot, de la Mare' (to E. Smyth).

October

9 (Fri) Wonders how to begin *RF*; has not read the recently published novels by A. Huxley, *Eyeless in Gaza*, R. Lehmann, *The Weather in the Streets*, and C. Morgan, *Sparkenbroke* (to O. Morrell).

11 Returns to London for the winter; begins to entertain again.

19 Visits E. Smyth at Woking, Surrey.

30 In her diary writes scene of visiting S. Colefax on the eve of her auction at Argyll House; later uses the passage as the basis of the final pages of 'Am I a Snob?' (1 Dec).

HOGARTH PRESS: Fritz Faulkner, *Windless Sky*; Millard Douglas, *The Co-operative Movement To-day and To-morrow*; Yuri Olyesha, *Envy*, tr. Anthony Wolfe; T. Reik, *The Unknown Murderer*, tr. Dr Katherine Jones; R. M. Rilke, *Sonnets to Orpheus*, tr. with intro. J. B. Leishman; R. Strachey, *Our Freedom and its Results by Five Women: Eleanor F. Rathbone, Erna Reiss, Ray Strachey, Allison Neilans, Mary Agnes Hamilton*; A. D. Whyte, *Lights are Bright*.

November

1 (Sun) In despair over *Y*, delighted when LW declares it 'extraordinarily good'; privately, however, he has reservations (see *LW* IV), and VW cannot bring herself to believe he is right (*D*, 4 Nov).

9 K. Martin asks VW to review Chesterton's *Autobiography*; George Barnes, of the BBC Talks Department, visits to ask VW to talk on Spenser: she declines both offers (but delivers 'Craftsmanship' on the BBC, 29 Apr 1937). Notes Madrid, under heavy bombardment, has still not fallen.

10 Dines with A. Stephen; meets Dr John Rickman, editor of the *British Journal of Medical Psychology*, enjoys not talking politics. LW has just finished reading B. Russell's *Which Way to Peace?*

(1936), and has, VW says, become an isolationist. (*D*; to J. Bell, 14 Nov; but see *D* n.)

11 Decides not to review *Miss Weeton: Journal of a Governess, 1807–11*, ed. E. Hall, but quotes from it in *3G*, ch. 2.

(Mid-month) Has cut *Y* from 700 to 420 pages; has been persuaded by S. Spender and W. Plomer to subscribe to the *Left Review*, and has written an article for the *Daily Worker* (14 Dec). Notes that A. Huxley is 'on the rampage' with peace propaganda, that F. L. Lucas attacks TSE in *The Decline and Fall of the Romantic Ideal* and that W. B. Yeats has just published *The Oxford Book of Modern Verse*, in which he gives high praise to D. Wellesley's poems (to J. Bell, 14 Nov).

13 C. Mauron visits. VW reads RFs translation of Mallarmé and the introduction by Mauron, impressed by the wit and clarity of his commentary.

14 Mauron to dinner; tells VW to advise J. Bell not to leave China in order to fight the Fascists (see Stansky and Abrahams for an account of Bell's involvement in the Spanish War).

15 Receives a package of photographs from Spain of dead children (which becomes a recurring motif in *3G*). Lord Robert Cecil, president of the League of Nations Union, visits to discuss the situation in Spain.

17 R. W. Chapman, editor of J. Austen, visits, and later in the week sends a copy of his edition of the manuscript of two chapters of *Persuasion*.

23 Begins *3G*; has finished 'Am I a Snob?'

25 Lunches with CB to meet the Princesse de Polignac (Winnaretta Singer, daughter of the sewing-machine millionaire, friend of Proust), with R. Lehmann, E. Sackville-West and Lord Berners.

27 Lunches at Claridges with E. Smyth, the Princesse de Polignac, French composer Nadia Boulanger, and former diplomat and authority on the Near East Sir Ronald Storrs; reads Gibbon for a bicentenary article (24 Apr 1937).

HOGARTH PRESS: S. Freud, *Inhibitions, Symptoms and Anxiety*, tr. A. Strachey; A. Stephen, *The 'Dreadnought' Hoax*; H. G. Wells, *The Idea of a World Encyclopaedia*.

December

Early this month, charts the progress of the 'Simpson affair' – the constitutional crisis brought on by Edward VIII's determination to marry the twice-divorced Mrs Wallis Simpson – which supplants Spain and Germany in the press (*D*).

1 (Tues) Reads 'Am I a Snob?' to the Memoir Club (*MOB*).
2 V. Dickinson sends VW typescript copies of 350 letters, written by VW to Dickinson in her youth.
10 Edward VIII abdicates; George VI succeeds.
14 'Why Art To-day Follows Politics' in the *Daily Worker*.
15 Attends meeting at A. Stephen's to discuss Spain; meets writer J. B. Priestley.
18 To Monk's House for Christmas. VW continues to work on Gibbon; LW reads history for his next volume, *After the Deluge*.
24 Visits Gibbon's grave, at Fletching, Sussex.
25 Lunches with the Keyneses at Tilton.
26 Promises O. Morrell she will read Djuna Barnes's *Nightwood* (1936) and Peter Delius's *Women in White* (1934, 1936); has been reading MacKenna (possibly Stephen MacKenna's *Journal and Letters*, ed. E. R. Dodds, 1936): likes his life but not his slang (to O. Morrell).

HOGARTH PRESS: Sir Arthur Salter, *Economic Policies and Peace*.

1937

EVENTS AND LETTERS. Spanish rebels destroy Guernica; Picasso paints *Guernica*, mural for Paris World Exhibition; riots take place in Sudeten area of Czechoslovakia; Lord Halifax visits Hitler – beginning of policy of appeasement; Duke of Windsor marries Mrs Wallis Simpson. W. H. Auden and C. Isherwood publish *The Ascent of F6*; J. Dos Passos, *USA*; E. Hemingway, *To Have and Have Not*; C. Odets, *Golden Boy*; G. Orwell, *The Road to Wigan Pier*; J. P. Sartre, *La Nausée*; J. Steinbeck, *Of Mice and Men*.

January

Early this month, while at Rodmell, works on Gibbon; exchanges visits with J. Stephen, the Robsons, the Keyneses, R. Lehmann and her husband, as well as with those at Charleston.

8 (Fri) Visits E. Robin and Dr Octavia Wilberforce in Brighton, to discuss Robins' book *Raymond and I* (1955).
10 Works on 'Fishing' (*M*), an article prompted by J. W. Wills's *My Sporting Life* (1936); notes death of S. Tomlin (5 Jan) and of H. Tonks (8 Jan).

16 Returns to Tavistock Square.
18 Lunches at CB's with his friend M. Baker, R. Mortimer, TSE and Virginia Brett, daughter of Viscount Esher.
22 M. West, manager of the Hogarth Press since early 1933, dies.
25 VW's fifty-fifth birthday.
27 Francesca Allinson visits to discuss her forthcoming book, *A Childhood* (Hogarth, Oct).
28 Begins work in *3G* again. Dines with the Hutchinsons to meet H. G. Wells, whom the Woolfs have not seen since he and LW quarrelled in March 1932; they talk of Compton Mackenzie, A. Bennett and TSE, who has been, according to Wells, 'the death of English literature' (*D*).

February

12 (Fri) Continues to work hard at *3G*, in part because she is fearful of the reception of *Y*. Concerned about J. Bell, who has resigned his professorship in China and intends to join the International Brigade in Spain, where J. Cornford was killed at the end of December.
13 Rodmell Labour Party, which includes writer Neil Lyons, meets at Monk's House; discusses the abdication crisis more than Labour politics.
14 Reads *The Final Struggle, Countess Tolstoy's Diary, 1910*, with extracts from Leo Tolstoy's diary, tr. A. Maude (1936).
16 S. Spender to tea and dinner; discusses his recent marriage and his intention to go to Spain to join his friend Tony Hyndman. VW attends performance of Chekhov's *Uncle Vanya*.
18 Has completed 38 pages of *3G*; puts it aside for a few days to work on a series of 'incidents' to be illustrated by VB (nothing comes of this project).
20 Visited by S. Graves and C. Isherwood, in London for rehearsals of his play *The Ascent of F6*; VW is pleased by his admiration of her and EMF (*D*).
21 Julian Fry (RF's son, who has a cattle ranch in British Columbia, Canada) visits.
22 Marquerite Yourcenar, whose French translation of *W* will appear later this year, visits.
24 Working hard on *3G*, apprehensive about forthcoming reviews of *Y*; reading Molière, *Le Misanthrope* (1667) and Colette's *Mes apprentisages* (1936).

27 D. MacCarthy visits, discusses *The Amberley Papers*.

March

1 (Mon) To Cambridge to attend performance of *The Misanthrope* (with L. Lopokova as Célimène).

2–7 Charts her 'spiritual temperature' in the face of the approaching publication of *Y* (*D*).

11 *Y* published.

12 Greatly relieved by positive reviews in *TLS*, *Time and Tide*, and particularly by B. de Selincourt in the *Observer* (14 Mar), where he declares that no writer of the time is as gifted as VW 'with power to divine and express the quality of infinity in all experience' (*M&M*). During the following week VW is occasionally cast down but on the whole excited and astonished that the book is being hailed as a masterpiece – much of it seems 'feeble' to her, and 'the scene in the college' ('1880') still makes her blush (*D*, 14 Mar).

13 To Charleston, to see J. Bell, who has just returned from China.

15 Considers recasting the deleted section of *Y* for the Uniform Edition (she does not do so).

21 Visits S. S. Koteliansky. Suffers for the next four days from headaches.

25 To Rodmell for Easter.

27 Begins G. Meredith's *Lord Ormont and his Aminta* (1894); finds it 'so rich, so knotted, so alive, & muscular', it makes her want to write fiction again (*D*).

28 Reads Gilbert White's *The Natural History and Antiquities of Selborne* (1798) and Edward Ward's *The London Spy* (1698); has ordered Robert Southey's *Commonplace Book* (1849–51), Edward, Earl of Clarendon's *History of the Rebellion and Civil Wars in England* (1705–6) and Walt Whitman's *Leaves of Grass* (1855).

HOGARTH PRESS: Bertrand and Patricia Russell (eds), *The Amberley Papers*; R. M. Fox, *Smoky Crusade*; Christopher Lee, *Poems*; Adolf Lowe, *The Price of Liberty: A German on Contemporary Britain*; VW, *The Years*.

April

1 (Thurs) Visits J. Case, who is dying.

3 Plans 'Craftsmanship'.

4 Returns to London, reads Balzac, attends performance of *A Midsummer Night's Dream* (with A. Bell as Ariel).
8 H. Walpole and C. Isherwood to lunch, the former 'nourishing a sorrow that his books sell too well and the intellectuals dont admire' (to J. Case).
16 To Monk's House for the weekend; works on an article on Gibbon's aunts ('Reflections at Sheffield Place', *NS&N*, 19 June).
24 'The Historian and "The Gibbon"' in *TLS*.
26 Attends performance of Paul Dukas's opera *Ariane et Barbebleue*, with R. Mortimer, M. MacCarthy and Desmond Shawe-Taylor, music critic for *NS&N*.
27 Attends meeting of Memoir Club: DG recalls a party in Florence when he was taken for JMK by the bankers in attendance; D. MacCarthy delivers a version of 'Shooting with Wilfred Blunt' (*Memories*, 1953); and EMF reads his introduction to T. E. Lawrence's letters (the edition is taken over by D. Garnett, pub. 1938).
28 Reads *Walter Leaf, 1852–1927: Some Chapters of Autobiography*, with a Memoir by C. M. Leaf (1932).
29 'Craftsmanship', talk broadcast in the BBC series *Words Fail Me*, (*Listener*, 5 Apr).

HOGARTH PRESS: Dr I. Harris, *Diet and High Blood Pressure*.

May

Early this month, gives a party at which J. Bell inveighs against the Bloomsbury 'habit of education'; bitter because at 29 he has no special training, only a 'vague literary smattering' (*D*, 4 May).

5 (Wed) D. MacCarthy visits to discuss the lecture he is to give on VW's father for the annual Leslie Stephen lecture at Cambridge, 26 May.
6 Attends exhibition of VB's recent paintings at the Lefevre Gallery.
7 The Woolfs cross to Dieppe, beginning a tour of western France. VW reads JMK's *Essays in Biography* (1933) and George Sand's *Elle et lui* (1859); visits Sand's house at Nohant; returns to Monk's House 23 May (*D*, 25 May).
27 Lady Simon, member of the governing body of Newnham College, Cambridge, to tea; discusses the question of Newnham achieving equality with the other colleges.

Hogarth Press: L. B. Pekin (pseud. of Reginald Snell), *The Military Training of Youth*.

June

1 (Tues) Works ahead on *3G* after five days of recopying and rewriting. *Y* has reached the top of the bestseller list in the *New York Herald Tribune*, where it stays for several weeks.

6 Returns to London; attends farewell dinner for J. Bell, who leaves the next day to drive an ambulance in Spain.

8 Dines at the Hutchinson to meet Duff Cooper, First Lord of the Admiralty, and his wife Diana.

11 D. Brace, of VW's American publishers Harcourt Brace, to lunch.

14 Dines with E. Bowen and her husband; meets A. Butts, American writer May Sarton, and scholar Maurice Bowra.

16 Finishes the 'education section: much re-arranged' in *3G* (*D*).

19 'Reflections at Sheffield Place' in *NS&N*.

21 M. Sarton to tea; speaks of *Y*, which she finds disappointing but greater than *W*, and of her own novel in progress, *The Single Hound* (pub. 1938).

22 Observes 'a long trail of fugitives', Spanish refugees from Bilbao, passing through Tavistock Square (*D*, 23 June).

23 Reads W. Congreve's *Love for Love* (1695) – a 'masterpiece'; wonders how her father could deny him feeling (*D*).

24 Attends meeting organised by the National Joint Committee for Spanish Relief to raise money for the Basque refugee children; pictures are auctioned, including one by Picasso, but VW finds it all 'very stagey empty & unreal', though enjoys P. Robeson's singing and her meeting with W. H. Auden (*D*).

25 Begins work on Congreve article.

28 Working on ch. 2 of *3G*; now sees it as a book of three chapters.

Hogarth Press: E. M. Delafield, *Ladies and Gentleman in Victorian Fiction*; N. Mitchison and R. H. S. Crossman, *Socrates*; L. B. Pekin, *Darwin*; VSW, *Joan of Arc*; M. Strachey, *Mazzini, Garibaldi and Cavour*.

July

Early this month, 'in full flood' every morning with *3G*.

7 Declines party at the Bussys' to meet painter H. Matisse.

9 Dines with S. Sydney-Turner at the Oxford and Cambridge

Club to meet the Beresfords and retired Treasury Counsel Sir William Graham-Harrison.

15 J. Case dies; VW notes 'how great a visionary part she has played in my life, till the visionary became a part of the fictitious, not of the real life' (*D*, 19 July).

20 Learns of death of J. Bell, age 29, killed by a shell fragment while driving his ambulance, 18 July; in the coming weeks VW devotes herself to VB.

22 'Miss Janet Case: Classical Scholar and Teacher', obituary, in *The Times*.

29 To Rodmell for the summer.

30 Writes out her thoughts on J. Bell (*QB* II, Appendix C).

August

Early this month, continues work on 'Congreve' and on *3G*; resumes reading for *RF*; negotiates with New York agent Jacques Chambrun over 'The Shooting Party' and 'The Duchess and the Jeweller'.

11 (Wed) Buys J. Jeans's *The Mysterious Universe* (1930); reads G. Sands's *Histoire de ma vie* (1854–5), W. H. Auden and Louis MacNeice's *Letters from Iceland* (1937) – 'mainly attitudinising' to E. Smyth, 19 Sep) – and manuscript of K. Nott's *Mile End* (Hogarth, Oct 1938).

29 Works on 'Congreve', which she has been finding very difficult, finishing it by 2 September.

September

2 (Thurs) Read J. Bell's 'War and Peace: A Letter to E. M. Forster' (included in *Julian Bell*, Hogarth, 1938), which she thinks the best thing she has read of his, and which helps her understand his point of view about being a soldier (to VB, 8 Sep).

16 Visits VSW at Sissinghurst.

18 'Snowed under' with RF letters and articles, cannot make up her mind whether to begin writing or not (to M. L. Davies).

19 Attends meeting of the Left Book Club in Lewes.

25 'Congreve's Comedies: Speed, Stillness, and Meaning' in *TLS*.

26 TSE, J. Stephen, W. Plomer and CB visit, which keeps her from writing the end of *3G*.

October

1 (Fri) Reads VSW's *Pepita*; thinks it 'more masterly and control-

led' than her *Saint Joan of Arc*, but detests the character of her mother (to VSW).

9 Receives the Modern Library edition of *TL*; objects mildly to the biographical references made by Terence Holliday in his introduction (to D. Brace).

10 Returns to London; for the last two weeks has been working every day from 10 a.m. to 1 p.m. on *3G*.

12 Finishes first draft of *3G*, a book she has been meditating since her visit to Delphi, 2 May 1932; 'my brain feels cool & quiet after the expulsion' (*D*).

19 Reading over 'The Shooting Party', sees the form of a new novel, the statement and restatement of a theme, 'singling out this & then that: until the central idea is stated', a form which might also fit her book of criticism (*D*; cf. *BA* and 'Reading at Random'). Begins R. Storrs' autobiography, *Orientations* (1937), but doubts she will finish it (*D*).

22 Notes LW has conceived a scheme for turning the Hogarth Press into a co-operative company.

HOGARTH PRESS: Francesca Allinson, *A Childhood*, with wood engravings by Enid Marx; Anna Freud, *The Ego and the Mechanisms of Defence*, tr. Cecil Baines; VSW, *Pepita*; V. Tree, *Can I Help You? Your Manners – Menus – Amusements – Friends – Charades – Make-Ups – Travel – Calling – Children – Love Affairs*, illustrated by Virginia Parsons.

November

1 (Mon) Reads W. Lewis's *Blasting and Bombardiering* (1937); revises ch. 1 of *3G*.

3 Reading RF's papers, feels it more and more impossible to write a conventional 'life' (to Pamela Diamond, RF's daughter).

11 Attends private view of DG's recent paintings.

12 To Cambridge, where LW speaks to the New Peace Movement on 'The Colonial Problem'.

27 Declines an invitation to join a committee to advise on the selection of books for the Pelican paperback series (to D. Kilham Roberts).

30 Still revising *3G*, which has occupied most of the month. Has been reading memoirs of Chateaubriand (1768–1848), *Deux livres des memoires d'outre tombe*, ed. M. Levaillant (1936): judges the work a 'masterpiece', but the author a 'detestable sham Byronic man' (to E. Smyth, 27 Jan 1938).

HOGARTH PRESS: *A General Selection from the Works of Sigmund Freud*, ed. J. Rickman; C. Isherwood, *Sally Bowles*; M. Klein and J. Riviere, *Love, Hate and Reparation*; Ella Freeman Sharpe, *Dream Analysis*.

December

Early this month, sends off ch. 1 of *3G* to typist.

13 (Mon) Thanks E. Smyth for *Maurice Baring*, but refuses, on policy, to comment (to E. Smyth). VSW dines, 'more matronly & voluptuous than ever' (*D*).

17 Attends H. Anrep's party, given to raise support for the new 'School of Drawing and Painting', later 'The Euston Road School'.

22 To Monk's House for Christmas.

25 Receives the Duke of Portland's memoirs, *Men, Women, and Things* (1937) from TSE (later writes to O. Morrell – the Duke's half-sister – 'the self complacency seemed omnipotent'; 19 Feb 1938). The Keyneses to lunch; JMK works himself into a fury talking about politics.

29 Returns to London.

1938

EVENTS AND LETTERS. Chamberlain meets Hitler at Berchtesgaden and Bad Godesberg; P. Buck awarded Nobel Prize; T. Wolfe dies. J. Huizinga publishes *Homo Ludens*; G. Greene, *Brighton Rock*; C. Isherwood, *Goodbye to Berlin*; T. Wilder, *Our Town* (Pulitzer Prize, drama).

January

Early this month, anxious about LW, who is ill; J. Lehmann proposes to buy a share of the Press.

9 (Sun) Finishes rewriting *3G*.

11 Thinks of writing 'An Ode to Whitaker' (*Whitaker's Almanack*, which she has consulted frequently in writing *3G*.

15 Takes *3G* to the typist; travels to Monk's House for LW's convalescence; VW is ill with influenza for several days.

25 VW's fifty-sixth birthday.

February

3 (Thurs) Thanks P. Morrell for his affection, and for his

admiration of *JR*, her own favourite, and of *N&D*, which nothing will make her reread (to P. Morrell).

4 LW approves *3G*, thinks it 'an extremely clear analysis' (*D*). D. Cecil to tea; has agreed to deliver the Clark lectures (at Cambridge) on Hardy, in 1941.

7 Considers ideas for an illustrated paper to be called *The Outsider* (cf. *3G*, ch. 3); works on the notes for *3G*.

19 Reads E. H. Young's *William* (1925); thinks her better than H. Walpole or H. G. Wells (to O. Morrell).

23 Signs agreement with J. Lehmann, selling her share in the Hogarth Press for £3000.

March

Early this month, works five hours a day to finish the notes and proofs of *3G*.

9 (Wed) Attends performance of Chekhov's *The Three Sisters* (with J. Gielgud and P. Ashcroft).

11 Busy correcting proofs; made slightly jealous by R. Macaulay's new book on EMF (Hogarth, Mar). Hitler annexes Austria; the Woolfs hear 'a snatch of dance music from Vienna' on their new radio (*D*).

21 TSE to dinner and then to see S. Spender's play *Trial of a Judge*.

22 Recasts the last page of *3G*.

26 Almost expecting to hear war announced – 'When the tiger, ie Hitler, has digested his dinner he will pounce again' (*D*).

31 Buys E. Fitzgerald's *Dictionary of Madame de Sévigné*, ed. M. Fitzgerald Kerrich (1914); LW works on his play *The Hotel* (Hogarth, 1939).

'The Shooting Party' in *Harper's Bazaar*.

HOGARTH PRESS: Libby Benedict, *The Refugees*; C. Isherwood, *Lions and Shadows*; R. Macaulay, *The Writings of E. M. Forster*; Edward Upward, *Journey to the Border*.

April

1 (Fri) Begins writing *RF*.

2 Satisfied that she has said her say in *3G*, begins making up a new work, 'Pointz Hall', ultimately *BA* (*D*, 12 Apr; see *Pointz Hall*, ed. Leaska).

5 Writes to VSW, asking if she has read G. Borrow's *The Zincali, or an Account of the Gypsies in Spain* (1841), and to Ling Su-Hua, wife of Professor Chen of Wuhan University and friend of

J. Bell, urging her to read the eighteenth-century English writers, and to write her biography (*Ancient Melodies*, Hogarth 1953; see also *L*, 27 July and 15 Oct).

12 Suspicious of the 'vulgarity . . . a certain insistence' in the notes to *3G*; has completed 20 pages of *RF* (*D*).

14 To Rodmell for Easter; reads Bernard de Mandeville's *The Fable of the Bees; or Private Vices, Publick Benefits* (1714).

20 Works on *BA* (Oliver and his dog).

21 Lady O. Morrell dies; VW writes obituary for *The Times*, 28 April.

26 Meditates on *BA*, in which she envisions 'all lit, discussed in connection with real little incongruous living humour. . . . "I" rejected: "We" substituted . . . we all life, all art, all waifs & strays' (*D*). Attends memorial service for O. Morrell.

28 Sends off final proofs of *3G*.

29 So absorbed by *BA* she cannot attend to *RF*.

'America which I Have Never Seen Interests me Most in this Cosmopolitan World of Today' in *Harper's International Combined with Cosmopolitan*.

May

3 (Tues) Struggling with *RF*: 'How can one cut loose from facts, when there they are, contradicting my theories? . . . But I'm convinced I cant physically, strain after an RA portrait' (*D*). Meets Libby Benedict, author of *The Refugees* (Hogarth, Mar 1938).

14–15 To Haslemere, Surrey, to stay with R. and O. Strachey. Declines J. Lehmann's invitation to write a story for *New Writing*.

(Mid-month) Anxious about the forthcoming appearance of *3G*, but conscious that Europe may be in flames, and her book, 'like a moth dancing over a bonfire – consumed in less than one second' (*D*, 24 May).

22 K. Arnold-Forster dies (*D*, 25 May).

26 Reads A. Davidson's *Edward Lear, Landscape Painter and Nonsense Poet, 1812–88* (1938); praises its suggestiveness (to A. Davidson).

27 Receives Elizabeth Nielson, an American 'entirely distracted by Einstein, & his extra mundane influence upon fiction', who is planning a doctoral dissertation on VW (*D*).

29 TSE to tea; talks of his visit to Portugal, and of his lecture on George Herbert at Salisbury, in aid of the cathedral.

'Women Must Weep', subtitled 'Or Unite against War', summary of *Three Guineas* in *Atlantic Monthly*.

HOGARTH PRESS: Dr R. Laforgue, *Clinical Aspects of Psycho-analysis*, tr. Joan Hall; R. M. Rilke, *Later Poems*, tr. with intro. by J. B. Leishman.

June

2 (Thurs) *3G* published to positive reviews: the *TLS* calls her 'the most brilliant pamphleteer in England'; B. de Selincourt in the *Observer* compares her to Matthew Arnold, and speaks of her 'deep wisdom'; Graham Greene in the *Spectator* calls it a 'clear brilliant essay', which, however, sounds a little 'shrill' when it touches morality or religion (*M&M*; see also *D* and *L* in early June, and VW's outraged rebuttal to VSW's charge of 'misleading arguments', 19 June).

9 TSE given an honorary degree at Cambridge by Lord Baldwin, the subject of the third illustration in *3G*.

16 Embarks on motor tour to Scotland and the Western Isles. While LW cleans spark plugs, VW reads in *The Oxford Book of Greek Verse in Translation*, ed. with introductions by T. F. Higham and C. M. Bowra (1938). Visits grave of W. Scott; visits Dove Cottage, Wordsworth's home 1799–1808; returns to London 2 July. (*D*, 16–20 June.)

HOGARTH PRESS: VW, *Three Guineas*.

July

3 (Sun) Works on *BA* (the portraits in the dining room).

5 Prepares the memorial volume of J. Bell's writings; tries to force herself back to the 'appalling grind' of *RF*.

7 Martin Freud (banker, son of S. Freud) and J. Lehmann to lunch. Lehmann asks VW to contribute to *New Writing*; she refuses, although he persists in the coming week (*D*, to J. Lehmann, early July; see also 15 May).

12 Meeting of the Memoir Club; D. Garnett read.

14 S. Buchan to tea; E. Playfair and K. Nott (author of *Mile End*, Hogarth, Oct) to dinner; Benedict Nicolson (son of VSW and H. Nicolson), J. Stephen and R. Macaulay come in afterward.

18 Meets with Sir W. Rothstein, whose *Men and Memories* (1932)

tells of his friendship with RF in Paris, in 1892 (quoted in *RF*, ch. 7).

19 Attends performance by the Ballet Russe de Monte Carlo.

22 Asks R. Trevelyan for information about 1893–6, during which he shared a house with RF (to R. Trevelyan).

28 To Monk's House for the summer.

Late this month, J. Buchan sends copies of his *Walter Scott* (1932) and *Oliver Cromwell* (1934); R. Hughes sends his *In Hazard* (1938).

August

1 (Mon) Works on *BA* (Mrs Manresa).

4 Tries to write about 'a lily pool' in *BA;* wants the novel to be a series of contrasts, and plans to end with a play. Forces herself to keep at *RF*.

6 Writes the meeting of Isa and Giles in *BA*. Sees tanks on manoeuvres: 'Small boys playing idiotic games for which I pay' (*D*).

7 Receives notes on RF from R. C. Trevelyan, sketches general plan of book in *D*.

13 To Pulborough for a performance of *Gammer Gurton's Needle* (with A. Bell).

17 Begins reading the fourteen volumes of Madame de Sévigné's letters in *Les Grands écrivains de la France* (1862–6) (see 'Madame de Sévigné', *DM*); has been reading *Memorials of Edward Burne-Jones* by G. B.-J. (his wife) (1904), and thinks it 'richer & warmer & more important' than EMF's biography of G. L. Dickinson, which could not mention his homosexuality (*D*).

18 Reads *Kilvert's Diary: Selections from the Diary of the Rev. Francis Kilvert* (1840–79), which W. Plomer is editing (1938–40).

22 In *BA* writes of the view described by Figgis's Guide Book.

23 Reluctant to lunch with JMK because his talk of Hitler unsettles her, making it difficult to work on *RF*.

28 Concerned about the Nazi build-up on the border of Czechoslovakia: 'L. is very black. Hitler has his hounds only very lightly held' (*D*).

29 In *BA* Giles thinks of Europe bristling with guns, like a 'hedgehog'. VW reads *The Diary of Lady Frederick Cavendish*, ed. John Baily (1927) – 'drab and dowdy' (to E. Smyth).

September

1 (Thurs) Notes attack on *3G* in *Scrutiny* by Q. D. Leavis, who

takes issue with VW's definition of the 'educated class' and dismisses the work as 'unpleasant self-indulgence' (*M&M*).

5 Looks up facts on RF and the Metropolitan Museum in New York. Notes beginning of rally of Nazi Party congress in Nuremberg – 'Everyone asks everyone, Any news?' (*D*).

11 VSW, S. Colefax, EMF and M. MacCarthy visit for Memoir Club meeting at Tilton; JMK reads 'a very packed profound & impressive paper . . . about Cambridge youth; their philosophy; its consequences; . . . The beauty & unworldliness of it' (*D*; 'My Early Beliefs' in *Two Memoirs*, 1949).

13 Depressed by praise of EMF's 'Credo' (*London Mercury*; Hogarth pamphlet, *What I Believe*, May 1939).

15 Chamberlain flies to Bad Godesberg to meet Hitler. Herbert Rosinski (formerly an instructor at a German staff college, now a refugee), dines with the Woolfs; predicts the Czechs will be sacrificed and 'war staved off for one year'. VW finds solace in writing *BA*. (*D*, 16 Sep.)

16 In *BA* Giles reflects on his position as 'audience' and his dislike of Dodge.

19 Continues with *BA* (William's and Lucy's eyes meeting in the mirror).

20 Sketches ch. 7 of *RF*, 'The Post-Impressionists'.

22 Reads Madame de Sévigné, and S. Sassoon, *The Old Century* (1938).

27 K. Martin to dinner, wretched about his editorial in *NS&N* which advocates appeasement, a position he subsequently reverses.

28 While looking up *Times* articles on Post-Impressionism in 1910, is warned to get her gas mask (*D*; to VB, 1 and 3 Oct).

29 Munich agreement signed by Chamberlain, Daladier, Mussolini and Hitler, giving Germany the Sudetenland.

October

2 (Sun) JMK to tea; reads from his article 'Mr Chamberlain's Foreign Policy' (*NS&N*, 8 Oct).

3 Plans to read *Troilus and Cressida*; had been trying to read Colette's *Sido* (1929), but was interrupted by the political crisis (to E. Smyth, 3 and 9 Nov).

6 Can only work on *BA* for an hour at a time, but as with *W* enjoys it intensely. E. Bowen sends her new book, *The Death*

of the Heart (1938), and Marie Mauron sends hers, *Le Quartier Mortisson* (1938).

7 Works on *BA* (William wanting to kneel to Mrs Swithin).

8 At 1911 in *RF*, asks VB how to deal with the love affair between her and RF (to VB).

9 To Tilton, where LW reads his play *The Hotel* to the Keyneses.

10 Hitler occupies the Sudetenland.

14 Considers a critical book based on her reading notes (see 'Anon' and 'The Reader', ed. Silver).

16 Returns to Tavistock Square for the winter.

18 Reads CB's *Warmongers* (1938), in which he asserts that living under tyranny is better than war (to QB).

19 H. Anrep dines; VW lends her £150, subsequently regrets it.

22 Works on the account of RF at Broussa, Turkey (*RF*, ch. 7; see Apr 1911).

25 Planning, reluctantly, to read E. Bagnold's *The Squire* (1938); felt *National Velvet* (1935) was 'a fake' (to E. Smyth).

28 While travelling Hogarth Press books in Hastings meets writer C. Kernahan.

30 Dislikes VSW's new poem, *Solitude* (Hogarth, Sep 1938).

31 Attends party at S. Colefax's with M. Beerbohm ('Orbicular. Jowld'), who talks of himself and C. Kernahan; S. Maugham ('his lips . . . drawn back like a dead mans'), who talks of A. Huxley's conversion; and C. Isherwood ('a slip of a wild boy: with quicksilver eyes'), who meets VW on the step (*D*, 1 Nov; to VB, 2 Nov).

Hogarth Press: Kenneth Allott, *Poems*; Margaret Cole, *Books and the People*; R. Palme Dutt, *The Political and Social Doctrine of Communism*; K. Nott, *Mile End*.

November

9 (Wed) Thanks E. Smyth for Colette's *Sido* and a book by Edith Somerville (to E. Smyth).

14 Works on 'The Art of Biography' (*Atlantic Monthly*, Apr 1939).

15 Reads Chaucer, Madame de Sévigné, and LS's *Elizabeth and Essex* (1928), for the article on biography. V. Tree dies (*D*, 16 Nov).

22 Rewriting 'Lappin and Lapinova', written 20 years ago; reflects on C. Connolly's criticism of her in his *Enemies of Promise, or How to Live Another Ten Years* (1938).

28 Works on 'Lappin and Lapinova'; LW works on vol. II of *After*

the Deluge, and *Barbarians at the Gate* (both pub. 1939). They dine at CB's where the talk is of T. E. Lawrence, whose *Letters,* ed. D. Garnett, have just been published.

Hogarth Press: Percy Arnold, *The Bankers of London*; *Julian Bell: Essays, Poems and Letters,* with contributions by JMK, D. Garnett, C. Mauron, C. Day Lewis and EMF, ed. Q. Bell; *New Writing,* New Series I, ed. J. Lehmann with C. Isherwood and S. Spender; VSW, *Solitude: A Poem.*

December

1 (Thurs) Resumes work on *RF,* having finished 'The Art of Biography' and 'Lappin and Lapinova'.

8 Gives tea to D. Cecil; attends 'disappointing' performance of *Twelfth Night* (with P. Ashcroft and Michael Redgrave).

12 Rewrites the 'transition page after 1918' in *RF* (end of ch. 9).

18 TSE dines; talks of his attempt to use a three-stress line in his new play, *The Family Reunion,* which contains, he says, flaws 'congenital, inalterable' – VW suspects these are in 'the department of humour' (*D,* 19 Dec).

19 Has brought *RF* to the year 1919, completed 120 pages of *BA,* to where the beldame recognises the mole; plans to write 220. Reads Chaucer, Madame de Sévigné, and 'the usual trash books' (*D*).

20 To Monk's House for Christmas.

24 J. Hills dies (*D,* 9 Jan 1939).

25 To Tilton and Charleston.

Hogarth Press (month of publication unknown): G. D. H. Cole, *The Machinery of Socialist Planning*; I. Origo, *Tribune of Rome: A Biography of Cola di Rienzo.*

1939

Events and Letters. Spanish Civil War ends; Italy invades Albania; Britain and France declare war on Germany; S. Freud, Ford Madox and W. B. Yeats die. R. Graves publishes *The Long Week-end*; Hitler, *Mein Kampf* (English tr.); J. Joyce, *Finnegans Wake*; J. Steinbeck, *The Grapes of Wrath* (Pulitzer Prize, novel); TSE, *The Family Reunion.*

January

5 (Thurs) Works on the account of RF and Josette in *RF*; reads

Madame de Sévigné, Chaucer, and LW's *After the Deluge: A Study of Communal Psychology*, vol. II (Hogarth, Sep).

15 Returns to Tavistock Square.

17 Reads TSE's announcement in the *Criterion* that he is resigning the editorship, bringing the journal to an end; notes the Spanish war is being won by Franco; reads the *Journal de Eugène Delacroix*, ed. André Joubin (3 vols, 1932). Takes four days' holiday from *RF* and works on the 'Barn scene' (after Giles kills the snake) in *BA*.

18 Visits Hertford House to view paintings by Bonington in connection with her work on *RF*.

23 Police find 340 rounds of ammunition, believed to belong to Irish terrorists, in Tavistock Square.

25 VW's fifty-seventh birthday; writer and sex-educationalist Dr Marie Stopes visits.

27 The Princesse de Polignac visits.

28 Visits S. Freud, and his children and Anna and Martin, at Hampstead; he assures her the situation with Germany would have been worse if Britain had not won the First World War. Attends fancy-dress party at A. Stephen's with TSE (as H. H. Crippen, who was hanged for the murder of his wife) and others. W. B. Yeats dies (*D*, 30 Jan).

29 Records fall of Barcelona.

30 Reads in J. Michelet's *Histoire de France* (15 vols, 1833–65) and Cecil Roth's *The Magnificent Rothschilds* (1939).

31 Writes 'The Telescope Story' (cf. 'The Searchlight', *CSF*).

February

6 (Mon) Reads D. Cecil's *The Young Melbourne and the Story of his Marriage with Caroline Lamb* (1939).

8 Through E. Bowen meets Irish writer Sean O'Faolain. Attends recital by the Busch Quartet at Wigmore Hall.

12 Visits Dickens' house at Gadshill, Kent, where he wrote *Great Expectations* (1860–1), which she has been reading.

16 Buys H. G. Wells's *The Country of the Blind and Other Stories* (1911), on TSE's recommendation.

28 Reads Shelley's 'Mont Blanc'; finds the language too 'nebulous' (*D*).

March

2 (Thurs) Speaks at an exhibition of book-jacket designs at the

Central School of Arts and Crafts. Dines with painters Claude and Elsie Rogers, journalist Tangye Lean, Dermod MacCarthy (son of Desmond and Molly MacCarthy) and others at VB's.

3 In *BA* writes, 'What's the origin of the expression, "A flea in his ear?"' (just after the audience reassembles). Is offered and refuses an honorary doctorate from Liverpool University.

10 Finishes the first 'sketch' of *RF*.

13 Lunches with Lady Diana Cooper.

15 Hitler enters Prague.

22 Finishes the eighteenth-century scene in *BA*. Reads TSE's *The Family Reunion*: 'the experiment with stylised chatter isnt successful. He's a lyric not a dramatic' (*D*).

23 Attends performance of *The Family Reunion*.

28 TSE, K. Martin and others to dinner; TSE talks of his lectures on Church and State (*The Idea of a Christian Society*, 1939), Martin of politics, saying war is inevitable, Madrid having fallen to Franco that day (*D*, 29 Mar).

30 Attends meeting of Memoir Club; CB reads on RF.

'Two Antiquaries: Walpole and Cole', review of *Letters of Horace Walpole to the Rev. William Cole*, ed. W. S. Lewis and A. D. Wallace, in the *Yale Review*.

April

6 (Thurs) To Monk's House for Easter.

7 Mussolini invades and annexes Albania.

10 To Tilton; JMK sees little hope of avoiding war now that Italy has taken Albania.

11 Plans to revise *RF* at the rate of two weeks per chapter. Reads Dickens' *Nicholas Nickleby* (1838–9) as a 'refresher' from the 'flu; reads Madame de Sévigné 'professionally'; has also been reading La Rochefoucauld, and 'Chaucer I take at need', as she has done since the previous December (*D*).

13 Has rewritten 40 pages of *RF*, and read 100 pages of Dickens: 'Literature – that is the shading, suggesting, as of Henry James, hardly used. All bold & coloured' (*D*).

15 Moving swiftly through *RF*, no longer thinks she will need two weeks per chapter; LW 'galloping' through *Barbarians at the Gate* (*D*).

17 Advises Su-Hua to continue with her memoirs, but agrees the English is a problem (to L. Su-Hua; see also *L*, 16 July).

18 Begins writing a 'sketch' for her memoirs, which over the next

year and a half becomes 'A Sketch of the Past' (*MOB*). Reads Chaucer and memoirs of Madame de la Fayette.
19 Articulates her theories of 'being' and 'non-being' in 'Sketch'.
26 Has completed 100 pages of *RF* – a quarter of the book – and hopes to finish in nine weeks.
28 Works on the 'marriage chapter' in *RF* (ch. 4). Reads account of Hitler's Reichstag speech.

'The Art of Biography' in *Atlantic Monthly*; 'Lappin and Lapinova' in *Harper's Bazaar*.

May

2 (Tues) Visits Dickens' London house (48 Doughty Street). Has discovered a form for 'Sketch': will include the present to serve as a 'platform to stand upon' in her recounting of the past (cf. *D*, 25 Apr 1940).
3 E. Bowen and C. Day Lewis to tea; the latter discusses the script he is writing for a documentary film on colliers. VW begins reading Dickens' *Our Mutual Friend* (1864–5).
4 Attends performance of J. B. Priestley's play *Johnson over Jordan*.
14 Reads Jeremy Taylor (author of *The Rule and Exercises of Holy Living*, 1651, and *The Rule and Exercises of Holy Dying*, 1651). M. Gertler dines; VW asks him about the impression RF made on younger painters.
15 Works on portrait of her mother in 'Sketch'.
21 Reads Richard Roberts *Portrait of Stella Benson* (1939), 'a drivelling book, judging from 10 pages' (to E. Smyth).
24 Gives dinner party for G. Keynes and his wife Margaret Darwin; E. Williamson and her 'underworld' friend Leonie Leontineff, and B. Nicolson come in afterward.
25 To Rodmell for Whitsun.
28 In 'Sketch' records her response to her mother's death.

June

5 (Mon) The Woolfs cross to Dieppe, tour Normandy and Brittany, returning to Monk's House 19 June.
18 Reads Colette's *Duo* (1934).
20 Works on portrait of S. Duckworth in 'Sketch'.
22 Returns to Tavistock Square.
23 Resumes work on *RF*, 'the appallingly difficult' Post-Impres-

sionist chapter (ch. 7). V. Ocampo visits; annoys VW by bringing photographer Gisèle Freund.

25 Visits VB; learns of M. Gertler's suicide (23 June, age 47).

26 Dines with CB and Cory Bell.

27 TSE and Frank Morley, fellow director of Faber and Faber, to tea.

28 Agrees to write an article on royalty for *Picture Post* (*M*).

29 Turns to 'Sketch of the Past' as relief from the Post-Impressionist chapter in *RF*; reads Pascal.

July

2 (Sun) LW's mother dies; VW feels regret although she always hated going to visit her (*D*, 3 July).

11 'Over all hangs war. . . . Dantzig. The Poles vibrating in my room' (*D*).

12 Works at *RF* with pleasure for the first time in weeks (ch. 8, 'The Omega').

13 Reads Pascal, Pater, and D. S. MacCall, *Confessions of a Keeper and Other Papers* (1931), which reprinted three articles relating to RF; reflects on the words of Spinoza which were read at RF's cremation and which she uses to conclude her biography: 'A free man thinks of death least of all things; and his wisdom is a meditation not of death but of life' (*D*).

15 Reads Freud's *Moses and Monotheism* (1939).

19 Takes up 'Sketch' for the first time since 20 June: reflects on relation of past and present; continues with portrait of S. Duckworth.

21 Reads R. C. Trevelyan's *Collected Works* (1939).

25 To Monk's House for the summer; quarrels with LW over building a greenhouse; over the next few days reads in *André Gide's Journal, 1885–1939* (1939), F. L. Lucas's memoir *Journal under the Terror* (1938), *Kilvert's Diary* ed. W. Plomer (1938–40), and the manuscript of E. Robins' memoirs, *Both Sides of the Curtain* (VW recommends it to Harcourt Brace, 10 Aug 1939; Heinemann publishes it 1940).

30 Writes Flavinda's speech for 'Where there's a Will there's a Way' in *BA*; wonders whether the book will compose, written at three-month intervals, 'But I'm all in favour of the wild, the experimental' (*D*).

August

2 (Wed) Stops smoking; finds this 'clears the brain – certainly the tongue' (*D*).

7 Works on ch. 10, 'Vision and Design', in *RF*. Notes that all books now seem to be surrounded by 'invisible censors', which she doubts Wordsworth had (*D*).

17 The Woolfs move the Hogarth Press to 37 Mecklenburgh Square, and on the 24th move their personal possessions there.

19 Reads Kenneth Clark's *Leonardo da Vinci: An Account of his Development as a Artist* (1939).

25 Records signing of German–Soviet Non-Aggression Pact (23 Aug), 'a disagreeable & unforeseen surprise'; expects announcement of war (*D*).

September

1 (Fri) Hitler invades Poland.

3 Britain declares war; VW sews black-out curtains, notes tha her work is more real to her than the war (*D*, 3 and 6 Sep).

6 First air-raid warning.

11 Tries to anchor her mind by reading Greek (Theophrastus).

23 S. Freud dies, age 83 (*D*, 24 Sep).

27 Reads R. L. Stevenson's *The Strange Case of Dr Jekyll and M Hyde* (1896).

30 'White's Selborne' in *NS&N*.

October

6 (Fri) Has finished copying out *RF*, although it still needs to b 'revised, compacted, vitalised' (*D*); composes article on Lewi Carroll (9 Dec). Reads Francis Steegmuller's *Flaubert and Mm Bovary*, and Jacques Emile Blanche's *More Portraits of a Lifetime 1918–38* (both 1939). Hitler announces his last offer to th Allies; G. B. Shaw argues in *NS&N* that Britain should mak peace with Germany.

7 TSE sends his *Old Possum's Book of Practical Cats* (1939); VV plans a dog story, 'Gipsy, the Mongrel' (which J. Chambrur New York literary agent, pays for, Feb 1940, but does nc publish; see *CSF*).

11 Reads A. M. Sayers' *Poems of Twenty Years* (1939).

13 To London for a week (the Woolfs now live at Monk's House, coming up to London usually once a week).

25 Reads G. Heard's *Pain, Sex and Time* (1939); decides he has nothing to offer once he has finished his historical account. Resolves not to read A. Huxley's *After Many a Summer* (1939), which develops Heard's ideas in fiction, and read Dickens' *Little Dorrit* (1855–7).

November

1 (Wed) Decides she cannot complete with the 'compression & lucidity & logic' of A. Gide's *Journal* in her diary.

2 *Reviewing* published as a Hogarth pamphlet; engenders controversy in *TLS* and *NS&N*.

5 Reads Erasmus, Plato, Dickens' *Little Dorrit*, W. Rothstein's memoirs, and Gide's *Si le grain ne meurt* (1926), amazed at the frankness with which he discusses his homosexuality (to D. Bussy).

11 'Reviewers', letter to the editor, in *NS&N*.

28 J. Lehmann spends the night, discusses his *New Writing* and his quarrel with S. Spender.

December

3 (Sun) VSW sends her latest book, *Country Notes*, which includes an account of her trip through Burgundy with VW in 1928.

9 'Gulping up' Freud's works (probably *The Future of an Illusion*, 1928, and *Civilisation and its Discontents*, 1930); finds them 'upsetting . . . & I daresay truly. If we're all instinct, the unconscious, whats all this about civilisation, the whole man, freedom &c ?' (*D*). Plans to read John Stuart Mill's *On Liberty* (1859). 'Lewis Carroll', review of *The Complete Works of Lewis Carroll*, in *NS&N*.

16 Declines S. Spender's invitation to write for *Horizon*, because it would conflict with her allegiance to J. Lehmann's *New Writing*, published by Hogarth.

17 Waiting to hear what will happen to the German battleship *Graf Spee*, trapped by British warships in the harbour of Montevideo (she blows herself up). Reading Freud's *Group Psychology* (1922), *Self-Portrait, Taken from the Letters and Journals of Charles Ricketts, RA*, compiled by T. Sturge Moore (1939), *Letters and Diaries of Henry, Tenth Earl of Pembroke and his Circle*,

1734–80, ed. Lord Herbert (1939), and G. Rylands' anthology *The Ages of Man: Shakespeare's Image of Man and Nature* (1939).

Over Christmas exchanges visits with the Keyneses; spends Christmas day at Charleston.

1940

EVENTS AND LETTERS. Germans enter Paris; Battle of Britain waged over England; Trotsky assassinated in Mexico; F. Scott Fitzgerald dies; E. O'Neill writes *Long Day's Journey into Night*, JMK publishes *How to Pay for the War*; G. Greene, *The Power and the Glory*; E. Hemingway, *For Whom the Bell Tolls*; Arthur Koestler, *Darkness at Noon*; T. Wolfe, *You Can't Go Home Again* (posth.).

January

2 (Tues) Thanks Vera Brittain for her *Testament of Friendship* (1940), a tribute to W. Holtby (whose *Letters to a Friend*, 1937, she had read earlier).

3 Still struggling with the revision of the Post-Impressionist chapter in *RF*. Reads J. S. Mill's *Autobiography* (1873); writes obituary of poet Humbert Wolfe in *D* (see May 1927).

6 Attends party for A. Bell's twenty-first birthday at Charleston; guests include the Woolfs, the Keyneses, M. Strachey and DG.

16 Attends concert at the National Gallery (emptied of pictures for duration of the war). W. Plomer and H. Walpole to dinner; Walpole reminisces about Conrad.

18 Attends performance of Wilde's *The Importance of Being Earnest* (with E. Evans as Lady Bracknell). Has been composing her lecture for the Worker's Educational Association ('The Leaning Tower', 27 Apr); plans to go on with the 'Omega' chapter (ch. 8) of *RF*.

25 VW's fifty-eighth birthday.

26 Condenses last chapter of *RF*; makes an attempt at the opening in *D*. Reads Edmund Burke's *Reflections on the Revolution in France* (1790).

27 'Gas at Abbotsford', review of *Sir Walter Scott's Journal*, vol. I, ed. J. G. Tait, in *NS&N*.

February

7 (Wed) Begins W. Holtby's *South Riding* (1935); having just finished *Little Dorrit*, judges Holtby 'a ventriloquist, not a creator' (to E. Smyth).

8 Dr Rita Hinden, secretary of the Fabian Colonial Bureau, visits.

9 Continues reading Holtby and reads manuscript of S. Spender's *The Backward Son* (Hogarth, 1940); finds them a relief from her evenings grinding at Burke and Mill. Feels her labour on *RF* is paying off.

14 TSE and S. Sydney-Turner to dinner; CB comes in afterward, and the talk is of civilisation, S. Spender's 'September Journal', which is appearing in *Horizon*, Yeats's *Oxford Book of Modern Verse* (1936) and other literary topics (*D*, 16 Feb).

15 Attends performance of E. O'Neill's *Desire under the Elms* – 'elemental situation bare of words; like a scaffold' (*D*, 16 Feb). 'The Dream', review of George Bullock's *Marie Corelli: The Life and Death of a Best Seller*, in the *Listener*.

23 Sends manuscript of *RF* to M. Fry; spends most of the next month in bed with influenza.

March

7 (Thurs) Reads H. Havelock Ellis's *My Life* (1940).

12 Finland signs peace treaty with the USSR.

(Mid-month) LW reads *RF*, thinks it analysis rather than history, but VW becomes convinced he is wrong, and both VB and M. Fry think it good (*D*, 20 Mar; to VB, 15 Mar).

21 Reads Lord Hervey's *Memoirs of the Reign of George II*, ed. J. W. Crokers (1848), and A. B. Goldenveizer's *Talks with Tolstoi*, tr. S. S. Koteliansky and VW (1923).

24 Enters M. Fry's corrections to *RF*. Reads J. Austen's *Sense and Sensibility* (1813) and Charles Darwin's *A Naturalist's Voyage round the World* (1905).

26 Transcribes letter from H. Walpole in which he asserts, 'But you *dont* write novels. . . . I am the *true* novelist' (*D*).

27 Reads Helena Gleichen's *Contacts and Contrasts* (1940).

28 Q. Bell dines before meeting of the Rodmell Labour Party, which has been meeting regularly since the Woolfs moved to Monk's House.

29 Reads Whymper (probably the new biography of climber Edward Whymper by Frank Smythe).

April

1 (Mon) To London; meets B. Dobrée, who thinks TSE's latest poem, *East Coker*, 'didactic' (*D*, 6 Apr).

6 Reads Sydney Smith's *Letters of Peter Plymley* (1807–8). Has been asked to write a play for the Rodmell villagers to act (she does not do so).

9 Germany invades Norway and Denmark.

18 D. MacCarthy to dinner; VW records his talk (*D*, 20 Apr). H. A. L. Fisher dies (*D*, 25 Apr).

23 VSW spends the night at Monk's House.

27 Delivers lecture, 'The Leaning Tower', to Workers' Educational Association in Brighton (pub. Nov).

May

8 (Wed) Tells R. Hart-Davies she had enjoyed R. C. Carter's *He and His* (1940).

10 Germany invades Holland and Belgium.

13 VW sends in proofs of *RF*; next day LW finishes *The War for Peace* (1940).

15 Reading Coleridge, has a theory that the contemporary editions of William Pickering (Aldine Press edition) 'reveal now aspects'; plans to continue with Shelley (to TSE). VW and LW discuss suicide in the event of an invasion (LW keeps a reserve of petrol in the garage so they can asphyxiate themselves with exhaust fumes).

20 D. MacCarthy and G. E. Moore visit; VW, VB, and Q. Bell discuss his influence and his famous silences – Moore claims he simply could not think of anything to say (*D*).

21 W. Plomer and TSE visit; VW struck by the latter's egotism after MacCarthy's geniality and Moore's 'candid childs eyes' (*D*, 25 May).

21–4 Visits with S. Colefax, and with S. S. Koteliansky, who seems deranged by the war.

26 Evacuation of Dunkirk begins, and continues until 4 June, with 340,000 being brought to England.

28 VW attends first air-raid meeting. Belgium surrenders, exposing the flank of the British and French armies retreating toward Dunkirk.

29 Begins work on *BA* again. Reads 'masses' of Coleridge and Wordsworth letters, and G. K. Chesterton's *Thomas Aquinas* (1933).

31 *BA* now 'bubbling'; writes 'Scraps, orts & fragments'. Begins reading Balzac's *La Comédie humaine* (1855).

June

3 (Mon) Awakened by a bomb exploding.

7 As the German offensive across the Somme continues, K. Martin, R. Macaulay, and the Woolfs discuss suicide.

8 Discovers her notes for 'Sketch', 19 July 1939; continues with J. Hills and his love for S. Duckworth. 'The Humane Art', review of R. W. Ketton-Cremer's *Horace Walpole*, in *NS&N*.

9 Correcting proofs of *RF*, 'It struck me that one curious feeling is, that the writing "I", has vanished. No audience, No echo. Thats part of one's death' (*D*).

10 Finishes *RF*, except for the index; the 'after book stage' is upon her (*D*). Italy declares war on Britain and France.

13 Sends off index to *RF*. Reads *Letters on Poetry from W. B. Yeats to Dorothy Wellesley* (1940), with her praise of VW; depressed by broadcasts by Lord Haw-Haw announcing German victory, 'the Wordsworth letters my only drug' (*D*).

14 Visits Penshurst with VSW; Paris falls to the Germans.

22 Reads R. Macaulay's latest novel, *And No Man's Wit* (1940), *Lady Bessborough and her Family Circle*, ed. Earl of Bessborough (1940), and Donald Bateman's *Berkeley Moynihan: Surgeon* (1940), and Shelley and Coleridge at night. Wishes she could invent a new critical method, more 'fluid' than her *CR* essays: 'The old problem: how to keep the flight of the mind, yet be exact' (*D*).

25–6 Disrupted by E. Bowen's visit, tries to 'centre' herself by reading Freud; feels 'loosely anchored' with only *BA* to work on, has so little sense of a public she forgets about *RF* coming out: the standards 'which have for so many years given back an echo & so thickened my identity are all wide & wild as the desert now. . . . We pour to the edge of a precipice. . . . I can't conceive that there will be a 27th June 1941' (*D*, 27 June).

July

5 (Fri) Reads Coleridge *Biographia Literaria* (1817) and her father's essay on Coleridge in *Hours in a Library* (1892).

9 Reads the last volume of E. Smyth's nine-volume biography, *What Happened Next* (1940); finds it less brilliant but more 'sequacious' (cf. Coleridge; to E. Smyth).

(Mid-month) Attends first-aid classes in Rodmell, as preparation for air attacks or invasion.

16 R. Strachey dies (*D*, 24 July). Review of *Hary-O: The Letters of Lady Harriet Cavendish*, ed. Sir George Leveson-Gower, in *NS&N*.

19 Hitler invites Britain to capitulate.

23 Reads her account of the Dreadnought Hoax to the Women's Institute in Rodmell.

24 Again feels there is 'no standard to write for: no public to echo back: even the "tradition" has become transparent'; tired of the 'notes' of Gide and of Alfred de Vigny's *Journal d'un poète* (1867), wants something more 'robust' (*D*).

25 *RF* published; VW feels connected with him, as if they together had given birth to her 'vision' of him. H. Read, in the *Spectator* (2 Aug) praises VW's new 'firmness and directness' but attacks RF's 'retreat into the private world of his own sensibility', as does D. S. MacColl in the *Observer* (4 Aug), but D. MacCarthy praises the work in the *Sunday Times* (4 Aug), and EMF, who VW feared had refused to review the work, declares 'Good book' in the *NS&N* (10 Aug), defending RF's and Cézanne's apples as 'symbols of civilisation' (*M&M*).

Late this month, reads Ruth Benedict's *Patterns of Culture* (1934), Augustus Hare's *The Story of My Life* (6 vols, 1896–1900), William Morris's *Chants for Socialists* (1885), and continues with Coleridge.

August

The Battle of Britain rages for the next two months, with daily air raids.

2 (Fri) Accepts J. B. Priestley's invitation to join a committee to campaign against the inclusion of books in the proposed Purchase Tax (a proposal which the Government later drops).

13 Replies to B. Nicolson, who is serving in an anti-aircraft battery and had criticised RF for living in a 'fool's paradise' (see 24 Aug).

16 Notes 144 planes brought down last night (this is the heaviest week of losses for the Luftwaffe, with the RAF claiming 496).

24 Types a carefully drafted letter to B. Nicolson, vigorously defending RF and Bloomsbury; sends a more moderate one (see *L* for draft and letter, and invitation to Monk's House, 2 Sep).

30 VSW phones from Sissinghurst, where bombs are dropping around the house; VW feels 'Now we are in the war' (*D*).

September

1 (Sun) Attends meeting of Memoir Club at Charleston; reads her account of the Dreadnought Hoax.
8 Reads Katherine Furse's *Hearts and Pomegranates, Story of 45 Years, 1875–1920* (1940).
10 Bomb drops on Mecklenburgh Square; a few days later it explodes, wrecking the Woolfs' house.
11 Works on Coleridge review (26 Oct); watches an aerial dog-fight over Lewes; listens to Churchill's warning of impending invasion.
12 Conceives (or 'remoulds') an idea for a 'Common History' of English literature, which would include biography (*D*; first mention of 'Reading at Random' or 'Turning the Page'; for the first chapters, 'Anon' and 'The Reader', see Silver).
13 The Woolfs travel to London to help J. Lehmann arrange the moving of the Hogarth Press and staff to Hertfordshire.
14 Reads Ifor Evans' *A Short History of English Literature* (1940) for 'Reading', as well as Henry Williamson's *Goodbye West Country* (1937) and Madame de Sévigné, though she finds the latter has gone stale with the 'mannered and sterile' Compte de Bussy (1618–93), who reminds her of L. P. Smith and TSE (*D*).
15 Asks W. Plomer for the latest volume of Kilvert's diary (see 25 July 1939); takes the 'unfashionable view' that Kilvert is 'more real than war' (to W. Plomer).
17 Looks at a volume of F. L. Lucas's criticism, which checks her impulse to write her own book ('Reading'); continues work on *BA*. Hitler decides to postpone the invasion and to concentrate on night bombing of London and other cities.
18 Begins new notebook, 'Reading at Random/Notes'.
21 Overcomes her rage at being beaten at Bowls (a frequent occurrence throughout Aug and Sep) by reading Michelet.
22 Continues 'Sketch' with portrait of T. Stephen and St Ives; notes that people now think of weather as it affects a possible invasion or raids on London, not as how it affects them personally.
26 'In flush' with *BA*.

October

2 (Wed) Reads E. Griggs's biography of Sara Coleridge (26 Oct).
12 In 'Sketch' explores her relation with T. Stephen.
17 Continues with *BA*. Receives *East Coker* (1940) from TSE: 'According to our compact, I say nothing of the printed matter' (to TSE).
19 'The Man at the Gate', review of *Coleridge the Talker*, ed. Richard Armour and Raymond Howes, in *NS&N*.
21 'Thoughts on Peace in an Air Raid' in the *New Republic*, New York.
22 Thinks about a prayer for the Victorian scene in *BA*.
26 Begins G. M. Trevelyan's *History of England* (1926); thinks it provides a service like Roman roads, but avoids the 'forests & the will o the wisps' – unlike the history she plans to write (used for opening sentences of 'Anon' and figures in Miss Swithin's 'Outline of History' at the end of *BA*); throws aside vol. 15 of Michelet 'with a glorious sense of my own free & easiness in reading now' (*D*). 'Sara Coleridge', review of E. L. Griggs's *Coleridge Fille: A Biography of Sara Coleridge*, in *NS&N*.
31 'Georgiana and Florence', review of *Two Generations*, ed. O. Sitwell, in the *Listener*.

November

1 (Fri) Revises 'The Legacy' for *Harper's Bazaar*, which in the event does not take it. Reads E. F. Benson's *Final Edition, an Informal Autobiography* (1940).
5 Excited by *BA*; cheered by the setbacks suffered by Italian forces in Greece.
7 EMF asks if he may propose her name for the London Library committee; VW refuses (see 9 Apr 1935).
14 Delighted that the river Ouse has been bombed, turning the adjoining field into an inland sea.
15 Having trouble with the end of *BA*. Reads H. Read's autobiography, *Annals of Innocence and Experience* (1940) – 'good cabinet making'; notes Coventry has been almost destroyed (*D*).
17 Notes the rhythm of *BA* 'became so obsessive that I heard it, perhaps used it, in every sentence I spoke', and so turned to 'Sketch' (continuing with an account of her father's rages and need for sympathy), which has a rhythm 'far freer & looser. Two days of writing in that rhythm has completely refreshed me' (*D*).

18 Finishes Read's autobiography; thinks of him, TSE, Santayana and H. G. Wells as 'little boys making sand castles. . . . I am the sea which demolishes these castles' (*D*).
23 Finishes *BA*, thinks it 'more quintessential' than her other novels; notes that it was written at intervals as relief from *RF*, and hopes to keep the same scheme, alternating 'Reading' ('a supported on fact book') with an imaginative work (*D*).
24 Begins 'Anon'.
29 Reads Ellen Terry's *Memoirs*, ed. E. Craig and C. St. John (1933), Edward Gordon Craig's *Ellen Terry and her Secret Self* (1931) and *Ellen Terry and Bernard Shaw: a Correspondence* (1931), for her sketch of Ellen Terry (Feb 1941). Has been made treasurer of the Women's Institute, Rodmell.
'The Leaning Tower' in *Folios of New Writing*, ed. J. Lehmann.

December
4 (Wed) Moves furniture and books from Mecklenburgh Square to Monk's House.
8 Notes the Greeks are driving the Italians out of Albania.
16 Exhausted by the struggle of writing 2000 words on E. Terry.
19 Reads R. C. Trevelyan's *Translations from Horace, etc., with Two Imaginary Conversations* (1940). Notes the meat ration has been reduced, sugar and petrol are scarce.
20 Buys E. Power's *Medieval People* (1924); works on the Shakespeare chapter in 'Reading'.
22 Visits the Keyneses.
23 M. Oxford, who has lately conceived a passion for VW, sends a statuette of Voltaire which she had intended to leave VW in her will (to E. Smyth, 14 Nov and 24 Dec).
24 Copying out the manuscript of *BA*, notes her hand is becoming palsied.
29 Reads Matthew Arnold's 'Thyrsis'; transcribes, 'The foot less prompt to meet the morning dew,/The Heart less bounding at emotion new,/And hope, once crush'd, less quick to spring again' (*D*).
31 O. Wilberforce offers VW a month's milk and cream in return for a copy of her next book, *BA*.

1941

EVENTS AND LETTERS. Germans invade Russia; S. Anderson and J. Joyce die. B. Brecht writes *Mother Courage and her Children*; N. Coward, *Blithe Spirit*.

January

1 (Wed) Reads the Elizabethans for 'Reading'. O. Wilberforce, who now comes fairly often, to tea.

9 Copies *BA*. Reads D. MacCarthy's new book, *Drama* (1941); finds it 'too sloppy & depending upon the charm of the Irish voice' (*D*).

12 Agrees with E. Smyth that an inability to write about sex limits autobiography; mentions being molested by her half-brother, an incident she had written about earlier in 'Sketch' (to E. Smyth).

13 J. Joyce (a week younger than VW) dies in Zurich, age 58; VW remembers TSE at Garsington wondering how anyone could write again 'after achieving the immense prodigy of the last chapter' of *Ulysses*, and her reading it in the summer of 1922 with 'spasms of wonder, of discovery, & . . . long lapses of intense boredom (*D*, 15 Jan).

20 Reads A. Gide's *La Porte étroite* (1909): 'feeble, slaty, sentimental' (*D*).

25 VW's fifty-ninth birthday.

26 Depressed by *Harper's Bazaar*'s rejection of 'The Legacy' and 'Ellen Terry' (to *Harper's*, 23 Jan, 3 Feb; 'The Legacy' pub. *HH*, 1943; (Ellen Terry', 8 Feb).

February

1 (Sat) Reads *Two Generations: Reminiscences of Georgiana C. Sitwell and Journal of Florence A. Sitwell*, ed. O. Sitwell (1940), and memoirs of Blanche Dugdale (*née* Balfour), *Family Homespun* (1940), and sixteenth-century literature for 'Reading'; finds it a jerk to shift to the eighteenth-century for her review of *Hester Lynch Piozzi* (8 Mar).

2 Protests to D. MacCarthy, who in his review of *The Leaning Tower* stated that she herself wrote from a tower (*Sunday Times*, 2 Feb), that she was much closer to the working man than he and all those who had gone to Eton and Cambridge (to D. MacCarthy).

4 Asks VSW for biography of Lady Clifford (d. 1676), whose diary VSW had published 1924, and any other Elizabethan biographer.
7 Sees Charlie Chaplin's *The Great Dictator*, finds it boring. Notes the Sitwells are 'proving their existence as poets in the Law Courts', suing Hamilton Fyfe and *Reynolds' News* for a review which stated 'oblivion has claimed them' (they are each awarded £350).
8 'Ellen Terry' in *NS&N*.
11 To Cambridge; visits P. Strachey at Newnham College. Next day visits the Hogarth Press (at Letchworth for the war).
17–18 VSW visits, lectures on Persia to the Rodmell Women's Institute.
26 Finishes *BA*; gives the typescript to LW to read.

March
1 (Sat) Trying to write on Elizabethan plays for 'Reading', feels this is the worst stage of the war, that 'we have no future' (to E. Smyth).
8 Thanks TSE for sending *The Dry Salvages*; marks H. James's sentence 'Observe perpetually', resolving to use her despondency (*D*). 'Mrs Thrale', review of James Clifford's *Hester Lynch Piozzi*, in *NS&N*.
10 Reads William Curry's *The Case for Federal Union* (1939).
13 The Germans have been dropping incendiary bombs along the South Downs, but VW remains more troubled by the fact that there is 'No audience. No private stimulus, only this outer roar' (to E. Robins).
14 VW and LW travel to London for the day, lunch with J. Lehmann and tell him of *BA*. VW asks for reading; Lehmann agrees to send some manuscripts for *Folios of New Writing*.
18 LW becomes alarmed at VW's condition: she recently came back wet from a walk and claimed to have fallen into one of the dykes (see *LW* v and, for an argument that one of her two suicide notes to LW was written on 18 Mar, see *L* vi, Appendix A).
20 Sends J. Lehmann the typescript of *BA*, asking him to give the 'casting vote' in deciding whether or not it should be published; she feels it 'much too slight and sketchy' but LW thinks it ready (to J. Lehmann).
21 Thinks LW's *The War for Peace* (1940) 'the only kind of thing

worth writing now'; finds she cannot read novels (to Lady Cecil).

23 Has worked through the manuscripts for *New Writing* as far as she can, but 'my head is very stupid at the moment' (to J. Lehmann).

27 The Woolfs travel to Brighton to consult Dr Wilberforce about VW's state; VW admits she fears going mad again, that she will be unable to write.

28 VW writes to LW that she has begun to hear voices, and that she is certain she will not recover; she then drowns herself in the river Ouse. Her body is found three weeks later and cremated 21 April 1941.

Leonard Woolf continued to live at Monk's House. In 1946 he sold John Lehmann's interest in the Hogarth Press to Chatto and Windus. Through the 1940s and 1950s, in addition to working on his *Principia Politica* (1953), he published collections of VW's stories and essays, as well as *A Writer's Diary: Being Extracts from the Diary of Virginia Woolf* (1953) and *Virginia Woolf and Lytton Strachey: Letters* (1956). During the next decade he edited the four volumes of VW's *Collected Essays* (1966–7) and published the five volumes of his *Autobiography* (1960–9). He died in 1969.

Vanessa Bell lived and worked at Charleston, with Duncan Grant, until her death in 1961.

Vita Sackville-West stopped writing poetry after the mid 1940s, but published biographies, novels, and books and articles on gardening until her death in 1962.

Clive Bell published *Old Friends: Personal Recollections* in 1956, the year the last meeting of the Memoir Club was held; he died in 1964.

Duncan Grant continued to paint until his death in 1978.

Index

Index of Titles

Essays and Poems

Books

Books – *continued*

GOSHEN COLLEGE - GOOD LIBRARY
3 01008669 0

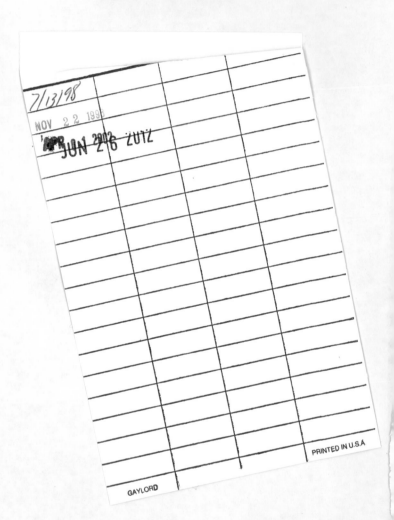